Scribe Publications
MAKING YOUR HOME SUSTAINABLE

Derek F. Wrigley, OAM, LFDIA, FRAIA, ARIBA, DA, studied architecture and town planning at Manchester University in the UK. In 1948 he emigrated to Australia and became a lecturer at NSW University of Technology, where he established the first building-science course in Australia. In addition to teaching, he has practised as an architect, industrial designer, and solar consultant — including designing and building six solar houses in Sydney and Canberra. He was a co-founder of the Industrial Design Council of Australia and was awarded Life Fellowship of the Design Institute of Australia in 1980. He is currently retired from formal practice and is researching applications for solar energy in building and experimenting with low-energy and low-resource retrofitting of existing houses.

MAKING
YOUR HOME
SUSTAINABLE

A GUIDE TO RETROFITTING

DEREK WRIGLEY

SCRIBE

Melbourne

Scribe Publications Pty Ltd
18–20 Edward St, Brunswick, Victoria, Australia 3056
Email: info@scribepub.com.au

Published in Australia and New Zealand by Scribe 2005
Reprinted 2006, 2007, 2010 (with updates)
This revised edition published 2012

Printed in Australia by Trojan Grafix.

National Library of Australia
Cataloguing-in-Publication data

Wrigley, Derek F.

Making Your Home Sustainable: a guide to retrofitting.

Rev. ed.

9781921844171 (pbk.)

1. Architecture and energy conservation–Australia.
2. Sustainable architecture–Australia.

728.370472

www.scribepublications.com.au

Contents

Author's Note

1-1 **Preview**
2   Introduction
3   Before you get too absorbed

2-1 **Context**
2   The need for this book
3   The broader picture
4   Retrofitting and location
5   The Mawson house

3-1 **Recognising retrofitting possibilities**
2   Before you buy an existing house
3   Solar access

4-1 **Free hot water**
2   Solar hot-water heaters
3   Location of absorber panels

5-1 **Improving windows**
2   Problem of fixed, northern eaves
3   Northern, adjustable sun shades
4   Obtaining effective shade
5   Sunshades as bushfire radiation shields
6   Sunshades for east and west windows
7   Double glazing
8   Curtains and convection losses
9   Internal blinds and summer heat gain
10   Natural daylighting for dark interiors

6-1 **Using wasted sunshine**
2   Fixed, southern reflectors
3   Geometry of fixed, southern reflectors
4   Reflector design considerations
5   Combined reflector/photovoltaics panel
6   A reflector project
7   Reflecting heliostat
8   Reflecting heliostat – solar geometry

7-1 **Rationalising your electricity consumption**
2   Electrical appliances
3   Electrical appliances – phantom loads
4   Improving the usefulness of refrigerators
5   Photovoltaics – the design process
9   Photovoltaics – the Mawson experience
10   Comparative PV generation/consumption
11   DIY or contract?
12   Integrated photovoltaics

8-1 **Mass and internal comfort**
2   Controlling internal comfort
3   How mass can help
4   Trombe-Michel walls
5   Timber floors
6   Concrete floors

9-1 **Insulation and internal comfort**
2   Insulation
3   Insulation and ventilation
4   Insulation of timber and concrete floors

10-1 **Ventilation and internal comfort**
2   Using natural, free ventilation in summer
3   Ridge and ceiling ventilation system
5   Heat losses and draughtproofing
6   Conservatories as heat sources
7   Conservatories

11-1 **Rationalising water usage**
2   Our profligate usage of water
3   Reducing our water consumption
4   Modifying our water-using equipment
5   Rainfall – the forgotten resource
6   The arguments for and against tanks
7   How much rainwater can we collect?
8   Where can we place tanks?
9   Sizes and location of tanks
10   Option 1 – tank input/output graph
11   Option 1 – tank flow analysis
12   Option 1 – the physical possibility
13   Options 2 and 3
14   Comparative analysis of Options 1, 2, and 3
15   So what is the best value?
16   Gutter guards, diverters, and filter bags
17   Low-cost variable toilet-flushing mechanism
18   Re-using domestic greywater
19   Direct and subsoil disposal of greywater
20   Re-using kitchen greywater
22   On-site subsoil drainage of greywater
23   Making suitable connections to existing greywater outlets

12-1 **Making a useful landscape**
2   A solar garden?
3   Natural, automatic shading
4   Deciduous trees
5   Deciduous vines and climbers
6   Lawn alternatives
7   Holding the roof down

13-1 **The Mawson results**
2   How do we evaluate the results of retrofitting?

14-1 **What if I live in a rented house?**
2   How tenants can reduce their fuel bills and stay comfortable

15-1 **Who benefits and who pays?**
2   Why should I retrofit?
3   Retrofitting and lifestyle
4   Which retrofit project should I do first?
5   How can we finance retrofitting?
       'Solarisation' by Dr Andrew Blakers
7   Technoclutter

16-1 **Useful information**
2   Glossary
4   Useful reading
5   Useful sources of general information
6   Clear and cloudy days in Canberra
7   Irradiation on inclined planes
8   Solar plotter 1 and 2
10   Checklist
15   Is housing design going in a sustainable direction?

Author's note

The aim of this book is primarily to encourage homeowners to modify their houses for their personal wellbeing, their pockets, and for the sake of the planet.

It is vital to the future of the world as we know it that concepts which enable us to reduce the production of greenhouse gases become better known and practised.

Consequently, I claim no rights on the designs in this book and hope that individuals will make as much use of them as possible. If any manufacturer wishes to develop any of these concepts, I would appreciate some discussion in order to maintain their design integrity and performance efficiency.

Many of these topics are interactive, cumulative, and very specific to their particular situation. The use of one may very well affect the use or efficiency of another, so professional advice should be sought wherever possible to ensure good integration.

Every effort has been made to ensure accuracy, but I hope it will be realised that this field of design and technology has changed rapidly over the last few decades and is still changing. You will appreciate, I am sure, that I cannot be responsible for any activities or their consequences carried out as a result of reading this book.

While some commercial products and services have been named in this book, I am not endorsing them and have no financial connections with any of them. I simply wish to explain their special characteristics in relation to the growing needs of sustainable living.

Lastly, the descriptions of the Mawson house projects are not absolutely final — they are works in progress — experiments into new ways of doing better with less, which hopefully will show that not all technology has to be high-tech or produced by industry. The home handy-person, with a modicum of skill and know-how, can often make significant changes to their home comfort.

Updating a book after several years is a salutory exercise in humility. Retrofitting makes us think deeper and work better because you can only blame yourself if things go wrong. I would not wish it otherwise, as the link between designing and doing is critical and unbelievably rewarding.

However, while this book has been extremely well received and has stimulated many to pick up their tools, the speed of national retrofitting incentives needs to be much faster if existing houses are to be made adequate to the challenges of global warming.

While I would like to think this book was mandatory reading for all politicians, nothing would please me more than to find a grubby, well-thumbed, dog-eared, scribbled-in copy in the nation's home workshops.

'The bottom line of vibrant, enduring urban regeneration is recognising that many different small things happening will eventually add up to a big change. The big projects — whether a Millennium Dome or a Detroit Casino — will never live up to expectations.

'The more modest ones invariably succeed.'

Roberta Brandes Gratz
Cities Back From The Edge

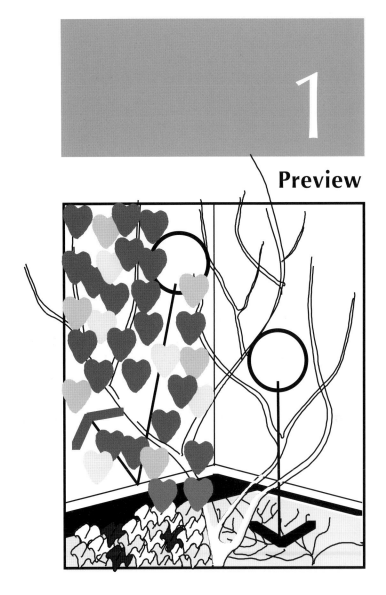

1

Preview

1-2 **Introduction**

1-3 **Before you get too absorbed**

Introduction

In 1991 personal circumstances caused me to move into a house designed by somebody else — a rather new experience for me. Trying to design a better mousetrap is in my blood, so the townhouse in Mawson, Canberra, provided a timely challenge: modifying an existing house to utilise natural rather than imported energies.

In this book you will find a sanitised version of the blood, toil, tears and sweat involved in retrofitting the Mawson house. The exercise has clearly shown me that it is possible to improve the energy efficiency of an existing house. In the colder months, both north- and south-facing rooms can be heated and cheerfully illuminated at the same time, and air conditioning is not necessary in summer. Visitors to the house in Mawson are amazed at the simplicity of some of the ideas that enable us to take control of our internal environment using natural, free energies. Above all, the improvements had to be simple because I had to make them myself — a cautionary tale.

We now have to accept that the old ways of constructing houses are no longer appropriate for the sustainable age. The architecture of Britain was transplanted in Australia in the eighteenth century with a strong carry-over influence from the climate of the northern hemisphere. Our forebears often regarded the sun as their enemy rather than their friend, and this attitude is still prevalent in the Australian housing industry. For example, verandahs are fine in summer, but when we can freely obtain warmth from the winter sun they are as useless as a northern window with the blind pulled down.

Our way of living must also change. Most houses built in Australia last century rely on fossil fuels to provide heat, light and cooling. We need to realise that these energy resources are limited and that we must embrace the concept of sustainability if our children are to enjoy what we have taken for granted. There is an urgent need to control global warming caused by our enormous consumption of fossil fuels, with its resultant greenhouse gas emissions. This cannot be achieved in the time available by designing and building more sustainable new houses — we have to improve the sustainability of the enormous numbers of existing houses. Hence the Mawson experiment to see what could be done.

My own education as an architect was strongly influenced by the Bauhaus in Germany — the pioneering German design school headed by Walter Gropius, and closed by the Nazis not long before I started studying architecture in Manchester. Both the Bauhaus and Manchester schools placed a strong emphasis on the practicalities of design — of learning how to lay bricks, or shape a piece of wood, and, in particular, how a building should be designed to suit its climatic conditions.

Our knowledge of the science of building has improved enormously since then, and today's architects owe a great deal to scientists at the Building Research Station in Garston, UK, and at the Commonwealth Experimental Building Station in Ryde, NSW. These scientists laid the groundwork for a practical understanding of how materials respond to weathering and other stresses, and of the thermal behaviour of buildings — all critical design factors if we are to build houses that are comfortable to live in. This knowledge has played a determining role in my efforts to make the Mawson house sustainable.

Looking back over the latter half of the twentieth century, it is sad to see that the gradual divorce of architecture from the housing industry has resulted in a huge number of houses that do not utilise this knowledge to provide comfort for their occupants. The fragmented nature of the housing industry has worked against the development of integrated housing. Architects are responsible for only a tiny fraction of house designs in Australia, and those who build and sell project houses rarely, if ever, have design qualifications or a demonstrable interest in utilising the latest research in the quest for sustainability. Why else is there now such a demand to remedy deficiencies by the installation of air-conditioners?

While I do perceive some signs of hope in the housing industry, I sense that real hope may well lie with the great army of Do-It-Yourselfers who are willing to have a go. I urgently want to try out new, more sustainable building ideas; and, in this spirit, the descriptions of the Mawson house projects are not absolutely final. They are works in progress — experiments into new ways of doing better with less which are simple, sustainable and as inexpensive as possible, and use recycled materials wherever practicable. Hopefully they show that sustainability does not have to be high-tech and that many remedies lie within the capabilities of ordinary people. By sharing the ideas used in the Mawson house experiment, it is my fervent hope that I can encourage others to do likewise.

My underlying motivation for this book is to do something practical towards a more sustainable world for our grandchildren. We, who have feasted on the best the world has to offer, really have no alternative but to make some effort now on their behalf — otherwise they will pay the cost.

Derek F. Wrigley

Before you get too absorbed ...

This book does not sit happily on the coffee table — its prime motivation is to help those whose social conscience tells them that all is not well with the planet and that there must be some way for homeowners to contribute to a solution. I hope that this book will smooth the path for you and perhaps stimulate you into making yourselves more comfortable using less energy, while at the same time helping to resolve some of the global problems to which we have all contributed. Existing houses represent some 95% of the domestic building stock at any one time, and almost all of them are badly designed for a changing climate and the coming energy crisis when fossil fuels become scarce and too expensive to use.

Time is not on our side — in 1992 the Union of Concerned Scientists warned us that we had about 20 years to turn the ship around before it became too late. Half of that time has now been dissipated with plenty of hot air and greenwash, but not enough action. We need lots of people to actually do lots of little things — if only to counter our governments, who are actively cutting back on funding research into renewable energies. I have been heartened by the 3500 interested people who have wandered through our Mawson house in the last few Sustainable House Days, and many separate groups, with their encouraging requests for information. Many visitors commented — "Why can't we buy houses like this one?" They stimulated this book.

There is indeed hope — because something can be done to every existing house. It is possible to retrofit economically; but, to be honest, it does call for a bit of cash and effort in most cases. There is also hope for those on limited incomes who may be renting a house. Section 14 in this book describes several ideas for keeping warm in winter and cool in summer, which are also beneficial to the environment and which cost nothing — not all sustainable technology has to be high-tech or produced by industry.

But despite the best will in the world, none of these broad areas of activity will thrive unless there is recognition by our various levels of government of the real need for sustainable building and that good levels of incentive are required to generate action.

To those who pointed the way ...

Writing this book has brought home to me how much we owe to those who have preceded us in the search for ways to harness natural energies for comfort and convenience in our homes. Many have been Australians who have pushed back the frontiers of knowledge by explaining the characteristics and usefulness of natural energies, developing new technologies, trying out new ideas, and who have illuminated the road to better ways of doing things:

Dr John Flynn, the original Flying Doctor, who designed and built his naturally air-cooled house in Alice Springs in 1924 — a simple technique that has been largely ignored in modern architecture.

Roger Morse in the 1950s with his development of solar water heaters at CSIRO, which led to the development of several large industries that export solar water heaters all over the world.

Ralph Phillips' seminal and extremely useful work *Sunshine and Shade in Australasia* when working at the Commonwealth Experimental Building Station at Ryde, NSW. An inspiring colleague who subsequently joined me in the development of the first building-science course in Australia at the School of Architecture at the University of NSW, Kensington, in the early 1950s.

J.W. Drysdale and other members of the Commonwealth Experimental Building Station at Ryde, NSW, who researched and published their Science of Building Notes in the 1950s. Their seminal research on the thermal performance of houses and utilisation of solar energy was extremely useful.

Steve Szokolay's book *Solar Energy and Buildings* really interested me in 1974 with his detailed collection of solar statistics which laid the foundation of many solar-collection techniques.

Professor Steven Kanef's research at ANU on the use of solar heat to dissociate ammonia, enabling it to be stored and recombined to form useful heat when needed.

Professor Martin Green's pioneering work on photovoltaic cells at UNSW.

Professor Andrew Blakers' researches have now produced the CHAPS (Combined Heat And Power System) and the highly efficient Sliver Cell photovoltaic panel.

Professors Robert and Brenda Vale, whose eminent work on autonomous housing has continued to this day.

'Sustainable development is development that meets the needs of the present without compromising the ability of future generations to meet their own needs.'

World Commission on Environment and Development,1987

'I don't believe ethical behaviour should depend on its paying.
   To suggest that doing right needs to be justified by its economic reward is amoral, a self-inflicted wound hugely damaging to corporate reputation ...
   Doing right because it is right, not because it pays, needs to be the foundation of business.'

Sir Geoffrey Chandler, Amnesty International

2

Context

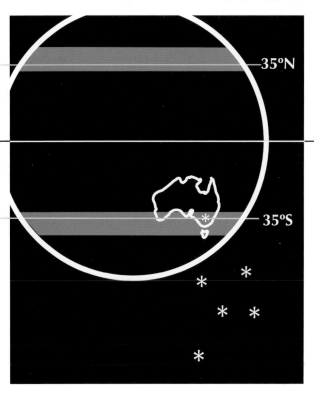

2-2   **The need for this book**

2-3   **The broader picture**

2-4   **Retrofitting and location**

2-5   **The Mawson house**

The need for this book

The need for an awareness of future problems
Scientific research is now much more readily available, and most people should now be aware of the global problems arising very largely from our use of fossil fuels. While some effects have unproven sources we cannot afford to ignore them — we have to adopt a precautionary approach.

The need for individual responsibility
Most of us have lived through the golden years of civilisation when measured by our standard of living and the convenience and comfort we enjoy.

We have, I believe, a moral obligation to pass on a better rather than a degraded world to our descendants, when the problems will be so large as to be insoluble or only treatable at enormous expense.

The need for awareness by designers and builders
While this book deals with the concept of making good the omissions of the past, I hope that those who are designing *new* houses will think some of the concepts in this book worthy of use. Some world-first ideas are shown, but no intellectual property is claimed. However, some recognition would be nice — perhaps a donation to charity ?

The need to encourage the use of natural energies
It is the writer's hope that house builders will think firstly about using free natural energies, rather than relying on the switch on the wall to solve the problems caused by ignorance of how the various building elements work.

The need for an integrated approach
All the elements of a building structure work in unison with the others, and together form a whole which is bigger than the sum of the parts.

A knowledge of this integrated collaboration can help to reduce costs, rather than assembling a heterogeneous collection having overlapping and expensive functions.

The need for a long view
We need to explore and develop new, simpler, building techniques and functions which do not damage the environment, have no detrimental effect on others, cost less to make, cost less to function in a long lifetime, and can be re-used or recycled when their useful life is over.

The need for affordability
As I write, there is much public concern that the cost of houses has reached the limit of affordability.

It is my belief that this can be mitigated by a more rational sense of relative values among designers, builders and potential house buyers — where life-cycle costs can be seen in true perspective and the purchase of a new house does not necessarily cut off the option of adding a future useful device such as a photovoltaic array which may perhaps not be affordable at the beginning — and usually not provided anyway.

The need for more detail
While this book cannot be a complete text book — technology is moving too fast for such a paragon of virtue — it does aim to be practical and useful, based as far as possible on practical experience and empirical research into what works and what doesn't. The latter is just as valuable as the former.

The need for regulation
We have reached an interesting stage in society's development where alternative technology is challenging the regulatory authorities with new and often better ways of doing what has been customary.

There are implied dangers in pushing the boundaries too fast, without adequate safeguards for public health and safety, and our public authorities must necessarily be cautious on our behalf.

Although I have crossed swords with building inspectors all my working life as an architect, I have lately changed my mind because of a new breed of regulators who appear willing to listen to new ideas rather than go by 'the book' and the way that things have always been done.

There is indeed hope for more environmentally aware housing and we should foster collaboration between the users and the rule-makers toward a more rational, scientific and humane regulatory framework.

The need for this book
There is a rapidly growing demand from the public — partly evidenced by the hundreds of people who have come to see the modifications made to our existing developer's house during Solar House Days organised by the ANZ Solar Energy Society and the Alternative Technology Association. Many wanted to know how the ideas could be applied to their own house.

This book shows that there are many ways in which the average handyperson can improve the thermal performance of their house, once the simple principles are understood.

Having designed, built and lived in five previous solar houses from 1949 to 1991, the move to a developer's house in Mawson, ACT, presented a marvellous opportunity to explore the challenging world of *retrofitting* and this book is one of the results.

The Mawson house is a medium-density Body Corporate dwelling built in 1984, of brick veneer (unfortunately), over a concrete slab on the ground, with a low-pitched, corrugated-steel roof. I am usually very critical of developers' houses, but I give credit to Gary Willemsen, who designed this group at Shackleton Park. The orientation, arrangement of rooms, windows and roof form take maximum advantage of the sun, making the job of retrofitting that much easier.

Nevertheless, it has been possible to improve its thermal performance and ventilation, to generate 15% more electricity than it consumes, and to become over 80% self-sufficient in water.

While stress is laid on keeping cool in summer and warm in winter at lower energy levels, we should not lose sight of the very pleasurable, subjective effects that internally penetrating sunshine has on our psychological wellbeing — of being in pleasant surroundings. The sun is a wonderful friend as well as an enemy — it is a matter of appropriate control.

I hope this book will enthuse its readers to the point of saying 'I *could* do that' and then on to 'I *will* do it'.

The broader picture

Solar Australia

There are many dire predictions about global climate changes — and there is now more than sufficient evidence to show that the continuing use of fossil fuels and their emission of greenhouse gases is a major cause of some of these changes. Equally, it is being recognised that eventually these fuels will become exhausted or too costly to use.

Australians in general have one of the most consumptive lifestyles in the world, and the designs of our houses have been based *and are continuing to be based* on the assumption that fossil fuels will always provide for our comfort and our convenience.

We have lost sight of the fact that natural energies which are freely available can contribute a great deal to our comfort more quietly and in a significantly cheaper way than energy-consumptive technology.

We have become almost totally reliant on electricity as a domestic convenience without realising that it is really a dirty, polluting and inefficient fuel *when generated from fossil fuels such as coal and oil.*

Natural gas, although cleaner burning, is still a non-renewable source.

As if that is not bad enough, only about a third of the chemical energy used to generate electricity actually reaches our power outlets — the other two-thirds being lost in generation inefficiencies and transmission over very long distances.

The logical answer to this problem, particularly in Australia, is now economically available to us in the form of *distributive generation.*

This means generating electricity where it is consumed, avoiding long-transmission losses. Every building with good solar access has the opportunity to generate its own electricity using BIPV (Building Industry Photo Voltaics), but this implies designing the building from the beginning to integrate this technology. It is not usually effective as a retrofitted, applied technique.

It is somewhat strange that Australia was, at one time, a world leader in the use of wind power in the bush.

We have an enviable record of innovation in the Coolgardie safe, solar cooling, solar desalination, solar water heating, solar-powered cars and solar-powered telecommunications, and research into the world's most efficient photovoltaic cells. These ideas, coupled with a marvellously sunny climate and a windy coastline, could have placed Australia in the driving-seat of solar-based technology.

Although the CSIRO made research contributions in housing during the last half-century, the housing industry has been slow to learn more effective ways of constructing houses, or to conduct its own research into improving climatic suitability. This is culpable behaviour.

Why is it that Australia, with abundant solar resources and rich in the skills of solar researchers, has not learned to fully utilise these sustaining devices and techniques? One problem is that we, somewhat ironically, have too much cheap coal and an abundant supply of natural gas — and a strong fossil-fuel lobby group.

These innovations could have established Australia as a commercial leader in the solar field, and one can only shake one's head in wonder at how these opportunities slipped through our fingers.

A huge, sustainable industry is being presented to us on a plate — an industry which can have a significant impact upon our production of greenhouse gases. If we do not take advantage of it *now,* our grandchildren will, in turn, shake their heads in incredulity at our lack of vision and our arrogant selfishness in not thinking about the future of our planet.

We have an urgent need to adopt this elegant piece of anonymous prose as our mission statement:

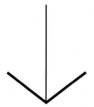

Our green buildings will not poison the air, nor the soul with artificiality.

Instead they will create delight when entered, serenity & health when occupied & regret when departing.

They will grow organically in and from their place, integrating people within the rest of the natural world, do no harm to their occupants or to the earth, foster more diverse & abundant life than they borrow, take less than they give back.

They will be not only be useful but an aesthetic and spiritual challenge.

My apologies to the anonymous author. Hopefully, it will breathe new life into a moribund industry which is putting profits before national well-being.

Retrofitting and location

Retrofitting

Retrofitting is a way of modifying an existing house to take advantage of the abundant natural energy which is all around us but insufficiently recognised by homeowners — and, unfortunately, most builders.

It is a sad fact that the housing industry has not learned to use building-science researches that have been carried out over the last 50 years. The car industry, on the other hand, has learned a great deal from research, and we have all benefitted from this by improved reliability, better fuel economy and interior safety — not so houses.

There are several ways we can improve the houses we live in to utilise the *natural* energies available to all of us, but unfortunately they usually involve spending money to rectify some of the design problems.

However, you might be able to console yourself with the fact that not only are you improving your personal comfort, but improving the resale value of the house — as well as saving money by reducing running costs and helping to reduce its daily impact on the environment.

Many Australian houses have been badly designed and sited for using the sun's movements to our benefit. Existing trees and subsequent unsuitable plantings around the house often make the situation worse, particularly as they grow above the roof line.

Every house and its landscaping is unique and has to be considered according to its own circumstances, so it is hoped that the principles and ideas in this book may help you to develop your own versions.

It is often asked, *"How long does it take to pay back the outlay?"* To which we might say, *"How long does it take to pay back the cost of a swimming pool — or a new car?"*— both of which require very expensive, continuing expenditure in upkeep and maintenance, with resulting deterioration of the environment.

A retrofitted house can produce very significant and worthwhile savings in annual running costs.

What price do you place on comfort — and of leaving a livable and less degraded world for your grandchildren?

Many of the retrofitting ideas described in this book show the principles of what can be done to a typical house in Canberra, often on a simple DIY basis. The average handyperson could tackle many of these techniques, which help to keep costs down, but some require professional help and cost more. Other ideas are described which I haven't tried, but they may stimulate you to find some new ways of reducing your energy bills.

Location

Canberra, Queanbeyan and surrounding towns lie in a cool temperate region, having relatively cold winters with many frosts, clear sunny days in winter, and warm to hot summers. Its humidity is moderate, and summer nights are pleasantly cool compared to many other areas.

Canberra residents realise that, despite a few extremes, this climate is one of the best in the whole of Australia — and these retrofitting ideas will help you to optimise this advantage.

Other relevant areas

Although most of the ideas have been built and tested in the Mawson house and in several other houses to suit the Canberra climate, they are applicable to a much wider area based loosely on latitude 35°S.

Canberra, of course, is at a higher altitude (570m) than any of the other major cities, which tends to give it colder extremes. Nevertheless, the upper and lower temperatures of the coastal cities would still warrant a high degree of retrofitting activity.

A relevant area would cover a band from Newcastle to Hobart and out west to Perth in Australia, where climates and housing construction techniques are not all that different. *(See chart 2-4.1 below.)*

Equally, the concepts could apply to a similar latitude (north or south of the equator) in other countries, particularly Europe and North America, with modifications to suit local techniques.

The main cities in the 35° latitude belt are shown with their climate zones as listed in Building Code Australia (1.1.1.2) (see **www.abcb.gov.au** for further detail)

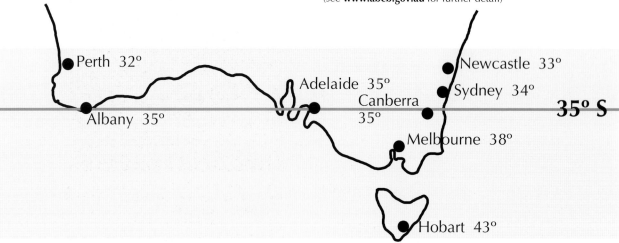

2-4.1 **Approximate areas of Australia which would be relevant to most of the retrofitted concepts described in this book**

The Mawson house
– an overview of some of the changes

The northeast corner

Large eucalypts have been kept on the southern side where they can give no shading problems to our solar collectors on the roof. They present no problem to neighbours across the street

Coolaroo sunshade over the study window in its fixed position

Boston Ivy on the east wall has lost its solid summer shade cover of leaves and lets the warming sun onto the brick wall behind in winter

One of two water tanks which supply house with ~80% of all domestic needs. To be vine covered

Intermittent sprinkler at each end of roof as a bushfire precaustion. Most water flows back into tank

The two rows of photovoltaic panels supply 110% of our electricity and shade the roof in the hot season Ridge vent is hidden behind the top row of PVs

Heliostat and fixed reflector panels are on the southern side of the house and cannot be seen from this viewpoint

Small eaves and open pergola allow entry of winter sun into northern windows. During summer a white Coolaroo shadecloth is attached over this space

Transparent conservatory roof allows light and heat into the kitchen and family room in winter. Deciduous vine and temporary shadecloth sheet provide adequate and delightful summer shade for outdoor eating and conversation

Large deciduous ash and maple trees on this bank are well away from the PV system, but help to keep the enclosed air volume cool in summer

October 2009

N

Some large eucalypts in this area (behind the photographer) are starting to give some shading problems for the PV system and may have to be pruned. This is going to be a big problem for many houses wishing to retrofit

All grass areas have been taken out and replaced with wood chips – with huge environmental and cost savings

The ornamental vine growing over the east court is supported on strained cables letting the sunshine through in winter and creating a large volume of cool shade in summer which serves to cool the house during the day and enters the house by buoyancy when the ceiling vents, windows and doors are opened around 6pm

2-5.1 The Mawson house seen from the north-east in spring. There is a reserve behind the photographer, close neighbours on the right and beyond, and a road on the left — all very tight planning, but very livable with adequate solar access.

Overview

The glossy magazines which cover house design, interiors and gardens tend to focus on novelty, the glamorous and the fashionable — often at a very superficial level — *but rarely do they describe those basic aspects of a livable, comfortable house that significantly reduces its demands on the environment we all share.* From ecological and sustainable points of view their emphasis is misdirected.

This book takes the opposite viewpoint, describing what has been done to improve year-round comfort for the occupants of an existing modest house in Mawson, a typical Canberra suburb. It deals with the art and science of *retrofitting — of improving an existing house and making it more sustainable.*

The house now captures the maximum of free, cheerful, warming sunshine in *all* habitable rooms — both north and south — by way of several innovative world-first items of reflective technology. It harvests and stores about 80 per cent of all the domestic water needs of two people and occasional visitors in two linked rainwater tanks (7200L).

The photovoltaic array generates 110 per cent of an average daily consumption of about 8kWh/day, ensuring a good financial return for the resident. To those who are concerned about the cost of making changes to their house, it has been estimated by one of our local real estate agents that for every dollar spent, on retrofitting, *two dollars* could easily be added to the asking price.

Each retrofitting aspect is described in the book, with suggestions about other ways of making savings for those who have the time, the energy, the desire and a few spare dollars — to help the environment.

From almost every point of view, retrofitting is a very beneficial activity.

It is a win-win-win situation for the environment, for our wallets (eventually) and for the physical and aesthetic amenity of our internal and external surroundings — (see results p **13**-2) — and, of increasing importance, it is very satisfying to know that it is helping to create a better environment in the future for our grandchildren.

2-5.2 The entry to the Mawson House, showing the overhead deciduous vine which is extremely functional in keeping the house cool in summer, yet helps to heat the house in winter.

It amply demonstrates our philosophy of wishing to walk *into* a garden rather than *onto* it. The daphne and star jasmine scents add a delightful sensory dimension in such an enclosed area.

Over 1.5 billion gallons of fuel are used each year by US truckers leaving their engines to idle overnight so they can keep the heating or air conditioning on.

Green Futures (Sept/Oct 2003)

Recognising retrofitting possibilities

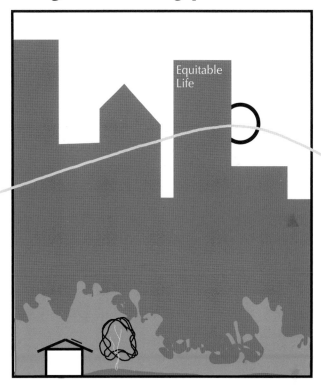

3-2   **Before you buy an existing house**

3-3   **Solar access**

Before you buy an existing house

This book started with the intention of helping owners to improve the comfort of their *existing* houses and to lower their consumption of fossil-fuelled energy. But, of course, the problem starts before that for those wishing to *buy* an existing house.

Will a *prospective* house be suitable for retrofitting?
An understanding of what is described in this book should forewarn you of *what to look for* if you are interested in helping the environment by retrofitting.

In buying an existing house it is more than likely that energy conservation and the utilisation of natural energies have not been considered other than token ceiling insulation, perhaps a token 'large' window on the north, and some mandatory insulation.

In reading this book you will see that there are many other aspects that could be considered if you are to get close to a comfortable low-energy house.

In looking around existing houses with the intention of buying, you should be aware of what has *not* been done to make the house comfortable in winter and summer and, equally importantly, what potential exists for rectification of the problems and the degree of expenditure involved.

In 2008, I and Professor John Sandeman compiled a five-page checklist to help readers select a greener, better house with lower running costs. The document was published by the ACT Minister for Planning. Download from: **www.natsoc.org.au**

Roofs

First, it would be safe to say that almost all existing domestic roofs have not been designed to accept these new technologies. This was excusable up to a few years ago, *but not now*. They have been designed down to a price and often to suit a prevailing fashion, but little thought, if any, has usually been given to the utilisation of natural energies — sun, wind, rain, etc.

Second, roof pitches have usually been determined by the material (tiles or metal decking), their capacity for waterproofing, and their appearance, rather than for the utilisation of solar technology.

House orientation (placing on the site in relation to natural attributes) is often ill-considered, making the placing of effective roof-absorbers difficult.

A typical, poorly oriented house such as sketched below will give some idea of how difficult it could be to place retrofitted hot water and photovoltaic panels on such a roof to obtain an effective return. The roof *pitch* (slope) is actually fairly good, enabling a 98% efficiency to be achieved when panels **A** and **C** are placed on the roof facing the viewer (approximately north). *(See chart p **16**-7 for efficiencies relative to orientation and tilt.)* **However, they would only provide about 2kWh/day.**

Array **B** *(facing east)*, although capable of being larger in area, would work at only 84% efficiency *(from chart)* and could perhaps contribute 2.4kWh/day, totalling about **4.4**kWh maximum generation per day — as against a probable consumption of perhaps 15–30kWh/ day, judging from the position and size of the house. **This would not be a very effective contribution unless the owners significantly reduced their consumption.**

In addition, the two windows on this north elevation would, due to the house being long and narrow, capture only a very small amount of winter heat from the sun. The large trees on the west would virtually mean that house would be in shade for most of the winter afternoon, with little penetration of warming sun.

A hot-water absorber placed at **D** (or on the long roof at **B**) would only be 84% efficient in absorbing radiant energy, and serious consideration would have to be given to a heat-pump system which relies on heat exchange from the air rather than solar radiation (p **4**-2).

The larger, western roof could well be too shaded by the existing tall trees in winter to place effective solar panels.

Several factors — proportions of site, poor orientation, unsuitable roofing design and large trees — will almost certainly result in large annual heating bills.

Knowledgeable purchasing will become increasingly vital when the energy crunch requires more thermally efficient house design.

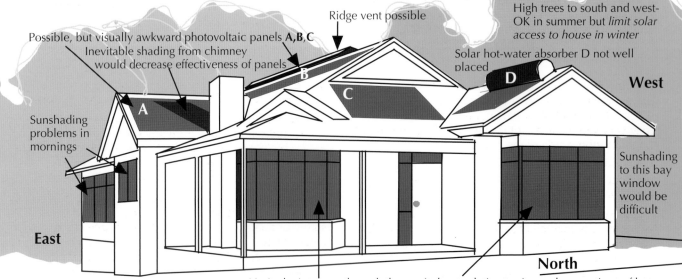

Ridge vent possible

High trees to south and west- OK in summer but *limit solar access to house in winter*

Possible, but visually awkward photovoltaic panels **A,B,C**
Inevitable shading from chimney would decrease effectiveness of panels

Solar hot-water absorber D not well placed

West

Sunshading problems in mornings

East

Sunshading to this bay window would be difficult

North

Limited winter sun through these windows relative to size and proportions of house

3-2.1   **This fairly typical house has a many-faceted roof which would make the location of *effective* photovoltaic panels very difficult. They would have to be split into small arrays, A, B and C which do not make them appear well integrated.**

Solar access – *is it possible?*

Solar access is a relatively new term in environmental design. It generally refers to *the degree of freedom that the sun has to shine on your land, and on the roof and walls of your house.*

A house without any trees or buildings around it would have total solar access, whereas the house shown in the photo *(3-3.1)* would have virtually zero solar access.

In wishing to modify your own house, or considering the purchase of an existing house, it is of critical importance to have some understanding of the amount of solar access you can expect.

The sun is a source of enormous beneficial energy which we do not utilise to the best advantage.

On a typical sunny day in Canberra the average house could be receiving about 400–500 kWh of solar energy per day, yet the consumption need for an average family in that house might only be around 2% of this freely available energy. What a waste!

There are problems of harnessing that energy, of course. In most cases it costs money to collect and store energy, but the efficiencies of receptive devices — eg. solar hot-water absorbers, and photovoltaics — are improving all the time. *It is now economically feasible* to incorporate these into our houses — as retrofitted items.

It is somewhat ironic, however, that after 200 years of planting trees to shade our houses and waiting for them to mature to a size where they can fulfil that function, we now have the technology to utilise these shaded roof areas to produce our hot water, electricity and daylight entry.

This shading problem will become a major issue in utilising solar energy in urban areas. W*e now have too many large trees close to our houses, yet we have no legislation to stop such ill-considered action.*

In particular, the problem of a *neighbour's* tall evergreen trees shading your roof can be a potential source of conflict and a legal can of worms.

Trees undoubtedly give us a lot of pleasure, but from a solar point of view the moving shade they cast can be a strong determinant of whether or not we even contemplate some retrofitting measures on our houses. Trees can make the difference between an efficient installation and not even starting.

In many retrofitting cases we will have to make some painful decisions — if we want to generate our own electricity from photovoltaic panels on our roof we may very well have to cut down some large eucalypts on the northern side of the house.

It is most unfortunate that the ACT government has now decreed that it is illegal to cut down or damage any 'significant' tree above a given size.

Such trees are capable of rendering any photovoltaic system totally inefficient and *not worth installing.* Each case will be reviewed on its merits when you apply for a 'Tree damaging activity' from Environment ACT.

There does not appear to be any legislation in Australia that gives a houseowner any right to solar access.

3-3.1 **This house has NO solar access and internal lights would be necessary during daylight hours. It is a romantic concept but quite unsustainable, gloomy and probably unhealthy.**

There is new legislation in the ACT to prevent new *buildings* from shadowing neighbours, but no mention has been made of the shading problem caused by *trees*. These must be considered if suburban houses and their occupants are to benefit from solar energy.

So the very first thing you should do is to evaluate the extent of your solar access by plotting the house to scale on your block of land, showing all trees on the northern side of the house between east and west which are growing above the gutter line or have the growing potential to do so. Also note any adjacent building if it it is capable of casting a sun shadow on the northern wall or the northern roof of your house.

(Ralph Phillip's book, Sunshine and Shade in Australasia, *would be useful on this issue: see p 16-4.)*

Plot the extent of the shadows every hour during a sunny mid-winter's day from any surrounding trees and/or buildings, as these shadows will help to determine the placing of any future solar device on your roof — or indeed whether you need bother at all.

This will give you the worst shading scenario, but it would be worth repeating the exercise around the spring or autumnal equinoxes. Make a note of the types of trees, and seek advice from a tree specialist as to its future growth potential and whether or not it can be topped without harming its growth or its form.

This is critical design data, serving as the basis of what is, and what is not, possible in modifying your house.

It has been estimated that to produce one litre of petrol would have required the organic growth of 23 tonnes of prehistoric plant material. Millions of years in production — used by a vehicle in less than an hour!

4

Free hot water

4-2   Solar hot-water heaters

4-3   Location of absorber panels

Solar hot-water heaters

Pioneering Australian technology — *ignored*

Solar hot-water heaters give the most effective return on investment, both financially and environmentally.

As heating water is often our largest consumption of energy, it is one of the mysteries of life that, with our sunny climate, solar heating is not mandatory for all Australian houses.

Good rebates are now available in all states.

The basic types of systems available

1 Tank on the roof, close-coupled to the absorber panels using a natural, thermo-syphon circulation between absorber panels and tank. *(This tank is badly placed in relation to the tree.)*

4-2.1 **Close-coupled tank and absorbers**

2 Panels on the roof with small circulating pump to a tank mounted in the roof or on the floor *or* panels on the roof with thermo-syphon circulation to a tank *in* the roof.

4-2.2 **Absorbers only, tank in the roof**

3 Heat-pump system with exchangers on the roof and a tank on the floor. It is claimed that the colour of the panels makes no difference to its efficiency.

4-2.3 **Heat exchangers, tank inside**

4 A compact fan-coil heat pump system which has no roof-mounted panels. It extracts its heat from the surrounding air, so should not be placed internally where this could produce uncomfortable temperatures. Compressor noise could be a problem indoors.

(3 and 4 are not strictly solar water heaters as they do not require direct solar gain.)

4-2.4 **Internal integrated HW unit**

4-2.5 **Evacuated tube collector with pumped connection to floor tank — pioneered in Australia, made overseas, and imported**

Selection of the model most suited to your house

This will depend upon:

1 The condition and age of your existing hot-water system. Tanks over 15 years old should be suspect, but it could be that it is only the sacrificial anode that needs replacing — check with your plumber before making any decision to replace.

2 Availability of suitable roof location, slope, orientation, and possible shading.

Roof *location* should be closer to the kitchen than to the bathroom (because of greater frequency of use) to reduce the amount of cold-water draw-off.

Roof *slope* of between 20º–40º would be fine, but the closer to your latitude angle, the better the insolation balance between winter and summer (35º in Canberra region). Panels could be tilted above the roof angle of course, but the ugliness increases pro rata. Avoid any odd angular positions — they can be *very* ugly.

Roof *orientation* (compass bearing or azimuth) should face between 30º east of north to 30º west of north for optimum efficiency. Beyond these limits efficiency falls off, and the cost/benefit analysis may become marginal.

The preferred location should have the least amount of *shading* from trees or buildings in the arc between 60º east of north to 60º west of north *(see 4-3.1)*. The sun is quite low in the sky outside these limits and the efficiency will be lower, partly due to highly reflective glass-top surfaces — evacuated tubes are better.

Obtain comparative quotes from the different suppliers who should advise on the following additional aspects:

1 Strength of roof structure *(tank on roof only, which can be very heavy when full of water)*.
2 Your demand for hot water *(size of family will determine the number of panels required)*.
3 The efficiency of the frost protection measures built into the system *(a good warranty is essential in the Canberra region)*.
4 Costs of new system *(and whether or not a new on-the-floor tank is really needed)*.

Location of absorber panels

Orientation of absorbers for maximum efficiency

It cannot be stressed enough to pick a roof position that receives the maximum amount of sun, avoiding shading from trees and nearby buildings. This may seem an obvious thing to say, but it is a surprising fact that several absorbers we have seen are shaded very severely during sunshine hours, making them much less efficient.

If other efficiency factors — such as angle of tilt or orientation — are not optimal *(see diag. below)*, a partially shaded position may well tip the scales against having solar hot-water absorbers in that location. If you are unsure about these factors it is as well to get some expert advice before you commit your money.

Remember that trees grow larger and if they are on your neighbour's land there could be future problems. Even trees up to 100 metres away could be a problem in the early morning or the late afternoon.

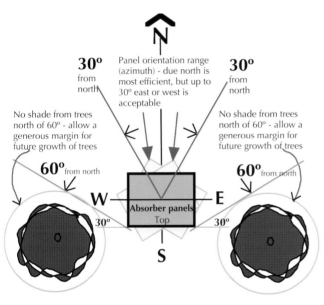

4-3.1 Range of absorber panel orientations and limits for trees or building shading on panels. Beyond ~60° from north the sun is at too low an altitude to be effective in winter, *but is still at a useful altitude in summer*. Make allowance for the actual orientation of the house which is probably not facing north exactly.

Aesthetic considerations

Opinions differ on the visual appearance of solar hot-water heaters on roofs which are part of the streetscape. *(See also Technoclutter p 15-7.)*

Suburban road design has not yet made allowance for the application of solar technology on roofs, and in a retrofitting situation we will not have very much choice due to the many limitations of existing conditions.

Tanks on the roof are ugly, obtrusive and irrational from a heat-loss point of view, unless painted black — which would only make them more obvious. They were an early, interim solution, and there are now better ways available.

Flat panels or evacuated tubes are visually acceptable if fixed parallel to an appropriate roof surface — but not if supported above the roof at an awkward angle.

Why did we choose a heat-pump water-heating unit for the Mawson house?

1 Our developer's house had a standard on-the-floor electric water-heating unit. It worked well, but consumed a lot of fossil-fuelled electricity. We then installed a small 20W circulating pump with sensors to control the pumping through some second-hand solar panels we were given for testing. They were laid on the 10° roof slope facing 15° west of north, but there were trees to the NW which gave some shadow in mid-afternoon above the 60° line. The unit functioned well in the warmer months and to a lesser extent in the colder months — and they were frost sensitive, despite the various precautions we took. We found we had to repair the absorbers virtually every winter due to frost damage.

2 For visual reasons we were not prepared to elevate new solar absorber panels to the ideal angle of 35°: on the only available roof space left after the photo-voltaic installation it would have looked really ugly.

3 The only position left was not a good one for a full day's insolation, being shaded by a large tree on a neighbour's block in mid-afternoon. Its efficiency would have been questionable.

4 We found that a Quantum heat-pump system could be installed for the same price and was not sensitive to its solar position or angle as it extracts its heat from the air — not the sun.

It uses a small amount of electricity (now provided by our photovoltaics), but significantly less than the standard water heater.

It was fitted to the south side of the house roof, and its colour was matched to the roof colour, making it virtually invisible.

It was the solution to the problem of our specific location, but all other things being equal we would have preferred absorber panels on the roof with a small circulating pump and a hot-water storage cylinder on the floor inside.

Environmental considerations

A major reason for the selection and use of a solar hot-water heater — beyond the fact that it saves the user money in the long run — is that its use will help the environment by reducing the amount of atmospheric pollution from the use of electricity by about 4 tonnes per year of CO_2. A solar hot-water heater could reduce your annual power bill for hot water by up to 75%. An instantaneous gas heater would be less polluting than electric heaters, but is better for low-consumption uses.

State and federal governments are now offering subsidies which reduce the cost of installing these solar hot-water heaters. They are also eligible for the creation of Renewable Energy Certificates (1 for each MWh saved = about $36) which can be cashed in to any energy retailer as part of their mandatory renewable energy target (MRET). You are allowed to accumulate them until you have an amount worth cashing in. However, RECs are now discounted at the time of sale of solar water heaters.

About 5–10% of household energy is used by appliances on standby.

Green Futures

5

Improving windows

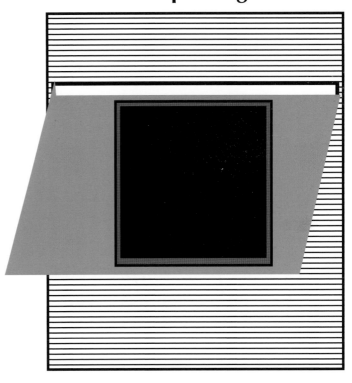

5-2   **Problems of fixed, northern eaves**

5-3   **Northern adjustable sunshades**

5-4   **Obtaining effective shade**

5-5   **Sunshades as bushfire radiation shields**

5-6   **Sunshades for east and west windows**

5-7   **Double glazing**

5-8   **Curtains and convection losses**

5-9   **Curtains and internal blinds**

5-10 **Natural daylighting for dark interiors**

Problems of fixed northern eaves

Most Australian houses have some form of fixed eaves, and numerous diagrams exist which specify suitable eaves projections to suit summer and winter mid-day sunshine *when facing north.* These diagrams are misleading if we are to take energy conservation into serious consideration in the colder climates such as Canberra: if the eaves do keep out the hot summer sun *they are inefficient in letting in the warming sunshine in winter because of the changing altitude of the sun at different times of the year.*

Since the advent of trusses and the elimination of brick lintels over windows, many windows are immediately under the eaves soffit lining, thus contributing to *winter shading* at the top of the glass which increases <u>heat losses</u> from the room during the day as well as at night.

To minimise this heat loss in winter requires us to minimise or eliminate this eaves shading *(see p 5-3).*

*(See also Solar Plotter 1 p **16**-8 to see how the sun's position changes during the year.*

Larger eaves

78°
mid-**summer**
noon

Fixed
cut off
point

32° mid-
winter
noon

55°
equinoxial
noon

**Better in summer
Worse in winter**

A

B

C

D

E   Early AM
& late PM

F   Heat loss areas
in cool months
during sunny
hours

Desirable
Warming noon
sun in cool
months

Undesirable
Entry of hot   Low angle
noon sun in   sun before
warmer months   & after noon

High density heat absorbing floor surface

5-2.1   Heat gain/heat loss areas of north facing window - large eaves designed to cut off noon mid-summer sun (**A**)

Advantages

- aesthetically more pleasing than a small eaves
- keeps out hot **noon** sun in Dec/Jan **only around noon** (**A**)

Disadvantages
- more costly in terms of extra roofing, extra soffit structure and lining
- still admits **undesirable** hot sun Oct - Mar and *before* and *after* noon (**B + C**)
- large areas of window are shaded on sunny winter days = creating heat **losses** instead of heat **gains** (**F**)
- excludes more daylight

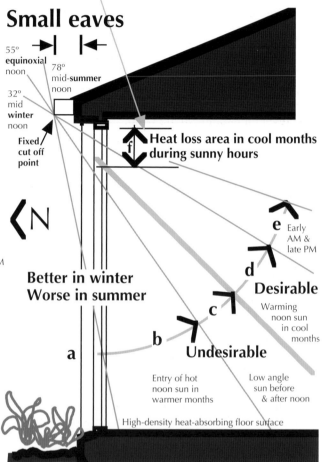

Small eaves

55°
equinoxial
noon

78°
mid-**summer**
noon

32°
mid
winter
noon

Fixed
cut off
point

〈N

f   Heat loss area in cool months
during sunny hours

**Better in winter
Worse in summer**

a

b

c

d   **Desirable**
Warming
noon sun
in cool
months

e   Early
AM &
late PM

Undesirable
Entry of hot   Low angle
noon sun in   sun before
warmer months   & after noon

High-density heat-absorbing floor surface

5-2.2   Heat gain/heat loss areas of north facing window — small eaves

Advantages
- reduces roofing cost
- admits ~**40%** more warming sun in cooler months
- reduces area of heat loss by about **70%** at top of window in cooler months compared to large eaves.
- admits maximum daylight

Disadvantages
- aesthetically unsatisfactory external appearance, unless shades are retrofitted *(see p 5-3 to 5-5)*
- admits about **60% more** undesirable sun in hot months, unless shades are retrofitted
- undesirable hot sun entry at **a** would be admitted for 3 weeks before and after 22 Dec *(summer solstice),*
- although heat loss area at **f** is smaller than for the large eaves example, it is still undesirable

It can only be concluded that, with a *moving* source of heat energy, a seasonally adjustable sun shade device combined with a small eaves is a much more satisfactory answer *(see p 5-3)*

Northern, adjustable sunshades

The need for *adjustable* sunshades

*(**Please note** -The comments on this sheet are **only** appropriate for windows facing within ~30° east or west of north)*

The Mawson house had an existing wooden pergola structure on north and south walls with battens on top which made the winter heat loss on the upper part of the window much worse — and a painting nightmare.

Some form of adjustable sunshading was required which was simple, cheap and only required minimum attention from the occupant.

The battens were removed and replaced with wooden frames covered with a relatively new shadecloth called Coolaroo which, due to its knitted (rather than woven) construction, enables it to keep out the hot sun and *refract* daylight through to the interiors.

The fabric enables the rain to fall through to keep the garden watered underneath, and it breathes sufficiently to prevent it flapping in the wind.

In autumn, when the hot days are finished, the panels are raised into a position ~45° above horizontal *(see diagram 5-3.1 above)* to allow all the warming sun to penetrate into the interior and warm it up for release and personal comfort in the evening — *if you have sufficient mass inside the house to take advantage of this heat transfer (see p **8**-3 for explanation of mass)*

Such a shade has been in use on this house for three years, and has proved to be extremely effective, cheap and attractive *(see diagrams this page)*

Spring and autumn days are the most difficult to shade as the sun can still be hot in early autumn and in late spring, but welcome cooler sun should be allowed to penetrate the house in early spring and late autumn. A compromise angle of 45° is about right during this period for the Canberra region.

The existing pergola on the Mawson house made it easy to fit the adjustable sunshades, but I recognise that not every house has such a convenient pergola.

From experience: The hinged, wooden-framed panels were very effective, but were rather heavy, and awkward to adjust from a stepladder. They also required repainting. I have replaced them with a large sheet of hemmed, eyeletted Coolaroo, which is less difficult to handle — and to maintain.

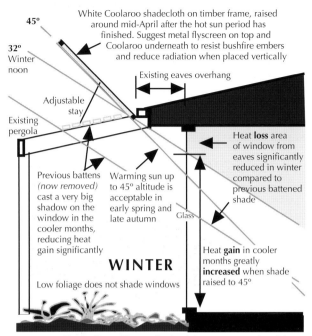

White Coolaroo shadecloth on timber frame, raised around mid-April after the hot sun period has finished. Suggest metal flyscreen on top and Coolaroo underneath to resist bushfire embers and reduce radiation when placed vertically

45°

32° Winter noon

Adjustable stay

Existing pergola

Existing eaves overhang

Previous battens *(now removed)* cast a very big shadow on the window in the cooler months, reducing heat gain significantly

Warming sun up to 45° altitude is acceptable in early spring and late autumn

Glass

Heat **loss** area of window from eaves significantly reduced in winter compared to previous battened shade

Heat **gain** in cooler months greatly **increased** when shade raised to 45°

WINTER

Low foliage does not shade windows

5-3.2 **Retrofitted adjustable sunshade giving more comfortable conditions during the colder months.**

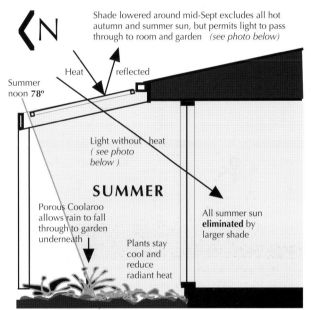

N

Shade lowered around mid-Sept excludes all hot autumn and summer sun, but permits light to pass through to room and garden *(see photo below)*

Heat reflected

Summer noon 78°

Light without heat *(see photo below)*

SUMMER

Porous Coolaroo allows rain to fall through to garden underneath

Plants stay cool and reduce radiant heat

All summer sun **eliminated** by larger shade

5-3.3 **Retrofitted adjustable sunshade giving more comfortable conditions during the hotter months.**

5-3.1 **Coolaroo sunshades in winter position, allowing maximum penetration of warming sun through the glass.**

5-3.4 **Northern Coolaroo sunshade in summer position, allowing light but no sun through the window. Compare to opaque canvas.**

Obtaining effective shade

The previous page showed the advantages to be gained in the use of simple, adjustable sunshades.

The use of the right shading material makes a significant difference to a shade's effectiveness; an opaque material is not, in my opinion, a good answer.

For over 200 years of Australian house design we have become conditioned to think that *shadow equals coolness*, and that dark interiors must automatically be cooler than *light* ones — an extension, perhaps, of seeking the shade of a tree on a hot sunny day.

But why should we suffer a dark, gloomy interior on a hot sunny day when we can enjoy coolness and light at the same time by using the benefits of materials technology?

In using the Coolaroo *white* fabric I discovered a very interesting side effect. It has the advantage of keeping out 95% of the heat (the infra red spectrum), but at the same time actually *enhancing daylight* penetration on blue sky days by its construction — which is not just a simple cross weave like other shadecloths, but a more three-dimensional, knitted type of construction which *refracts* the light

If you compare the light radiation from a clear blue sky with the light radiation coming through a sunlit white sheet of Coolaroo *(see 5-4.1),* you will see a *greatly intensified* transmission of white light. At a guess I would think it easily adds 50% to the quantity of light coming into the window — reducing any need to switch on the lights for reading.

We have found this quality to be quite delightful — compare it to the dark shadows and loss of view from the traditional roller awnings shown on the right.

Other types of blinds

There are other commercial ways of retrofitting shades to existing windows.These are usually roller or awning-type telescopic shades which use heavy duty, opaque canvas or plastic in either plain colours or striped.

These are much less effective:

1 Opaque materials create quite substantial shade, letting through very little light (or none at all), which makes the room inside rather dark.

2 Most awnings at an angle to the wall are not effective in keeping out hot low-angle sun in early morning or late afternoon. The awning should extend at least 500mm beyond both sides of the window, depending on its orientation *(see p 5-4.2 below).*

3 They are not 'set and forget' systems, requiring adjustment at different times of the day for real effectiveness.

4 If a near-vertical canvas blind is used which is close to a hinged window it would reduce its opening capacity and (including sliding sashes) its ventilating effectiveness.

5 They need to be professionally fitted, and cost more.

6 All blinds of this kind obscure the view to some degree, *which defeats the purpose of having a window.*

In travelling around Canberra looking for examples, I have been amazed at the large number of inappropriately installed sunblinds where occupiers are missing out on a lot of warming sunshine and using much more electricity, both of which are contrary to sound ecological design principles — and detract from the achievement of pleasant living conditions.

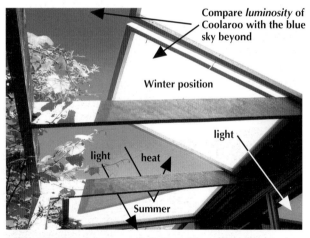

5- 4.1 **Winter and summer sunshade positions with white Coolaroo - the antithesis of opaque canvas awning blinds** *(shown at right).*

'Coolaroo'

This white *knitted* fabric is a significant advance on canvas and is available in hardware shops. Colours are available, but they are not as effective as white.

Made of long-life High Density Polyethylene (HDPE), It is porous, letting rain through to gardens below, and does not flap in the wind.

Coolaroo is suitable for use as awning blinds, but I found the awning manufacturers in Canberra would not consider anything but their own syndicated materials — a good solution stymied because of a seemingly restrictive trade practice.

5- 4.2 **The usual type of canvas blind which keeps out the view and the light as well as the sun is not the best of solutions.**

Both of these photos were taken in <u>mid-winter</u>!

5- 4.3 **Canvas awning blinds + venetians + curtains certainly begs the question — why have windows?**

Sunshades as bushfire radiation shields

Bushfire precautions

The 18 January 2003 bushfire which burnt out some 500 homes in the Canberra suburbs should cause architects and builders to reconsider their approach to window design.

The detailed results of an enquiry are still awaited, but it would seem that radiation from the intense firestorm resulted in either cracking of the glass, allowing entry of more oxygen to any internal fire, or the radiation passing through the glass was able to create volatile gases from various surface finishes.

Either way, intense radiation can create problems, so it would be circumspect for the serious retrofitter to consider some means of protection for their existing windows.

There is one question, however, which defies an answer — how far does one go to protect windows for an event which may not even happen again ? What is reasonable in these circumstances? How big a tail is needed to wag a dog?

Several devices are now on the market, including some that have appeared in the aftermath of this fire.

If they could have an *interim* use — such as burglar retardants, closing up for holidays, etc — there would be more of an incentive to install them.

The commonly used canvas roller awning would give a little protection, but only for as long as the canvas remained intact. Either direct flame or radiation could incinerate canvas or plastic very quickly, so this is not a satisfactory solution.

European wooden shutters hinged on each side of the window could be a delaying measure for small windows, but could be expensive for large sliding doors and fixed panels — and not fireproof.

The secret would seem to lie in the devices having a multiple use so that they are useful for daily living — such as light or heat control — and can quickly be turned into radiation screens during an emergency.

Joan Webster, in her excellent book, *The Complete Bushfire Safety Book (see p 16-4 for details)*, states that *metal* flywire 'has long been known to stop flying embers, reduce heat stress on windows by 27% and delays cracking of glass from radiant heat.'

Its biggest advantage is that it is cheap and is easily installed if adequately framed, and there is somewhere to store the frames when not in use. Considering the low frequency of bushfires in suburban areas the storage problem could be difficult for some. What is wanted is a means of having it permanently on hand *with no storage requirements* so that it is *immediately available* in the case of imminent fire.

An extension of the Coolaroo sunshade system *(see pp **5**-3 and **5**-4)* with a metal flyscreen addition on the upper surface may solve the problem. By dropping the frame down to a vertical position in a bushfire it then protects a half-height window, and with the addition of a hinged flyscreened frame it could then protect a full-height window *(see diagram **5**-5.2)*.

Although not a 100% protection device it has several advantages and could well make the difference between disaster and survival.

Experiments with my existing sunshades have shown that the addition of a copper flyscreen sheet results in only a small loss of daylight when in the summer position. The Coolaroo should then be placed on the inside of the frame.

The additional hinged screen would only be needed in case of a full-height window, and could be hinged to the bottom of the main sunshade. It would only need to be sheeted with the flyscreen material as it is a fire-radiation screen rather than a sunshade.

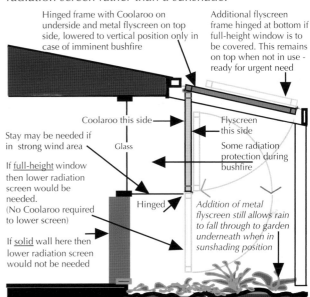

Hinged frame with Coolaroo on underside and metal flyscreen on top side, lowered to vertical position only in case of imminent bushfire

Additional flyscreen frame hinged at bottom if full-height window is to be covered. This remains on top when not in use - ready for urgent need

Coolaroo this side

Flyscreen this side

Stay may be needed if in strong wind area

Glass

Some radiation protection during bushfire

If <u>full-height</u> window then lower radiation screen would be needed.
(No Coolaroo required to lower screen)

Hinged

Addition of metal flyscreen still allows rain to fall through to garden underneath when in sunshading position

If <u>solid</u> wall here then lower radiation screen would not be needed

5-5.2 **Retrofitted adjustable sunshade/radiation screen in place when bushfire is imminent. Storage of screen is no problem.**

5-5.2 **Prototype double fire screen in lowered position, protecting full window height. Nearest sunshade is in winter position.**

Sunshades for east and west windows

East- and west-facing windows normally require different treatment from northern windows because of the lower angles of the sun in the early morning and late afternoon. There can be exceptions, however.

The usual conventional answer is to install vertical internal blinds or external canvas awning blinds which open to a low level.

In both cases they usually obscure the view and significantly reduce the light levels inside as well, which defeats the purpose of having a window in that situation *(see section on blinds p **5-4**)*.

In addition, the use of vertical blinds or curtains *inside* the house is less effective because the sun's heat has *already entered* the interior, and convected heat from the blind or curtains heats up the room space.

In our Mawson house we were not prepared to sacrifice a lovely easterly view of a bush reserve, or daylight quality, so we compromised with a larger horizontal Coolaroo shade at the window head level.

The compromise is that only a little early-morning summer sun with low heat intensity penetrates the window, and it is filtered by some tall trees. By mid-morning the sun has become hotter and the shade becomes fully effective because of an extended overhang to the northern end of the shade. By 1.00pm the sun has gone from that wall *(see diagram 5-6.1)*.

In autumn, winter and spring the early-morning sun is highly desirable, penetrating right into the house. It is filtered by the trees, with very little warmth to it, but with a lot of cheerfulness. The shade does not block any of this, but does exclude almost all of the hotter sun in late morning in early autumn and late spring.

The shade is hinged at the wall and suspended by wires from the roof, and can be raised to a mid-winter position, which permits a bit more mid-morning sun.

As with the similar shades on the northern side of the house, the white Coolaroo fabric allows the light to penetrate the room — in fact, we believe it even *increases* the quantity of light when the shade is sunlit because its knitted construction tends to refract the visible component of sunlight. This is quite an interesting and seemingly unrecognised property of the material.

Being similar to the shades on the northern wall, this gives a good sense of unity to the house.

The January 2003 firestorm has made us more aware of the need to protect our windows from the severe radiant heat that can penetrate glass and start internal fires *(see comments p **5-5** on this important requirement)*.

When modifed with the metal flywire on top *(see construction note opposite)*, the frame will be lowered into a vertical position in front of the glass should a bushfire threaten, there being quite a lot of bush on the eastern side of the house.

I believe this type of shade in this position can be very satisfactory and conventional wisdom is not always the right answer. Be prepared to think your problem through and come up with a different and better solution to suit your particular circumstances.

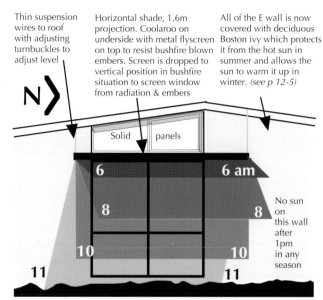

Thin suspension wires to roof with adjusting turnbuckles to adjust level

Horizontal shade, 1.6m projection. Coolaroo on underside with metal flyscreen on top to resist bushfire blown embers. Screen is dropped to vertical position in bushfire situation to screen window from radiation & embers

All of the E wall is now covered with deciduous Boston ivy which protects it from the hot sun in summer and allows the sun to warm it up in winter. *(see p 12-5)*

No sun on this wall after 1pm in any season

5-6.1 Mid-summer (22 Dec.) sunshade shadows on NE window.

5-6.2 Sun in the late morning (equinox). Note the very pleasant diffused quality of the light under the shade.

Construction and performance

This shade is quite large — about 3m x 1.5m — and was originally in timber, designed to be raised up at an angle in winter, and lowered to a vertical position in front of the window in the event of a bushfire (we have a eucalypt reserve on that side). Neither activity has been necessary so far and, as the timber frame needed too much maintenance, it was re-made in extruded aluminium sections (70mm x 20mm) with a flyscreen groove, which made the fixing of the Coolaroo very easy.

The extra embodied energy in the aluminium has been more than justified by the elimination of maintenance, due to the powder-coated surface on the aluminium.

The shade has been very successful in keeping about 95% of the hot summer sun out, letting in all of the cool, lower-angle sun around the equinoxes, and enabling the necessary daylight and beautiful views to be enjoyed. What more could be asked?

Double glazing

In the UK, most houses are now double glazed, and many of them also have central heating (now renamed as hydronic heating). Given the UK climate, with its long, cold winters, it certainly pays to prevent heat loss through windows, and that is why double glazing has become so popular. Their window sizes also tend to be a little smaller than ours and consequently the total cost is proportionately smaller.

The position in the Australian cool temperate zones, such as the ACT and Tasmania, is not quite as extreme as in the UK. Our cool season is not quite as long, and it is not so wet and miserable, but we do have greater daily temperature fluctuations and more abundant, cheery sunshine. All of this adds up to the fact that the effectiveness of double glazing is not so obvious as in the UK.

Nevertheless, while double glazing can be appropriate here, it should be borne in mind that, although it does slightly reduce heat intake from outside in summer, it is mainly effective in reducing heat *loss* from house interiors.

Glass has the wonderful property of admitting almost all of the short-wave radiation from the sun; but it is also very effective at blocking the escape of long-wave radiation from house interiors and furnishings after they have been heated by the sun.

To reduce *outward* radiation two sheets are better than one, particularly when they are separated with sealed edges and an inert gas between them, which reduces convective losses. They are even better with a low E-coating *(see below)*.

Heat losses occur because the inner glass will be at room temperature and the outer sheet at outdoor temperature — ideal for establishing convection currents, which convey the heat outwards. The size of the gap between the sheets is critical to this heat transfer: 19mm is regarded as ideal, and the transfer becomes less efficient as the gap gets smaller or larger.

Double-glazed units have to be measured precisely for specific window openings — and they are not cheap. There are several forms of double glazing with varying degrees of efficiency; it would seem that you get what you pay for.

The science of double-glazed units can get very technical. As a book could be written on this topic alone, you should undertake further reading or seek advice before you try to decide whether or not to install double glazing. The following aspects should be considered:

1 The ratio of window area to the external wall area of the room: the larger the glazed area the more effective (and expensive) the double glazing will be.

2 How well the other walls are insulated.

3 Expected temperatures indoors and out.

4 Length of the heating season within which the double glazing would be effective.

5 Cost of double glazing and its anticipated payback period, expected reduction in heating and cooling bills, etc.

6 Heated rooms v unheated. North v south?

Argon- or nitrogen-filled sealed double-glazing units are much more expensive than single glazing, particularly as we tend to have larger glazed areas than in the UK.

A cheaper way, but one that is not quite as effective, is to install a second sheet of glass if the window framing has an appropriate rebate. Stegbar windows, which are common in Canberra, offer this possibility. Despite its reduced effectiveness compared to sealed units (due to the large gap), we believe that, mainly because of its lower cost, this is worth doing.

If you feel you can handle glass, it is possible to DIY; but this requires careful, accurate measuring and documentation to ensure no mistakes or breakages, which immediately start minimising the savings.

Rather than fussing with mitred wooden beading to hold the sheets in, we made small clear acrylic blocks, about 10x10x4mm, with a small hole in the middle to take a brad. Three cubes to each side of glass (nine per pane) and soft foam draughtstripping in the rebate ensured a neat seal with minimum work.

It is important to eliminate condensation in the space between, and this is easy to do with one small plastic container containing silica gel crystals (you often get little packets of these crystals in your bottles of pills from the chemist). These absorb any movement of moisture content in the trapped air, preventing it condensing on the internal glass surfaces. We have had no hint of condensation over the last four years.

A further advantage of double glazing is its ability to reduce the transmission of external noise, but the use of opening sashes will completely nullify this benefit. Don't rely on double glazing for soundproofing if you like open windows.

A third method is called Winter Windows, consisting of a thin film of clear plastic press-fixed with double-sided adhesive tape to the rebate in the window frame, and then stretched and shrunk taut by the gentle application of a hair-drier. The film is virtually invisible, an easy DIY job, and a very low-cost solution.

The latter two methods rely on keeping the warm interior air away from the cold external sheet of glass, and are reasonably effective in doing this. However, because of the large gap, they do not completely prevent convection currents being set up between the sheets.

If a cost/benefit analysis were worked out I feel sure that Winter Windows would win hands down, but they are not child or dog proof!

Low E-glass
This is a good technological development which reduces heat loss through glass by a special coating on the external side of the internal glass of a sealed, double-glazing unit. This coating reflects back into the interior the long-wave heat energy from the furnishings and internal stored mass while still allowing the sun's short-wave energy to enter the house from outside during the sunshine hours.

The low-E coating can be either soft or hard — the soft one is only suitable for use within a double-glazed unit. Manufacturers do not recommend its use as single glazing, as its effectiveness results in increased condensation and its soft coating can be damaged.

Curtains and convection losses

Internal window coverings perform several functions in making a house more comfortable to live in.

Curtains are probably the most popular, by reason of their visual softness and convenience in transforming a rather cold, black hole in the wall at night time into something visually warmer and more private.

Curtains also provide a very effective means of reducing heat loss at night and, to a lesser degree, radiant heat gain during sunny days.

Their very nature makes them less than fully efficient, having difficult edges all around which leak air, enabling heat loss by convection currents to take place. The biggest loss is due to the cold sheet of glass cooling down the adjacent air, causing it to fall by its increase in density, thus causing a partial vacuum which sucks in warmer air from the higher part of the room. This sets up a convection current with its outlet at the floor level and its inlet around the pelmet area.

This simple physical principle is responsible for a large proportion of the heat loss from a room.

A test with a smoking incense stick at night when the room is warm and the curtains are closed will give a good indication of the draught intensity. Allow the air currents to stabilise by avoiding too much body movement — the currents are very delicate and easily disturbed. The use of an indoor/outdoor thermometer will also give you some idea of the temperature difference between the draught and the room in general.

The first improvement must essentially be to make the curtain fabric airtight, otherwise no amount of sealing around the edges (see later) will be effective.

Lightweight artificial fibres or loosely woven see-through fabrics are the least effective in preventing heat loss. Tightly woven, dense, woollen/cotton fabrics will provide better resistance to the *lateral* passage of warm air toward the colder window glass.

Over the last few decades some excellent linings have become available which are virtually *airtight* and light in colour. This helps to limit their ability to absorb the sun's heat which has penetrated the glass.

If there is an indication of downdraft, try the following edge treatments:

A common solution with full-height curtains is to place one, or preferably two, 'sausages' — sand-filled cylinders of soft plastic with a cloth covering, say about 75mm diameter — against the curtain hem (see diagram *5-8.4*). This helps to retain the air pocket, reducing the outflow of cold, dense air.

The usual commercial door 'sausage' may not be adequate as the diameter would need to be enough to cover the folds in the cloth — and it is probably not long enough anyway.

Sealing the vertical edges with Velcro strips will further increase the containment effect (see 5-8.3). It would need to be *sewn* to the curtain edge as the adhesive is not effective in sticking to fabric. This method has the advantage of not needing daily adjustment, but the pull cords at the end would need to be left outside the closure.

If the sides and bottom are well sealed it may not be necessary to seal the top edge of the curtains, but an incense test at the hem should show if there is still a downward air movement.

If there is still some air movement *(which equates to heat loss)* there will be a need to restrict air entry at the top of the curtains. Pelmets are the most usual answer, but due to the nature of gathered or pleated curtain tops they are not very effective. A better arrangement would be to seal the top entry of warm air near the curtain track — either by thick cardboard or by a soft foam strip. *(See 5-8.1.)*

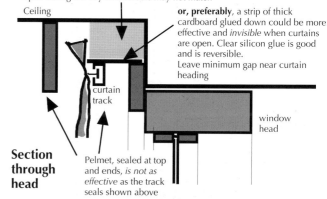

A long strip of soft foam plastic could seal this gap to prevent convection losses - it should be as close to the curtains as possible. A neat job is required as the face is visible when the curtains are open during the day and colours may not match

or, preferably, a strip of thick cardboard glued down could be more effective and *invisible* when curtains are open. Clear silicon glue is good and is reversible.
Leave minimum gap near curtain heading

Ceiling

curtain track

window head

Section through head

Pelmet, sealed at top and ends, *is not as effective* as the track seals shown above

5-8.1 **Ways of reducing warm-air entry at the top of curtains**

Section through curtain track

Continuous angle strip

Why can't a curtain track manufacturer make a sealed track?
It would be more effective than a pelmet in stopping convection

5-8.2 **A suggestion to curtain-track manufacturers**

NOTE: a manufacturer has taken on the challenge, and a section is now available.

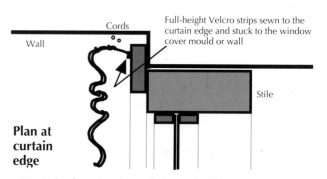

Cords

Wall

Full-height Velcro strips sewn to the curtain edge and stuck to the window cover mould or wall

Stile

Plan at curtain edge

5-8.3 **A simple seal at the vertical curtain edges**

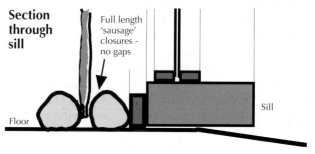

Section through sill

Full length 'sausage' closures - no gaps

Floor

Sill

5-8.4 **Sealing the bottom edge of the curtain**

Internal blinds and summer heat gain

Half-height windows and winter heat losses

The same techniques can be used to reduce downdraught as shown on p **5**-8, except for the sill detail.

If the head and sides are sealed as fully as possible, and the centre overlap has some Velcro pieces to hold the curtain material in tight contact — particularly at the top half of the curtain — it should prevent a convection current from establishing itself between the curtain and the glass.

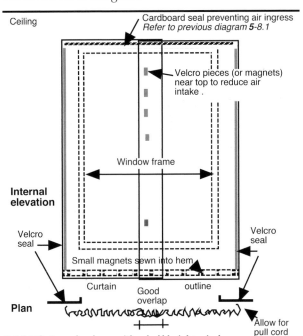

5-9.1 **What can be done with a half-height window to reduce convection downdraught**

There is a distinct possibility that a convection current will establish itself at the window-sill level. This is a difficult edge to seal, due to the gathered curtain material, but sewing small, strong magnets into the hem with a corresponding steel strip fixed to the wall may make a good-enough seal.

A further option is to fit a winter window film or go to the expense of installing double glazing, either of which should significantly reduce any heat loss.

Hinged, solid, internal insulated shutters would need to have sealed edges to be effective, and should be designed so as not to interfere with any curtains which cover them.

Internal blinds and summer heat gain

It is important to understand that incoming solar heat is short-wave radiation, which easily passes through the glass and heats up the internal air and furnishings. This internal heat is re-radiated back to the window as long-wave radiation, which is largely blocked by the glass. This is why greenhouses heat up.

Prevention of heat gain in summer by *internal* blinds and curtains is rather futile in that the radiation has *already gained entry* into the room and cannot escape. Only blinds which are *reflective* on their external surface have any real chance of reducing this problem by reflecting the short-wave radiation back through the glass (see **5**-9.2).

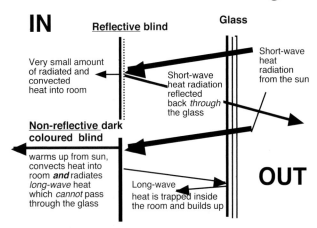

5-9.2 **Why reflective blinds work and non-reflective do not**

A few common types of internal blind

Pull-down roller blinds The old brown Holland material cuts out the daylight (and the view) and serves as an absorber of the radiant heat, becoming a radiator in its own right. The use of white-translucent fabric improves the situation by increasing the reflectivity and transmitting the daylight.

Tinted, transparent-film roller blinds will reduce the glare and give a coloured view, but the darker tint will absorb some heat and the long-wave re-radiated heat is still on the inside of the glass and can't get out.

The recently introduced *reflective* films, however, can be more effective, reflecting *short-wave* radiation which can escape through the glass (see **5**-9.2).

The roller blind gives a good degree of flexibility, as the height of the blind can be adjusted very easily. From a heat *loss* point of view they have little value unless the top and side edges are sealed.

Drop-down accordion blinds Using a patented Verosol accordion-pleated fabric, which is reflective on the outside face, these blinds can be effective in reflecting the short-wave radiation back through the glass.

Although the air space within the horizontal accordion pleats is useful in limiting heat transmission either way, the open ends could reduce their insulating value.

Vertical-strip, pull-aside, adjustable-angle blinds Their main value is in reducing direct solar transmisssion. If the material has a reflective external face, some advantage will be gained, but the variable angle of the strips reduces the efficiency due to the increasing angle of incidence on the glass.

Venetian blinds An ingenious device for *controlling light quality*, they do little to reduce heat gain or loss.

Roman blinds These have somewhat better insulating properties, but still have the problem of sealing the edges adequately. White material is to be preferred to increase their reflectivity. Dark colours will increase their heat absorbency. They are bulky when not covering the window, and do not have the visual character or 'warmth' of gathered curtains.

Preventing solar heat gain is more effectively done by external shading as any absorbed heat remains outside.

Natural daylighting for dark interiors

Although simple roof lights have been mentioned as a combined feature in the section on ceiling ventilation (see p **10**-3), there are other ways in which natural light can be obtained in dark corners of the house — which helps to reduce the use of electricity.

A weakness of roof lights in the past has been that they admitted the sun's heat fairly readily. New designs and materials have helped to reduce this tendency; but in the case of uncoupled solutions (roof lights *separate* from ceiling lights, e.g. transparent roof tiles), good roof-space ventilation would help to resolve that problem.

Clear glass or acrylic tiles (see **5**-10.1) have been available for many years, and are an unobtrusive and waterproof way of letting light into the roof space and through ceiling lights to the interior of the house.

They are very easy to insert in place of the terracotta or cement tiles, and they require no flashing, but it would be wise to take a sample tile with you when buying them, just to make sure they have the same profile.

However, if there are more than three or four tiles to be inserted, some sort of heat shield may need to be fitted. White Coolaroo stapled to the battens underneath would be an unobtrusive way of reducing the amount of heat penetrating to the ceiling lights. It would reduce the amount of light by a small amount, but not significantly.

An exciting development is the use of LEDs (light-emitting diodes), which consume far less power than traditional lights, used as ceiling-light panels powered by a fibre-optic cable connection to a parabolic solar collector on the roof. LEDs are non-toxic and have a very long life, high luminosity, and less heat — the ideal light in certain circumstances. Location can be very flexible.

Alternatively, at roof level an acrylic UV-stabilised dome light (see **5**-10.3) can be used with a reflective light shaft below. The dome light can be either clear or opal, the latter slightly reducing the amount of light passing through. An internal heat flap can also be fixed.

Another light-transference device is the Solatube (the original Australian invention), which has a clear acrylic hemisphere at roof level, with a round, reflective light shaft which is flexible enough to be placed in awkward positions. However, some light loss is likely when roof light and ceiling light are too displaced laterally. Dust can also collect on the crinkly inner sides of the tube, reducing its efficiency over the years.

The easiest solution for a roof light in a corrugated-steel roof is to cut a hole the size you want and insert a piece of clear acrylic or polycarbonate of the same profile with plenty of overlap all round (see **10**-3.1 and **10**-4.1). A frame of stretched white Coolaroo on top will effectively keep the heat out in summer.

Acrylic light-catching devices are not fire resisting and could facilitate the entry of glowing embers in a serious fire. Some form of metal flyscreening separated from the acrylic surface would be essential, but there would be a small loss of light.

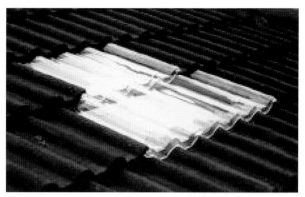

5-10.1 **Clear acrylic or glass tiles can be used in lieu of the usual terracotta tiles to admit light into the roof space**

5-10.2 **LED lights powered by fibre-optic cable from a solar roof collector**
<www.opticfibrelighting.com.au/contact-us.html>

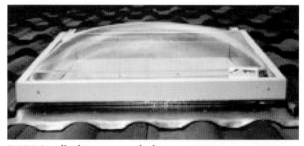

5-10.3 **Acrylic dome** <www.skydome.com.au>

5-10.4 **The original Australian Solatube** <www.solatube.com.au>

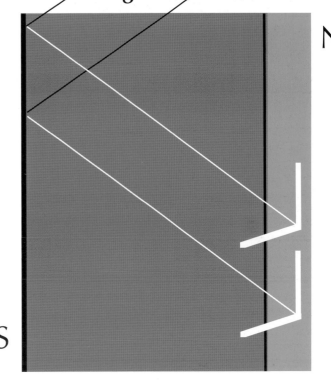

6

Using wasted sunshine

6-2   **Fixed southern reflectors**

6-3   **Geometry of fixed southern reflectors**

6-4   **Reflector design considerations**

6-5   **Combined reflector/photovoltaics panel**

6-6   **A reflector project**

6-7   **Reflecting heliostat**

6-8   **Reflecting heliostat**

Fixed southern reflectors

In 1997 I realised that a lot of sun was available on the *southern* side of the house which was only being utilised by the garden.

A simple test with a mirror showed that the sun's heat and psychologically desirable sunshine could easily be reflected into the *southern* rooms.

The 10° pitch of the roof enabled the sun to rise over the ridge at a relatively early hour, giving a good number of useful sunshine hours during the day.

Polished stainless steel panels are readily available from manufacturers of sinks and a trial panel of 1m² showed the enormous benefits to be gained.

The trial encouraged me to install three 1m x 1m panels fixed to the existing pergola outside our south-facing bedroom. Now, for seven months of the year, they reflect very welcome sunshine into the room.

These have never been touched since the day they were erected in 1997, and have continued to provide 'free' heat and sunshine at absolutely no operating cost. We now have a dark blue bed cover which helps to warm the bed throughout the day. The bedroom never receives any fossil-fuelled heat in winter.

The reflectors are 1.9m away from the window and *automatically* correct the position of the reflection without the need for any mechanism — as the sun gets higher in the sky (and hotter) in early spring the reflections gradually retreat *outside* the window.

In design terminology this is certainly an elegant solution — costing *nothing* to operate, and requiring *no* adjustment nor any maintenance by the occupier.

By mid-April the weather becomes cooler and the sun starts to make an effective contribution to the *psychological* and *actual* warming of the bedroom, and does so right throughout winter until early autumn.

The reflections, of course, move sideways and vertically, as does the sun during the day, so to obtain maximum benefit the reflectors need to be wider than the window to reflect the early-morning and the late-afternoon sun *(see diagram 6-2.2 opposite)*.

One interesting by-product has been that the panels are almost invisible, reflecting not only the sun but the surrounding sky, clouds and trees, which makes the panels merge into the background. They are polished on the reverse side also, so that their partial invisibility works both ways.

A cost/benefit analysis shows that this technique is simple and cheap, and a 'new' form of solar technology which can utilise otherwise 'wasted' sunshine to provide heat and cheerfulness into *south*-facing rooms of an *existing* house. It is estimated that it reflects 1.13MWh of heat into the room over the heating season.*(See results on p 13-3.)*

It is not a panacea for *all* southern windows, as a careful evaluation of the solar geometry has to be undertaken to establish the optimum extent of the panels and their aesthetic implications.

We do have a problem with growing trees on neighbour's land and also on an adjacent reserve — a problem which will have to be faced in the future.

Life wasn't meant to be *that* easy.

Stainless steel reflectors fixed to pergola
(outlined for better visibility)

South facing bedroom window
(Double glazed)

6-2.1   **Internal sunshine in main bedroom at 1pm,** *early* **winter.** In *mid*-winter the whole bed is sunlit and quite warm.

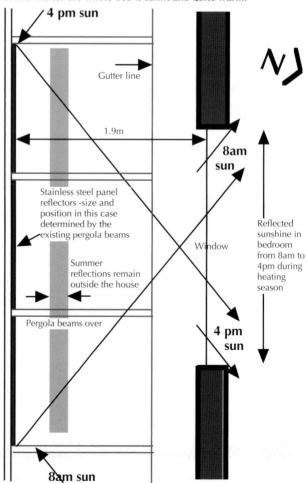

6-2.2   **Plan of window /reflector relationship.**

Geometry of fixed southern reflectors

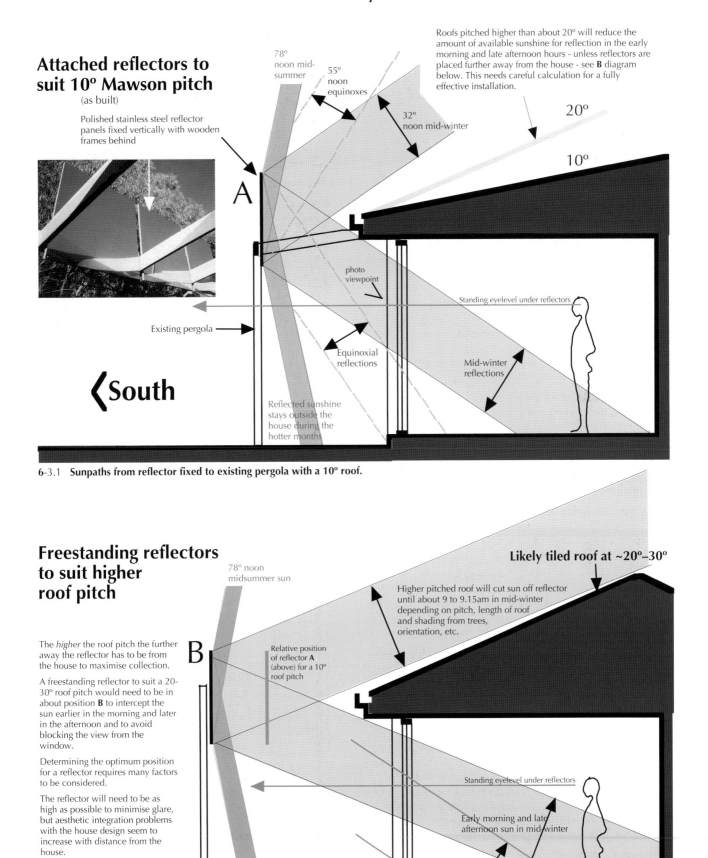

Attached reflectors to suit 10° Mawson pitch
(as built)

Polished stainless steel reflector panels fixed vertically with wooden frames behind

A

South

Existing pergola

photo viewpoint

Standing eyelevel under reflectors

78° noon mid-summer

55° noon equinoxes

32° noon mid-winter

Roofs pitched higher than about 20° will reduce the amount of available sunshine for reflection in the early morning and late afternoon hours - unless reflectors are placed further away from the house - see **B** diagram below. This needs careful calculation for a fully effective installation.

20°

10°

Equinoxial reflections

Mid-winter reflections

Reflected sunshine stays outside the house during the hotter months

6-3.1 **Sunpaths from reflector fixed to existing pergola with a 10° roof.**

Freestanding reflectors to suit higher roof pitch

The *higher* the roof pitch the further away the reflector has to be from the house to maximise collection.

A freestanding reflector to suit a 20-30° roof pitch would need to be in about position **B** to intercept the sun earlier in the morning and later in the afternoon and to avoid blocking the view from the window.

Determining the optimum position for a reflector requires many factors to be considered.

The reflector will need to be as high as possible to minimise glare, but aesthetic integration problems with the house design seem to increase with distance from the house.

78° noon midsummer sun

B

Relative position of reflector A (above) for a 10° roof pitch

Likely tiled roof at ~20°–30°

Higher pitched roof will cut sun off reflector until about 9 to 9.15am in mid-winter depending on pitch, length of roof and shading from trees, orientation, etc.

Standing eyelevel under reflectors

Early morning and late afternoon sun in mid-winter

Noon mid-winter sun

Reflected sunshine stays outside the house during the hotter months

6-3.2 **Sunpaths from reflector adjacent to a tiled roof of about 20–30° pitch. Note that the further away the reflector is from the house the more the reflection will move laterally across the window, so a wider reflector may be advisable.**

Reflector design considerations

Design steps

1 Determine which south-facing rooms could benefit from reflectors. Windows facing up to 30° east or west of south can still benefit, but with decreasing efficiency the further they are away from due south.

2 Low-pitched roofs under about 20° are better. Over 20° becomes more inefficient due to the roof cutting off the low-angle winter sun, although the higher sun in late autumn and early spring (about 20° to 40°) is still very desirable insolation.

3 Wide windows (>2m) are more suitable than narrow windows (<1m) because of the lateral movement of the sun during the day.

4 Full-height windows benefit more than half-height windows, allowing reflections below eye level.

5 A pergola outside the window about 2m away from the wall will be a big advantage. If there is none, some form of structure will be needed to fix the panels to. Don't forget wind stresses.

   The further away from the wall the reflectors are, the greater the lateral movement of the reflection, and the less time there will be for effective sunlight penetration into the room. Over about 3m from the window might be regarded as a limit. There will also be more glare evident when reflections become closer to horizontal.

6 It is important to draw a cross section of the roof and the room to scale — about 1:50 (similar to drawing **6**-3.1) — so that both the incoming and the reflected rays of the sun can be plotted, and the optimum height of the reflectors determined.

7 You will also need to draw a plan of the room, to scale with the reflectors, showing your determined distance from the window (see drawing **6**-2.2).

   This stage will determine any lateral displacement from the centre of the window to accommodate any variation of aspect away from due south. If the window is due south, the reflectors should be symmetrical with the window.

   If the window is facing more to the east, and you like morning sun in the window, place the reflectors to the east of centre — and vice versa.

   Your preferences come into play here, but it may well be that existing pergola beams may determine the position of the reflectors — as in my case.

   If you wish to take advantage of early-morning and late-afternoon sun (and the roof ridge enables you to do so), it will be necessary to make the width of the reflectors wider than the width of the window.

8 At this stage, if not before, it would be wise to find out who can supply you with cut sheets of polished stainless steel and what thicknesses.

   My sheets were 0.7mm thick, and I would not recommend anything thinner unless it is stiffened at the back to prevent wind movement, which creates disturbing visual reflections in the room. My panels were approximately 1m square, fixed to a wooden frame about 75mm x 20mm, lapped, glued and screwed at each corner — and well well painted. Intermediate framing would be necessary if the metal is any thinner than 0.7mm.

The panels are screwed to the wooden framing with small, binding head-plated screws in holes. This allows expansion movement of the panel, which gets rather hot during the day. If there is no expansion room the panels will almost certainly buckle in the heat and distort the reflected image.

9 The wooden frames should be bolted or coach-screwed to the pergola or other support very firmly, as wind pressure can be quite severe. The attachment method shown in **6**-4.1 *(below)* has proved suitable over five years, showing no failure signs.

Conclusions

These fixed reflectors are probably the most cost-effective of all the solar devices and certainly the easiest to construct. Cost on a DIY basis was under $250, but they have contributed well over 1MWh of heat energy over a six-month heating period.

They have functioned most effectively, with absolutely no adjustment or maintenance having been needed.

They have provided excellent *psychological* and physical benefits for rooms on the southern side which would otherwise have been sunless.

From a sustainability point of view, the energy invested in their manufacture vs. green energy created over what should be a long lifetime is excellent.

They are easily made by a competent handyperson, and recycling of components should be excellent.

Their appearance was a little unusual at first, but has now mellowed into an acceptable part of solar architecture.

The only disadvantage is that they are only useful during the cooler months, but this is in the process of being overcome by a new type of reflector/photovoltaic reversible panel which will be useful over the full year *(see p **6**-5)*.

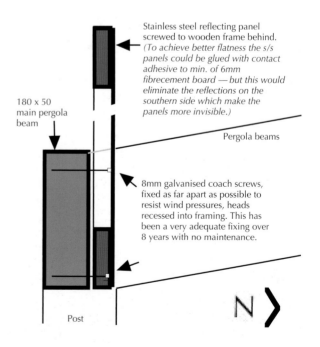

180 x 50 main pergola beam

Stainless steel reflecting panel screwed to wooden frame behind. *(To achieve better flatness the s/s panels could be glued with contact adhesive to min. of 6mm fibrecement board — but this would eliminate the reflections on the southern side which make the panels more invisible.)*

Pergola beams

8mm galvanised coach screws, fixed as far apart as possible to resist wind pressures, heads recessed into framing. This has been a very adequate fixing over 8 years with no maintenance.

Post

N

6-4.1   **Fixing reflectors to pergola**

Combined reflector/photovoltaics panel

The genesis for the combined panel was the fact that the three fixed panels outside the main bedroom window *(see p **6**-2)* were only useful during the cooler months of the year — ie. 50% efficiency — and the addition of back-to-back photovoltaics was an opportunity to make it useful for 12 months.

This is an evolutionary step. In no way does it denigrate the value of the original fixed panels, which were extremely good value for money in view of their original low cost.

The reversible panel rotates on a horizontal axis to expose photovoltaic panels to the northern sun in summer, adjusted to achieve optimum absorption and generation *(see diagram **6**-5.4)*.

The panel now has a 100% duty cycle — and possibly **more** if we can achieve the *28%* gain from the PV panels when facing *south* in winter, which is theoretically possible. *(See Irradiation chart p **16**-7.)*

The panel holds six 42W Uni-Solar PV panels, which should add a further 252W to our existing 2300W array = 2552W total, which should then generate about 14 kWh/day in summer and hopefully a little above our usual 7 kWh/day in winter *(see 2003 results p **7**-10)*.

6-5.3 **Sun in the south-facing bedroom from the vertical reflector outside at about 11am on a winter's morning.**

Double glazed windows reduce heat loss

Silica gel crystals eliminate condensation on glass

6-5.1 **PVs facing north generate electricity** *(not optimised in photo).*

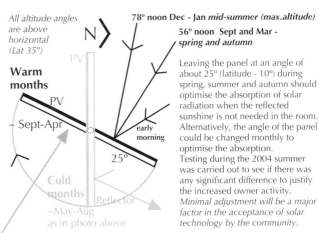

All altitude angles are above horizontal (Lat 35°)

PV

Warm months

PV

~ Sept-Apr

early morning

25°

Cold months

Reflector

~May-Aug as in photo above

78° noon Dec - Jan *mid-summer (max.altitude)*

56° noon Sept and Mar - *spring and autumn*

Leaving the panel at an angle of about 25° (latitude - 10°) during spring, summer and autumn should optimise the absorption of solar radiation when the reflected sunshine is not needed in the room. Alternatively, the angle of the panel could be changed monthly to optimise the absorption. Testing during the 2004 summer was carried out to see if there was any significant difference to justify the increased owner activity. *Minimal adjustment will be a major factor in the acceptance of solar technology by the community.*

6-5.4 **PV panel angle in warmer months (reflector not in use)**

Possible alternatives

A small problem with the panels so far has been the difficulty of obtaining a perfectly flat reflected image.

The reflections from the heliostat and the fixed panels so far have some concentrations of sunlight due to very slight warping of the reflector panels.

On the Pearce project *(see p **6**-6)* the reflectors were glued onto 6mm fibre-cement sheets. This helped a little bit, but they were still not smooth, flat reflections, as can be seen from the lower photo *(**6**-6.1)*.

Use of brushed stainless steel to achieving a diffusing effect was somewhat disappointing, as the linear brushed texture seems to concentrate the reflection into a narrow strip of light which was unacceptable.

Another possibility is the use of glass mirrors, which can now be supplied by Miralite in Canberra — a commercial offshoot of the ANU experiments in parabolic reflectors used at Whitecliffs, NSW, a few years ago. Cost not available.

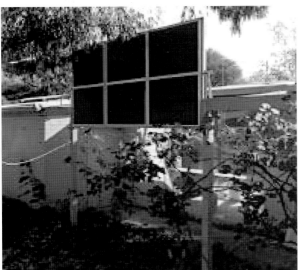

6-5.2 **Reflector facing north showing sun in bedroom. South facing PVs may generate some useful electricity during winter.**

A reflector project

The first application of the reflector system was made at a house in Pearce, ACT, in 2002, where a south-facing elevation with three half-height windows and a 22.5° tiled roof never received any sun.

In the top photograph, the right window is the kitchen, then living-dining room, and a bedroom on the left.

The neighbour to the north had planted some blue gums on their eastern boundary and some casuarinas in the south-west corner, which effectively meant that some early morning and late afternoon sun would shade some reflectors.

The neighbour would not top any of the trees or remove any — a possibly common scenario — but the client felt that even restricted sun from 11am to 3pm was worth the expenditure (proved correct).

The living room and bedroom windows were enlarged to full height to make more effective use of the vertical travel of the reflection and a pergola structure erected, on which eight reflector panels were fixed.

Two changes were adopted over the Mawson trial — the stainless steel panels were backed with 6mm fibrecement to give a more evenly reflected image (not fully satisfactory) and the panels were hinged along their centres to allow for any possible seasonal adjustment (which has been done once).

The array shown in photo **6-**6.3 is even more successful, with panels that can be swung horizontally in summer, giving a better view of the garden and shading the planting underneath. Both occupants are very happy with the extra warmth and cheerfulness in their previously cold southern rooms.

6-6.2 The southern sun has transformed these previously sunless rooms at 6 Whitelaw St, Pearce, ACT (2002).

Note the virtual invisibility of the reflectors

6-6.3 Temperature in these rooms is often raised 8° above normal on the coldest winter day at 55 MacNamara St. Pearce, ACT (2004).

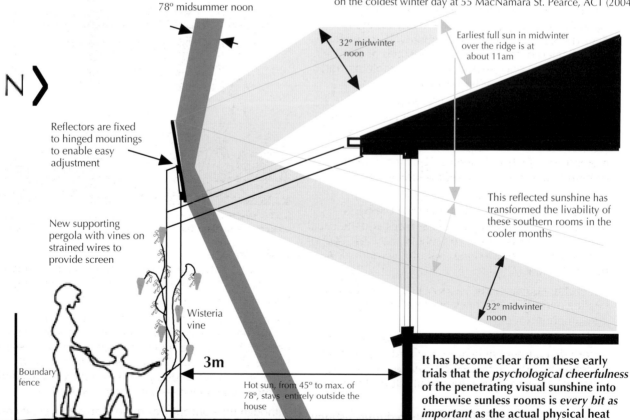

78° midsummer noon

32° midwinter noon

Earliest full sun in midwinter over the ridge is at about 11am

N

Reflectors are fixed to hinged mountings to enable easy adjustment

New supporting pergola with vines on strained wires to provide screen

Wisteria vine

This reflected sunshine has transformed the livability of these southern rooms in the cooler months

32° midwinter noon

Boundary fence

3m

Hot sun, from 45° to max. of 78°, stays entirely outside the house

It has become clear from these early trials that the *psychological cheerfulness* of the penetrating visual sunshine into otherwise sunless rooms is *every bit as important* as the actual physical heat input (which is considerable).

6-6.1 **Section through Whitelaw St house showing reflector relationship and some sun angles.**

Reflecting heliostat

Do you recall when you first learned that the sunflower followed the sun on its daily path across the sky to maximise its absorption of the sun's rays?

A heliostat is only a man-made version of the same principle in that it electro-mechanically tracks the sun to *reflect* the warming radiation and light into a room on the *south* side of the house during all sunny hours.

Its aim is just like the fixed reflectors described on p **6**-2, the major difference being that it reflects the sun *at 90° all day long* into one room, warming and lighting a room which otherwise would not receive any sun at all during the colder months.

Apart from the warmth and the light there is significant value in the *psychological* feeling of well-being when the room is flooded with sunlight.

It is a marvellous sensation and should not be underestimated, particularly when the sun is also beaming in from the north side in the living room and the two rays meet in the middle of the house.

I should stress at the outset that this is *not* a project for people just wishing to improve the thermal performance of their house. It is purely an experimental project to test the idea of heating the southern side of a house. TThe results obtained indicate that the concept of southern reflection is valid in both new and retrofitting situations.

The tracking heliostat was designed as a *useful sculpture* for use in our particular situation, and I think we can claim to have made the first domestic heliostat in the world.

In essence it is a large, reflective sculpture which rotates 1.875° every 15 minutes from 6am, tracking the sun until around 5pm and slowly tracking back again to its starting point of 6am ready for the next day. Tracking mechanisms for photovoltaics which are activated by *sensing* where the sun is at any particular time have several inherent problems, and this regular tracking system overcomes them.

Most of the stainless steel panels were cut from the three fixed panels I experimented with in 1998 over the dining room window, so they were recycled, as were the gears in the actuator and the window-winder motor from a Datsun Bluebird. Only the column support and its concrete footing were new.

Conservative calculations based on the 4m² of reflector panels indicate that, over the Canberra heating season, allowing for glass losses and the usual cloud cover in May, June and July, some 2.84MWh of heat should be reflected into our dining room *at 90°* during the sunny hours.

That is the equivalent of 15.7kWh/day over the whole heating period, or 1.5 times our *total* daily electrical consumption.

Regrettably, this is in excess of the house's capacity to absorb that amount of heat, so my next project is to increase the mass in the dining area to absorb and store that amount of heat for useful return during the evening.

However, the internal air temperature during a sunny day ranges between 20–24° which, together with the cheerful sunshine, makes the room very pleasant.

6-7.1 **The heliostat. Note how the reflected foliage makes the heliostat merge into the landscape — a feature which has reduced its visual impact significantly.**

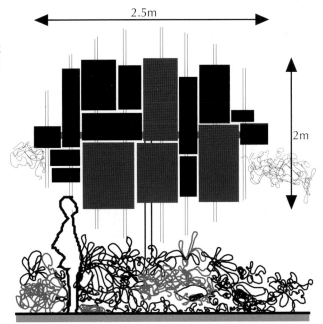

6-7.2 **Design concept of heliostat, utilising recycled panels and supporting structure. The aim was to make it a 'useful sculpture'.**

Design analysis

This is a prototype, and was commissioned for service on 20 May 2002. After the expected early teething problems it is now performing very well.

Some glare is evident when sitting at the dining table facing the heliostat. Ideally, the reflectors should have been higher, but the structure would then have been too high and dominant. It is functionally efficient and decorative in the landscape, but is not recommended for the uncommitted — only for the enthusiast.

Although the concept was mine I must give great credit to Richard Saberton, who masterminded the mechanics and David Anderson, who pioneered the electronics.

Reflecting heliostat - *solar geometry*

An electro-mechanical windlass fixed on top of the roof operates the heliostat by stainless steel cables wrapped around a spirally wound drum, activated by cogs from a car gearbox and a window winder motor. It is controlled by an electronic clock set in the wall below.

Every 15 minutes a pulse rotates the drum to move the heliostat 1.875° which exactly matches the apparent movement of the sun. This ensures that the reflected sunshine is *always at 90° to the dining room window*.

In winter the reflection floods the room during all sunshine hours; in spring and autumn the reflection during most of the day is just about at the external wall line, but in early morning and late afternoon when the outside temperature is lower the low angle sun penetrates the room, which is very cheering.

In the warmer months when sun penetration is not desirable the sun's higher altitude keeps the warming reflection outside the house - it is a wonderful symbiotic relationship.

The reflected beam can, if required, be moved by the electronic controller to the left or right *at any time* into the living room or the family room to add cheerfulness as well as heat to these areas - it's tantamount to "playing God", which always intrigues our visitors.

The project has been well worth doing, but rather fiddly and not for the average houseowner with little interest other than basking in the warm sun.

The penetrating sun has been absolutely marvellous, particularly at lunchtime. Trees are now blocking the early breakfast sun, but unfortunately they are on an adjacent reserve and can't be touched.

There is some glare from this device because it is twice as far away from the house with a lower angle of reflection than the fixed panels which have no glare problem. This is a small disadvantage, but the warmth and cheerfulness more than compensates.

Storing the gained heat

The heat from the heliostat is more concentrated and more constant than from the fixed panels and is more effective in heating up the room. Being a brick veneer construction there is inadequate mass in the house and the heat tended to raise the *air* temperature more than heat the surrounding *walls*. Room temperatures often reach 24°C during winter but was inadequately stored for use in the evening time.

I have solved this partially by erecting (2006) a high mass, precast concrete slab facing on the stud and plasterboard wall which faces the window and doesn't occupy much floor space.

The slabs are 800mm high x 250mm wide x 50mm thick with their weight being carried by the concrete slab and the stud wall behind simply preventing any lateral movement. There is a gap of 10mm behind the slabs which I hope will induce convection currents to distribute the gained heat around the room at night.

Even though the wall is not quite complete (May 2006) some of the slabs have reached 49°C around 3pm and my next step is to finish the wall and attach Thermochron temperature recorders so that I can graph the thermal variations during winter days.

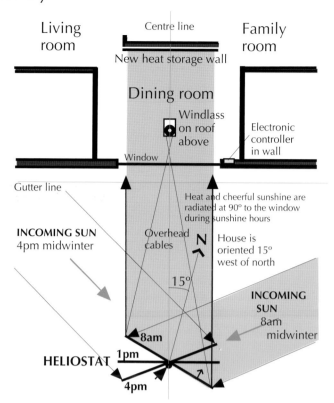

6-8.1 **Plan of heliostat showing midwinter rotational limits**

The apparent movement of the sun is 15° every hour from east to west so the reflector movement is half = 7.5° every hour.

The controller sends an electronic impulse to the motor to make the heliostat rotate 1.875° every quarter hour (7.5° divided by 4).

This movement is quite independent of any cloudy weather (a problem with optical trackers) so the heliostat is always pointing toward the sun.

After sunset the heliostat moves back to its sunrise starting point ready for another sunny day.

6-8.2 **The precast concrete heat storage wall** *(see plan above)*

7

Rationalising your electricity consumption

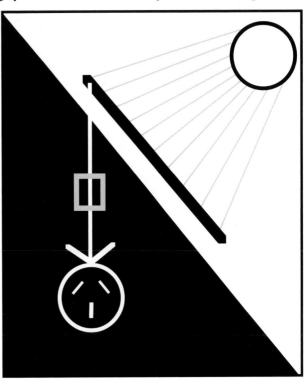

7-2   **Electrical appliances**

7-4   **Improving the usefulness of refrigerators**

7-5   **Photovoltaics – the design process**

7-9   **Photovoltaics – the Mawson experience**

7-10   **Comparative PV generation/
        consumption**

7-11   **DIY or contract?**

7-12   **Integrated photovoltaics**

Electrical appliances

If we are serious about wanting to help the environment, our retrofitting zeal should extend to a critical look at how we consume electricity — assuming, of course, that it is generated in the traditional way by coal, oil or natural gas, as most of it still is and probably will remain for a long time yet.

It will be many years before we can say that all our electricity comes from renewable sources such as wind, wave power, biofuels, photovoltaics and hydrogen, but all of these technologies are under urgent development.

Even Denmark, which is well advanced in terms of renewable energy generation, is only achieving 20% of its total need from wind turbines.

No matter what the source, conservation of energy will still be necessary for many decades, and if every household played some role in reducing its consumption we could start to have some impact on greenhouse-gas emissions.

Domestic electrical appliances have infiltrated our homes in enormous numbers over the last 50 years, and their convenience to us is something we will not willingly forego. It is now so easy to flick a switch to perform some task which consumes a kilowatt of energy in one hour, without sparing a thought that 0.9kg of CO_2e is being emitted at the power station.

The fact that it is several hundreds of kilometres away makes no difference in global terms — the polluting emissions from the smokestack have no respect for geographical boundaries.

Reducing our consumption really will make a difference *if we all do it*. So how do we start ?

Water heater

This is most likely your greatest consumer, unless you have a gas-fired model which still pollutes directly into your *immediate* atmosphere about 25-30% of the greenhouse gases produced by an electric water heater.

What you can do: an electric water heater would typically consume about 27% of your total electricity consumption, and is probably still producing hot water with no apparent problems.

The cylinders are always insulated, some better than others, but another wrapping of insulation around the outside and the top would help to reduce heat loss, electricity and money, not forgetting the short, exposed bits of copper piping emerging from the cylinder which feel hot. Some pipe lagging would help there — (see pp **14** -2 and **14**-3 on advice to tenants).

If your cylinder is over 15 years old it may be time to consider installing a solar water heater.

Refrigerator

Probably this is your next biggest consumer. *P 7-3* gives you a few clues as to how to reduce its electricity consumption.

However, if your refrigerator is nearing the end of its economic life, perhaps you could consider investing in a low-energy refrigerator which are now appearing on the market.

Apart from initial cost, sizes and features, the most significant factor from an environmental point of view and your wallet is the *running cost* in kWh per year.

Running costs per year for an average-sized refrigerator could vary from about $70 to $177, representing a range of discharge into the atmosphere of between 67kg and 171kg of CO_2e per year. Electrical products change so rapidly that I cannot hope to cover all types.

Regular reviews are published in CHOICE magazine which are an excellent guide, but we must start to think about comparisons based on the environmental consequences as well as the financial cost. Contact your electricity supplier as well to see what local advice it can give you.

The water heater and the refrigerator are usually the big electrical consumers in any house, and it would pay you (literally) to make careful comparisons.

Take note of the energy-rating system now being used by energy-consuming items — the more stars the better, with a maximum of 6.

The sticker on the front of the item will also tell you how many kilowatt-hours it will consume in one year, but CHOICE has found in its testing that these figures are often underestimated.

To translate kilowatt-hours into pollution terms:

  1 kWh of electrical energy = 0.968 kg of CO_2e

  1 MWh = 968 kg = ~1 tonne CO_2e

Electrical space heating

If you are heating your draughty, wooden-floored, poorly insulated living areas by any type of electric heater (even if on an off-peak rate), you might as well be pouring your money down a bottomless hole in the floor. It is inefficient and very polluting.

Heating by natural gas is more environmentally friendly and, in the absence of all the other conservation measures mentioned elsewhere, is your only realistic option for the time being.

Stand-by (LED) lights

These are sneaky 'phantom' leakages of electricity which are consuming electricity all the time and could account for a continuing 5–10% of your electricity bill.

All that need be said here is: *regard any appliance as surreptitiously consuming your precious power, adding to your electricity bill and polluting the atmosphere if it is plugged into a power outlet which is switched on.*

This is particularly important if you are relying on batteries to store the power generated from your photovoltaic array, as every watt is precious.

The answer seems to be: **switch OFF at the power outlet when not using any appliance.**

However, take care, as some appliances, like videos, have memory devices and integral clocks which can be lost if switched off at the power outlet.

It is salutary to think back to, say 1950, before the electronic revolution, when all we had were electric lights, perhaps a radio, a one-bar electric radiator, an electric iron and a very simple telephone. Compare that list with what you have now. (See p **16**-17.)

Electrical appliances – *phantom loads*

Beware the silent consumers

Our 'need' for convenience and a mythical saving of time has led us all into a situation where electricity is being consumed all the time for no real purpose.

The little red or green lights from light-emitting diodes (LEDs) are ubiquitous. Virtually every appliance seems to have one, and it has been calculated that some 5–10% of our electricity bills are due to these 'phantom' or 'ghost' loads. Multiply your own load by all the houses (and offices) in Australia and it will amount to a *very substantial waste of power* — along with its accompanying pollution, if fossil fuels are being used at the generating source.

In themselves, LEDs are often simple warning lights which show that the appliance is *'alive'*, consuming very little power — of the order of 0.032W.

But if they signify that the appliance is on *stand-by*, it means, in effect, that the electronics are being kept warm for an immediate start, so the appliance is virtually ON all the time, consuming more power, often to little purpose. Which are which?

The major culprits are items such as TV sets, office photocopiers, faxes and computers — the list seems to grow daily. Let us look at a few examples:

Television - if on *stand-by* it could be consuming about 10 W, which would work out at about 87kWh per year. At, say, 10c/kWh, this would be costing you about $8 every year, even though there is no picture or sound. Warm-up time from a cold start is, however, only a few seconds anyway; so keeping it 'warm' would seem to be an unnecessary waste of electricity. If you switch on and off with an infra-red remote control it has to remain on 'ready' in order to receive a command.

Videos - are probably consuming about 5 W, particularly as most have a digital display showing the time as well as some of the electronics waiting to be 'woken up'. Take care, though — if you switch it off you might delete your settings. Read the manual.

DVDs, Zip disc players, and **CD players** - more often use liquid crystal displays, which use much lower power at around 1-2 W.

Sound systems - any that have a remote control are probably using 1–5 W.

Radios - generally turn right off, but some may leave the mains power running through the transformer's primary coil using a few watts, and only switch off the secondary transformer output voltage.

Burglar alarms - generally a trickle charge maintains the internal battery, drawing about 0.07 amps, which might equate to about 16 kWh per year.

Computers - those with CRT screens would continue to draw around 60 W when on standby and the screen has gone blank. Flat LCD screens would be consuming around half that.

Modems - don't actually have a stand-by mode, and are simply on or off.

Printers, scanners - are likely to be using about 20W when on stand-by. Laser printers have a heated fuser which cycles on and off in stand-by mode.

Photocopiers - these are often left on stand-by during office hours to save staff time when copying, and are probably consuming ~10-30W every hour.

Faxes - the machines that use laser printer technology have a fuser that is maintained at 130°C, which would waste around 30 W or more when on stand-by; the ones which use thermal paper consume ~5-10 W when idle.

Computers - with their plethora of attachments, such as modems, printers, scanners, burners and players of various kinds, are all potential phantoms unless a 'switch off if not needed' mindset is adopted.

Clothes and dishwashing machines, most computers and microwave ovens - often consume about 5W *continuously* if the power point plug is live. They contain EMC filters (required by law), which are there to suppress radiation frequencies that can interfere with radio and television reception — using about 44kWh pa simply because the power point is left switched on. *These should be switched off at the power point.*

Other household items which, although small, cumulatively enlarge your power bill, could include:

Extension lead multi outlets (~0.1W)
Electric toothbrushes (~0.1W)
Electronically controlled gas heaters (if it has a temperature display ~5-10 W)
Small battery chargers, transformers etc.
Clocks on ovens, radios, TVs, etc (~5 W)
Halogen lights - the light switch normally cuts the input to the transformers
Sound proximity lights (~0.01W)
Electronic timers in power outlets - (~2W mechanical; near zero for LCD digital types)
Mood lighting controllers - (normally switched off but use a little power if the light has been turned right down on the knob)
Phone answering machine - (~5W if on all day)
Illuminated door bell push button - (transformer 5W)
Breadmaker - (~5 W if plugged in)
Irons - (normally switched off, but safer to pull the plug)

You can start making an immediate $ saving (and kg of CO_2e) by turning off all your phantom appliances around the house. You can also save if you switch off your electric or gas water heater when your family goes away on holiday — even if only for a few days.

New appliances Next time you are in need of a new appliance, think before you buy — do you *really* need a new one? Can the old one be repaired? Is there an alternative piece of equipment which will do the same job? (e.g., boiling water for coffee on the gas stove at 75% less CO_2e emissions than from an electric jug).

By listing our Mawson phantom loads and adjusting our mindsets to switching off, we have now reduced our household consumption for two retired occupants to 10.45kWh per day. It could be even lower, but writing this book on the computer for many long hours has consumed around 1kWh/ day. (Fortunately, the PV array generated 8.05kWh/day in 2003 - *see p 7-10.*)

To conclude, you can save now by switching off at the power outlet to lower your consumption, and your need for a large photovoltaic array will be reduced.

Improving the usefulness of refrigerators

Making the refrigerator more efficient

The fridge in the kitchen tends to be taken for granted by most people, yet it can be one of the greatest consumers of electricity in the house, apart from the traditional electric hot-water storage heater.

The external, insulated walls of the fridge have tended to become thinner over the years, and this is where the room heat gains entry into the cold interior.

There are two modifications you could do to improve this situation. If your fridge is in an alcove with room around it, an additional 25mm slab of expanded polystyrene would increase the R value of the side, walls and top.

Making use of the waste heat in winter and exhaust it in summer

The heat given off at the back of the refrigerator is very useful in winter, but it contributes to the heat level in the kitchen in summer — probably convincing you to install an air conditioner!

A modification to the fridge *(see diagrams below)* with a controllable vent and exhaust flue to the outside would save electricity and give you more comfort.

Close the vent in winter to keep the heat in and open it in summer to let the heat out. Two seconds of activity = six months' improved comfort.

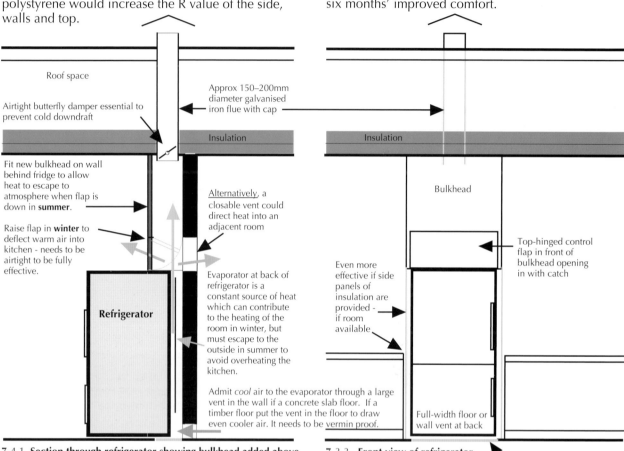

Roof space

Airtight butterfly damper essential to prevent cold downdraft

Approx 150–200mm diameter galvanised iron flue with cap

Insulation

Fit new bulkhead on wall behind fridge to allow heat to escape to atmosphere when flap is down in **summer**.

Alternatively, a closable vent could direct heat into an adjacent room

Raise flap in **winter** to deflect warm air into kitchen - needs to be airtight to be fully effective.

Refrigerator

Evaporator at back of refrigerator is a constant source of heat which can contribute to the heating of the room in winter, but must escape to the outside in summer to avoid overheating the kitchen.

Admit *cool* air to the evaporator through a large vent in the wall if a concrete slab floor. If a timber floor put the vent in the floor to draw even cooler air. It needs to be vermin proof.

Insulation

Bulkhead

Even more effective if side panels of insulation are provided - if room available

Top-hinged control flap in front of bulkhead opening in with catch

Full-width floor or wall vent at back

7-4.1 Section through refrigerator showing bulkhead added above

7-3.3 Front view of refrigerator

The other way in which to take advantage of the gentle, constant heat given off at the back is to make a fruit-drying system or a damp-washing drier on top of your fridge — it is extremely efficient in winter.

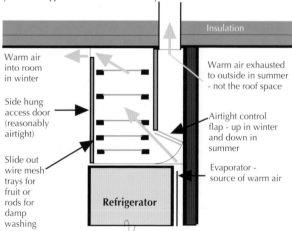

Insulation

Warm air into room in winter

Warm air exhausted to outside in summer - not the roof space

Side hung access door (reasonably airtight)

Airtight control flap - up in winter and down in summer

Slide out wire mesh trays for fruit or rods for damp washing

Evaporator - source of warm air

Refrigerator

7-4.2 Using the refrigerator's waste heat to dry fruit, warm dishes, or dry the washing on a wet day!

Adding a cool air inlet vent at the back will increase the evaporator efficiency substantially — up to 20%.

A new fridge?

Eventually we all seem to reach a point where we 'need' to change our refrigerators, for one reason or another. Perhaps we should now ask ourselves: '*Do we really need to?*', '*Can it be postponed?*' '*Will a new model be more energy-efficient than my old one?*'

If you *really* have to dispose of it, make sure that the refrigerant gas will be safely collected rather than allowed to escape into the atmosphere. It is a potent contributor to the world's ozone layer problem.

The refrigerator is a major energy consumer in the house, so make sure that your new model is energy efficient — that it has 5 or 6 stars. Compare the electrical consumption figures. Several new models are coming on the market which have lower consumptions and are better insulated. If you have natural gas installed in the house, consider having a gas refrigerator, which is environmentally more friendly.

Overview of photovoltaic arrays

What are photovoltaic arrays?

A number of photovoltaic panels (PVs) when installed on your land or on your roof becomes an array, enabling you to use the sun to generate your own electric power.

The PVs generate a DC current, and an inverter changes it to 220–240V AC for use by all your existing appliances.

Those of us who are already connected to the grid can install a PV array to generate power during the day and use the grid during the non-sunshine hours.

This is a 'grid interactive system', and no batteries are needed.

Any surplus generation that you can't use goes *automatically* into the grid, and your electricity supplier will credit you with the amount you export.

However, if you live outside town and are not connected to the grid, you will need a 'Remote Area Power System' (RAPS), which involves batteries.

A grid interactive system has the disadvantage that, if the grid goes off, your system goes off as well, but I believe that there is a new system which overcomes this problem.

Types of panels

There are two basic types of PV panels — amorphous and crystalline. Each have their own characteristics which need evaluating very carefully.

Crystalline panels give more output /m², but output diminishes with higher temperatures and they are sensitive to shading from other buildings and trees.

If you are very short of roof space, crystalline will give you greater output /m², but they also cost more.

Amorphous panels, on the other hand, are not as sensitive to shading, do not reduce power output as much when hot, cost less per panel, and, as there is no glass involved, are not susceptible to hail damage. In addition, they have a slightly textured surface which reduces low-angle reflection and increases absorption. They need more area of panels to achieve the same output as crystalline. I chose amorphous and have had no cause to regret it.

There are several other factors which must be considered before you decide which type to buy, so do your homework and evaluate all the factors that relate to *your* particular situation.

Ventilation at the back of the panel seems to be necessary to keep the panel temperature down.

Inverters

There are several manufacturers with differing sizes of inverters on offer, and most have a display panel which shows how much is being generated at any time, how much has been generated in the past, etc.

The AC power from the inverter then goes to your existing meter box, where your electricity supplier will have installed a special two-way meter which records what your array is producing, what your house is using, and what surplus you are providing to the grid.

This is known as nett metering, and is becoming the standard practice around Australia.

Why we should be promoting renewable energy ...

Before getting down to the physical details of designing and installing the photovoltaic system, it is important to understand why governments are trying to stimulate the uptake of PVs.

In principle, encouraging everybody to install PVs on their roofs is the right thing to do. We need to change our electricity generation from a centralised generation system, with its huge generation and distribution losses (~33% each) and high levels of pollution, to a *distributed* system in which electricity is *generated very close to where it is consumed*. This has the enormous potential to reduce transmission losses and pollution levels.

PVs seem to be very expensive when viewed as capital costs only but, when seen holistically, a different picture emerges. The question also needs to be seen as a moral issue because our actions (or inactions) today will determine the future enjoyment of life for our offspring — *How much do I love my grandchildren? What degree of commitment do I have to doing something about global warming? What lower energy level can I comfortably live with, and what can I afford to pay now to save later?*

More importantly, you will immediately be helping to reduce pollution to the extent of ~1kg of CO_2 for every kWh you generate. At the mercenary level, you will be making substantial savings on your electricity bills over 20–30 years, and even making a profit.

Federal and state governments are all coming up with different financial programs to wean us all away from the use of 'dirty' electricity. It is now more complicated than ever, with federal Solar Credits (June 2009) plus federal Renewable Energy Certificates (RECs) plus variable state Feed-In Tariffs (FITs).

As this book is sold all around Australia, I run the risk of misleading all of my readers by giving examples based on varying financial incentives, so I can only deal with the basics and suggest that you do some Google searches for relevant up-to-date information.

What is important is that we keep a long-term view in mind about what our ultimate objective must be — and I can only refer you back to the statement you read on p **2**-3 — which is a few steps closer to really sustainable housing that is less damaging to our environment.

To justify the trust that our children have in the decisions we make now, on their behalf, we have *no* moral option but to design houses which generate more carbon-free renewable energy than they consume — close to where it is consumed (the excess being sold to those who are in no position to do so, e.g. apartments).

But who is doing effective research on this? Governments? Vested interests? Coal-based power companies? The housing industry? The real-estate industry? *Porcine aviators?*

The following design process may help ...

The design process

Several practical aspects need consideration in the early design stages to assess the feasibility of PVs. Understanding them could save you a lot of work.

1 - What is a reasonable daily electricity consumption figure for your household?

Make a list of all your electrical items, their wattages in kilowatts (kW), multiplied by the length of time they are switched on *in one day*. This will give you a figure in kilowatthours (kWh). To give you a guide, there are normally two people in our house and, in 2008, we consumed an average of 8.8kWh per day. We don't live spartan lives, but we are careful about using compact fluorescent globes throughout the house, gas for cooking, no external lights on at night, etc.

The lower your electrical consumption, the less need you have for a large PV array, so your first major step should be to *realistically* assess your *needs* v. your *wants. Statistically, however, our electrical 'needs' are growing every year — computers, accessories, etc.!*

2 - Are you familiar with the sun's movements?

You really need to understand the geometry of optimising the placing of your future PV panels on your roof and reducing shading problems from trees *before* you get any quotes from installers, as you will need to evaluate and compare their quotes — and know what questions to ask. *This aspect is very important, as it could easily squash your thoughts on making your own electricity.* In principle, you should aim at pointing the face of the panels as close to north as possible. There are many books on solar geometry, but a seminal work written by Ralph Phillips at CSIRO, *Sunshine and Shade in Australasia*, will help *(p **16**-4)*.

You will need to be familiar with the daily rise, fall, and lateral movement of the sun from east to west, and the differences between these movements in the *four seasons*. Hopefully, your house orientation has an *azimuth* close to north (compass *bearing* in relation to *true* north — not *magnetic*), so you will only have to make a decision about the optimal angle of *tilt (or altitude — see diagrams **7-7.1**, **7-8.1** & **2**, and the accompanying p **16**-7 about tilt)*.

3 - Does your roof have suitable orientation, tilt, and area for a PV array?

Do you have a pitched roof of 'reasonable' size facing within 30° either side of true north? Beyond 30° your array will become less efficient *(see **4**-3.1)*.

PVs are all rectangular in shape — sizes varying with the manufacturer — so look at your northern roof area and imagine a rectangular group of panels between ridge and gutter, allowing for about 500mm all round for access. Rectangular solar panels fit much more easily on gabled roofs — physically and aesthetically — than they do on hipped roofs with hips and valleys.

Measure this total area in square metres (m²) and multiply by a rough average of 95W/m² (PV panels vary from about 42W/m² (amorphous) to 150 W/m² (crystalline) and you will get some idea of the wattage potential of such an array.

4 - Does the generation match the consumption?

Multiply the potential wattage by the number of useful sunshine hours per day — about 5 in Canberra, 4.5 in Melbourne — so if you have 20m² available for panels x 95W/m² = 1900W (or 1.9kW) rating x 5 hours = 9.5kWh potential *generation* per day (8.5kWh in Melbourne).

Relate that to your estimated daily consumption that you calculated in question 1 to see if they match. *(Check also the chart on p **16**-7 to see if the roof orientation is effective.)* If there is a shortfall and the roof area available is the absolute maximum you have then you will have to consider a higher-wattage crystalline type of panel, or accept that you can't achieve 100% match between generation and consumption — *or reduce your consumption, which is not really difficult.*

5 - Are you able to DIY (with mandatory electrical installation help) or will you need to employ a contractor to install everything?

Since the last edition of this book, many new supply and installation companies have entered the market, installation techniques have improved enormously, and imported PV panels from South-East Asia have flooded the market. Don't think of doing it yourself unless you are confident in your ability.

6 - Will you be able to afford it?

Since the last edition, the situation has changed quite substantially, with competition bringing prices down. Installation costs by accredited professionals have dropped from $14/watt of installed capacity, which was common in 2000, to around $4/watt in 2011. As electricity costs are increasing, there is now much greater incentive to install this type of technology. Consequently, the various governments have had to rethink their financial positions on encouraging the public uptake of distributed generation of electricity.

The return on investment can be quite variable between states, with lowered Feed-In-Tariff returns and increasing electricity tariffs (which must continue to rise), but balanced by lower capital outlays. Pay-back periods are being reduced, giving a comfortable feeling that you are doing the right thing for a better environment for your children.

Despite the financial volatility, the old message still holds: do your homework, understand the basic principles, join the Alternative Technology Association and read their excellent magazine *Renew*, shop around for advice, get at least three quotes from installers and electricity suppliers, and visit their installations to see if they have applied the solar principles which are still applicable.

7 - Tree shading

Are there any high trees to the east, north, or west which could *potentially* shade your array? Evergreens would be a problem, but deciduous trees could be OK. Can you top them to reduce their height? Are they on your land or your neighbour's? Even trees in the near distance can be a problem, so carefully plot significant trees between about 60° east and 60° west of true north *(see **4**-3.1, which applies to PV arrays and to solar water heaters)*.

The design process *(cont.)*

Trees outside these limits are of no great concern, as they may only shade the array when the sun's angle of incidence will be so obtuse as to be almost useless for generating electricity. *Remember, however, that trees have a habit of growing taller unless really mature.*

8 - Roof shading

The diagrams on the right will give you an indicative idea of how shading from roof elements might occur on absorber panels on a typical pitched roof with gabled and hipped extensions. *(Consult irradiation chart on p 16-7.)*

Note the larger morning shadow at **A** from a gabled roof compared to the smaller shadow at **B** from a hipped end, even though the hipped roof is higher.

The higher the pitch of the roof, the more shading would occur. A 10°-pitched roof would have much less shading, but the angle of the sun would be very low, contributing reduced energy to the panels.

These diagrams are indicative only — showing that there is likely to be a problem which would need a carefully dimensioned analysis before committing yourself to considerable expenditure.

The simple gabled roof has several advantages over the previous complicated roof: it has a large uninterrupted area available for twice the number of absorber panels, there is more freedom to vary the pitch to suit the latitude, and the panels are aesthetically more integrated into the form of the house — they look a little less like an afterthought *(see 2-5.1)*. The wiring would also be simpler and cheaper, particularly as it must be carried out by a licensed PV installer.

9 - Pre-tender knowledge about PV panels

The differences between crystalline and amorphous panels were briefly discussed on p **7**-5, but it will pay to do your own space analysis so that you can maximise your use of the available roof areas.

Crystalline panels certainly take up less roof space (which also saves on mounting costs) and you should be able to obtain a higher output from a smaller and perhaps more difficult roof space. But amorphous panels have other advantages, such as the larger area giving you more roof shading in summer conditions. As usual, it's a case of swings and roundabouts.

Panel output per sq.m., tilt, positioning of panels on a 'fractured' roof *(see 3-2.1)*, and azimuth must all be juggled for an effective outcome. Irradiation chart **16**-7 will be useful in this process.

10 - Getting quotes or DIY?

Now that you have more understanding of how PV systems work, it would be time to get two or three quotes from authorised installers in your area.

There are now several photovoltaic installers in our Yellow Pages (under Solar Energy Equipment), but you can get a list of accredited installers from the Clean Energy Council website, or from your local Alternative Technology Association, or the Australian Solar Energy Society *(see p **16**-5 for contact details)*.

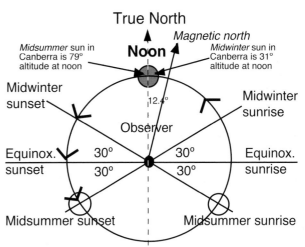

7-7.1 **Diagram of sun's daily movements at 35° latitude. Use with your house plan to get an indicative idea of possible shading problems such as shown below — adjust *altitude if different* latitude**

All PV panels shown will be less shaded if roof pitch is less than ~20°, but of course, their absorbance of solar radiation would be lessened in winter

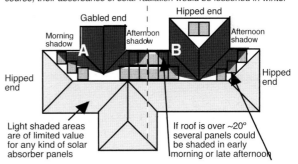

7-7.2 **PV shading problems with pitched roofs over ~20° with aesthetically poor arrangements of panels**

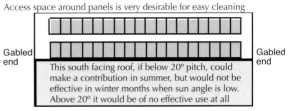

7-7.3 **A well-integrated array with no roof shading problems**

This is a specialised field and you must use an accredited installer, at least for the wiring up and inverter installation.

Be warned that roof pitches over about 20° become more difficult to work on, and safety harnesses are now required — so if you are not used to that sort of thing, it is advisable to get the specialists in. Factors like frost in midwinter and excessive heat in midsummer may well make you feel it is worth paying somebody else to do it.

The design process *(cont.)*

11 - What is the best tilt angle for your array?

A PV panel works best when it is pointing directly at the sun for as long as possible during the day, but in a suburban situation it is often not an economical or an aesthetic solution.

The keen enthusiast will probably delight in building a *tracking* array — a timing device which enables an array to follow the sun. But for an array of any useful domestic size — say >1kW — a tracking system would be an added expense and an aesthetic problem, both of which would most likely make such a PV system too expensive for most people.

A fixed array is the most usual answer to a domestic situation. The roof is a prime area for an array — it is reasonably available, away from most casual damage, usually with a pitch of ~20°, and hopefully oriented within a few degrees of true north.

In designing a new house, a skilful architect could integrate the needs of a PV array with those of the house. But in the case of a retrofit situation, there are several compromises that have to be considered.

Previous sections have dealt with azimuth and shading aspects, so the optimum angle of tilt of the panels (altitude or degrees above horizontal) now needs to be considered if you are to get value for your money.

A fixed array has variable effectiveness. When pointing to true north, its collecting efficiency is least at sunrise and sunset, and best between 9am and 3pm; similarly with tilt, and its relationship to the sun's movements during the day and its seasonal variations. Chart **16**-7 will be very useful here.

A fixed array will have times when it will be very inefficient and others when it will be excellent, so its tilt needs to optimise these variations (a tracking array would be excellent *all* the time — but more expensive and more prone to technical glitches).

If a fixed array is tilted at an angle equal to the latitude of the house (35° in Canberra), it would collect radiant energy equally in winter and summer.

Any increase or decrease from that tilt would make the array less efficient in summer or winter respectively.

12 - Do you use more electricity in winter or in summer?

The biggest uses are water heating, refrigeration, space heating or cooling, and cooking. Using gas (if available in your street) for water heating, space heating, and cooking will not only reduce your electricity bills and reduce your polluting emissions, but will change your *seasonal* electricity demand — which will be a factor in deciding the tilt of your array. The remaining heavy-demand area is space cooling, which can be eliminated by adopting the ceiling/roof ventilation techniques described on pp **10**-2 to 4.

We opted for a gas connection for our back-up space heating and cooking top. As our water heating is by heat pump, and there is no cooling load in summer, we do not have any great difference between winter and summer loads. Consequently, a 35° array tilt would have been the theoretical optimum.

If your long-term demand is more likely to be in *winter*, the optimal tilt should be about 5° to 10° *higher* than your latitude, or the converse.

Optimal tilt is very much a compromise, and other factors such as appearance may very well be just as important.

In our case, the roof was at 10° pitch, and to put the array at 35° or greater was not an option on grounds of aesthetics and wind-loading. We could not accept the thought of such a dominant, ugly array on our roof — it would have offended our neighbours and our body corporate, would certainly not encourage others to follow suit, and would have required the back row of panels to be much higher or further apart to avoid shading from the front row, with greater wind loading and extra substructure *(see grey panels in diagram below)*.

The efficiency loss between 16° and 35° is about 2%, which we felt was quite an acceptable compromise, so we settled on 16° — determined largely by physical access to the junction boxes on the undersides of the panels. We accepted the fact that it would be extremely efficient in summer, but not so efficient in winter. This has proved to be the case, as it has generated 9–17kWh/day in summer and 6–10kWh per sunny day in winter against a fairly constant average load of ~9kWh/day, creating a summer surplus greater than the winter loss (see 2008 output graph p **7**-10). *All in all, we now generate about 15% more electricity than we consume.*

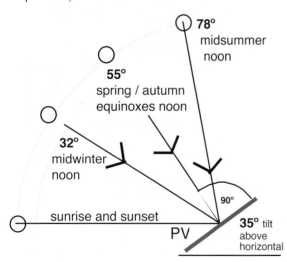

7-8.1 **Theoretical optimum tilt of PV array at latitude 35° giving equal insolation winter and summer** *(see 2-4.1)*

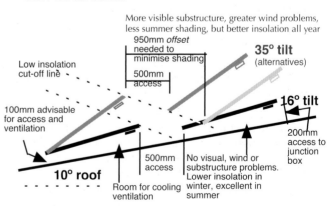

7-8.2 **Array tilt geometry at 16° and at 35° (= latitude = 2% more efficient)**

The Mawson photovoltaic array

Our specific circumstances

At Mawson in 1999, when contemplating the need for PVs, a number of factors needed to be balanced:

1 Potential roof shading by trees at both ends
2 Two existing roof vents and a TV aerial
3 A sub-optimal low roof-pitch of 10°
4 The aesthetics of an effective absorber tilt
5 Our need to obtain maximum shading value from the array in summer months
6 Our need to keep an area of roof available for a future PV extension
7 A 20-year-old electric hot-water storage system
8 A *very* consumptive in-slab electric space heating system
9 A free natural gas connection offer available at the time from ActewAGL
10 The federal government subsidy of $8250 available through the recently introduced PV Rebate Program
11 The need to get busy to avoid the start of GST on 1 July 2000 (a saving of over $1500)
12 Could I do most of it myself?

In July–August 2000 we installed 36 US64W Canon, amorphous photovoltaic panels on a DIY basis on the Colorbond corrugated-steel roof of the Mawson house.

The panels are hailproof (plastic, no glass), have three spectrally selective layers to improve absorption, are less heat sensitive, and are more tolerant of shading.

The roof was (fortunately) an appropriate size and it faced 15° west of true north, which was good. Its slope of 10° was not ideal, however — 35° would have been better, giving a more balanced output over winter and summer in relation to the sun's differing altitudes.

However, as we are very sensitive to the aesthetics of applied technology to the outside of buildings, we compromised with an extra 6° slope, which also allowed for easier access to the junction boxes under each panel. Our rationale was that if others see an ugly structure on a roof they get a negative impression, which may put them off installing such a system.

Installing the panels at an optimum 35° would have meant that one row would have shaded the other in winter *(see diag 7-8.2)*; there would have been less shading of the roof underneath in summer; and it would have meant more wind problems, more visible supporting structure, more cost and more ugliness. As it is now, it covers 53% of the northern roof area and integrates well with the house structure.

Chart **16**-7 shows that our array is 96% efficient, which is quite acceptable.

In the absence of any manufacturer's instructions on how to fix the panels to the roof, we chose Dexion galvanised angles for convenience and cost.

The panels were only 9kg each, but it was important to distribute their overall weight as equally as possible over the roof trusses — and equally important to firmly fix them to the *trusses* rather than to the roofing *battens* which were only nailed to the trusses.

As uplift from strong winds could easily take the panels and the roof covering away from the trusses, the panels were firmly coach-screwed through the roofing with

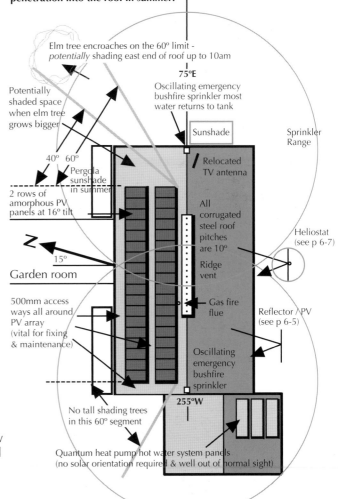

The eucalypts in the top left of the photo have grown taller and are now giving too much shade around 9am. They are on a reserve & permission will be needed to trim or remove them.

The trees on the right are not too much of a problem because the sun is very low & the solar gain is ineffective in the early hours

75° E house axis

Raised sunshades (discarded trial model) are shown in the winter position. Now Coolaroo panels which allow more daylight in summer

Ridge vent naturally ventilates the whole house (*see p 10*-3 &4)

36 - Canon US 64W amorphous panels tilted at 16°, mounted on galvanised Dexion framing

7-9.1 2.3kW photovoltaic array. Note the amount of shading on the roof surface from the panels which significantly reduces heat penetration into the roof in summer.

Elm tree encroaches on the 60° limit - *potentially* shading east end of roof up to 10am

75°E

Oscillating emergency bushfire sprinkler most water returns to tank

Sunshade

Sprinkler Range

Potentially shaded space when elm tree grows bigger

40° 60°

Pergola sunshade in summer

2 rows of amorphous PV panels at 16° tilt

Relocated TV antenna

All corrugated steel roof pitches are 10°

Ridge vent

Heliostat (see p 6-7)

Z

15°

Garden room

Gas fire flue

Reflector / PV (see p 6-5)

500mm access ways all around PV array (vital for fixing & maintenance)

Oscillating emergency bushfire sprinkler

255°W

No tall shading trees in this 60° segment

Quantum heat pump hot water system panels (no solar orientation required & well out of normal sight)

7-9.2 Roof plan of Mawson house showing the increasing value of the roof area in the sustainable house

100mm hex. head galvanised coach screws, which gave a 30mm 'bite' into the hardwood roof trusses at 900mm centres. This structure has survived some severe winds, confirming how critical wind uplift is.

Comparative PV generation/consumption — Mawson

COMPARATIVE EFFECTIVENESS SINCE COMMISSIONING PVs IN AUGUST 2000

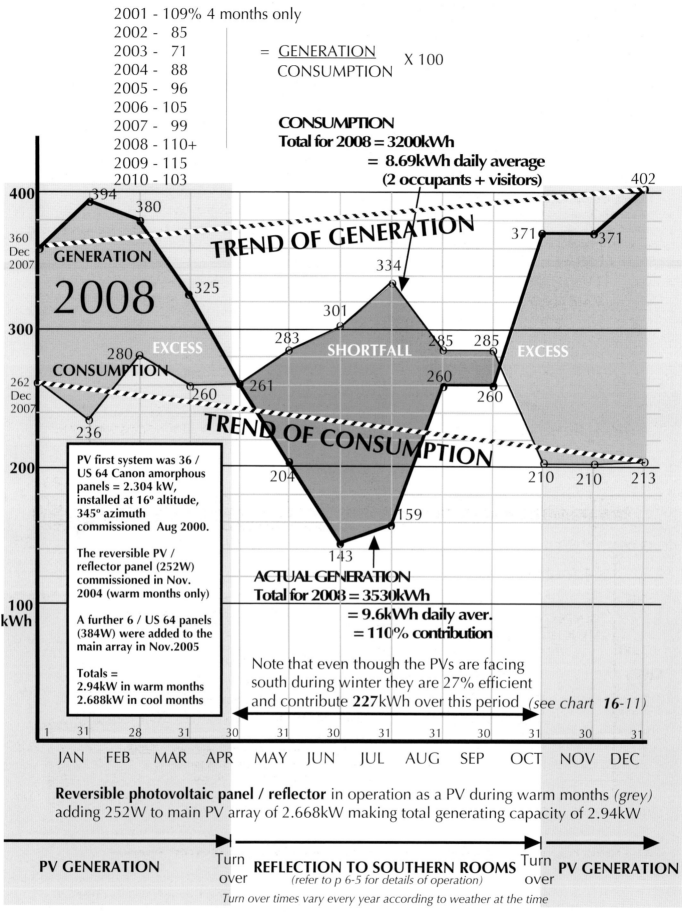

2001 - 109% 4 months only
2002 - 85
2003 - 71
2004 - 88
2005 - 96
2006 - 105
2007 - 99
2008 - 110+
2009 - 115
2010 - 103

$$= \frac{\text{GENERATION}}{\text{CONSUMPTION}} \times 100$$

CONSUMPTION
Total for 2008 = 3200kWh
= 8.69kWh daily average
(2 occupants + visitors)

GENERATION
2008

TREND OF GENERATION

EXCESS

CONSUMPTION

SHORTFALL

EXCESS

TREND OF CONSUMPTION

PV first system was 36 /
US 64 Canon amorphous
panels = 2.304 kW,
installed at 16° altitude,
345° azimuth
commissioned Aug 2000.

The reversible PV /
reflector panel (252W)
commissioned in Nov.
2004 (warm months only)

A further 6 / US 64 panels
(384W) were added to the
main array in Nov.2005

Totals =
2.94kW in warm months
2.688kW in cool months

ACTUAL GENERATION
Total for 2008 = 3530kWh
= 9.6kWh daily aver.
= 110% contribution

Note that even though the PVs are facing
south during winter they are 27% efficient
and contribute **227**kWh over this period *(see chart 16-11)*

Data points: 394, 380, 325, 280, 260, 262 Dec 2007, 236, 261, 283, 301, 334, 285, 285, 371, 371, 402, 204, 143, 159, 260, 260, 210, 210, 213

360 Dec 2007

400 | 300 | 200 | 100 kWh

| 1 | 31 | 28 | 31 | 30 | 31 | 30 | 31 | 31 | 30 | 31 | 30 | 31 |
| JAN | FEB | MAR | APR | MAY | JUN | JUL | AUG | SEP | OCT | NOV | DEC |

Reversible photovoltaic panel / reflector in operation as a PV during warm months *(grey)*
adding 252W to main PV array of 2.668kW making total generating capacity of 2.94kW

PV GENERATION | Turn over | **REFLECTION TO SOUTHERN ROOMS** *(refer to p 6-5 for details of operation)* | Turn over | **PV GENERATION**

Turn over times vary every year according to weather at the time

7-10.1 Monthly PV generation and consumption readings for 2008 showing excess export to grid over ~5.5 warmer months

DIY or contract? / Mawson PV trends

Lessons to be learned by the DIY enthusiast

Things have changed a lot since I started to install my PVs in 2000. There are now many more accredited installers, and prices seem to have come down to as low as $8–$10/W, compared to about $14.

Nevertheless, the cancellation of the $8000 federal grant has made life harder for the person who wants to do their bit — and DIY could still be attractive to those who are good with their hands.

The bureaucracy is now catching up with a fast-moving industry, and roof safety is now a requirement which the DIY enthusiast didn't have to consider in the 'old days' of 2000.

There are now many OH&S regulations and codes of practice relevant to working on roofs, and the DIYer would be wise to learn the easy way — things like safety harnesses, guard rails, ladders, safety meshes, etc. now need to be considered carefully. Working on a tiled roof of 20°+ pitch is no joke on frosty mornings or hot summer afternoons. Luckily, my roof was corrugated steel at 10° pitch, so it was easy to walk on, and tools mainly stayed where I put them. I now realise that I wouldn't even consider working on a tiled roof — leave it to the experts!

Lightning can seriously damage a photovoltaic array, but no instructions were given by the manufacturers, and very little seems to have been written about this essential aspect.

The cost of a strike could be potentially huge, so take the precaution of having a lightning rod at the highest point. I placed a 5mm stainless-steel conductor at each end of the ridge, separately wired to earthing rods so that any strike charge goes to earth *without going through any of the panels*.

Your accredited electrician should be aware of all these requirements. I can assure you that there is a big peace-of-mind factor which comes into play whenever an electrical storm occurs.

For some good information try:

wwwstaff.murdoch.edu.au/~mcalais/FlashprotectPV/

Warranty

Our panels have a 20-year warranty, so make sure you have the original receipt in a safe place with all the manufacturer's contact details on hand.

Trends in the generation and consumption of renewable electricity at the Mawson house
this is a most interesting graph of trends

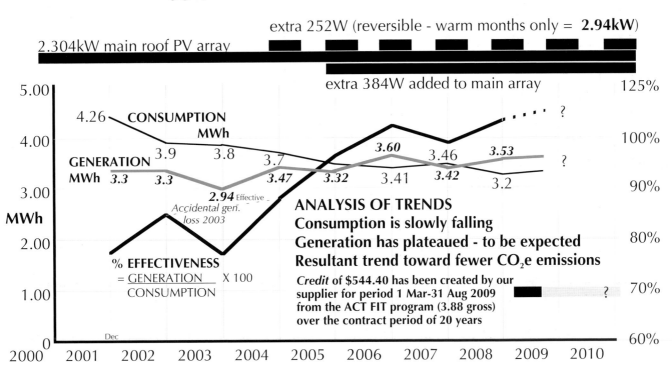

7-11.1 **Monthly PV generation and consumption readings for 2001 to 2008 showing rising generation over consumption**

Integrated photovoltaics — *the next rational step*

The dawn of a more integrated era

At the beginning of the 21st century we are still at the Model T Ford equivalent in the integration of solar-energy collection technology in suburban housing.

We are not thinking straight. We are still designing renewable energy technologies to be stuck onto the nearest suitable surface — the domestic roof — *instead of leapfrogging to the real problem of making domestic roofs themselves the solar-absorbing surface.* We are still hung up about what houses should look like, and they usually look like the ones we are used to!

We are at the dawn of an exciting period. Global warming is presenting us with the most marvellous *opportunity* we will ever have to design and develop new, autonomous houses, in which more energy is generated than is consumed, with as light a carbon footprint as possible, and which use no fossil-fuelled energies. But we are having to go through a painful period of change — of knocking the rough edges off technologies and making them integrate with the public concept of acceptable architecture, whatever that may turn out to be.

Australian universities have been at the forefront of developments in fundamental photovoltaic technology, and have produced some world-class thinking — only to find that the housing industry is not receptive to new ideas, blinkered by traditional continuation of one of the most unsuitable roof techniques ever developed — the clay-tile pitched roof which, with its many hips and valleys, was never designed to take PV panels.

Roof design is now the new solar frontier, and its potential needs to be recognised.

Germany (with only half the sunlight that we enjoy in Australia) has become a world leader with its development of integrated PV roofs, seen below in Freiburg.

7-12.1 **Residential units in Freiburg, Germany, built around 2000, with integrated, watertight solar roofs, creating 'solar surplus housing', of 445kWh capacity. Architect: Rolf Disch**

Even more integrated commercial models are coming onto the Australian market, in which the PV panels double as the roof — pioneered by Peter Erling of PV Solar Energy, St Peters, NSW.
<**www.pvsolar.com.au**>

7-12.2 **An elegant design solution: make the photovoltaic panels integral with the roofing — but it could go one step further**

Distributive generation — the 'down under' system

This means that electricity generated locally is used locally — with negligible transmission losses.

Australia's centralised generation of electricity loses about one third of the power simply by the transmission losses over very long distances. These are *enormous* losses, paid for by every consumer as part of their electricity bill, *but our environment also pays a price* from the creation of the enormous volume of CO_2e — due to the use of fossil fuels, a major contributor to environmental damage.

Housing in Australia is responsible for at least 20% of the total carbon emissions by way of emissions during manufacture and construction, and (the largest part) from the running costs over the life of the houses. It has been estimated in my latest book, *Low Energy Affordable Housing*, that about 90% of the polluting emissions from houses could be prevented by more careful design and by more aware styles of living.

The Mawson house, described in this book, already generates 10% more (carbon-free) electricity than it consumes in any one year, saving about 3.5MWh or 3.4 tonnes of CO_2e every year *(see graphs 7-10.1 & 11.1)*.

However, better design of *new* housing has little potential in the race against time to prevent global warming — unfortunately, it is too little, too late — but the *retrofitting of existing houses* and the re-education of all occupiers does have a chance of making a difference.

Existing houses represent about 95% of all housing at any one point in time, which is why it is important that readers of this book start planning to put these ideas into practical reality.

Having bought this book, you are obviously an intelligent and conscientious member of society. You have now assumed a measure of responsibility by becoming more aware of the problems we face and by actually putting these measures into practice. But first, gain a deeper understanding of the next chapters — they are the basis of most retrofitting activities ...

8

Mass and internal comfort

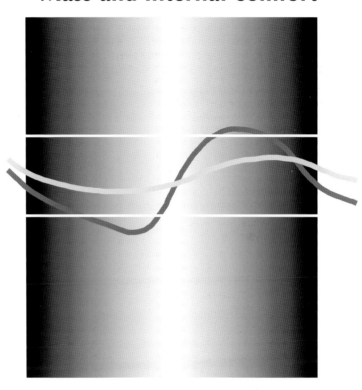

8-2   Controlling internal comfort

8-3   How mass can help

8-4   Trombe-Michel walls

8-5   Timber floors

8-6   Concrete floors

Controlling internal comfort

The value of internal mass in a cool climate

It has become common house-building practice to have external brick-veneer walls with internal walls of stud and plasterboard construction.

While it has some advantages for the builder it does not work well for the owner, in that the construction has very low internal heat capacity — it does not absorb gained heat from the sun very well, and does not help to smooth out the daily temperature variations to give the occupants more comfortable living conditions. *(See curve 1 below.)*

In fact, building research has now shown us that the brick-veneer wall is completely the wrong way round for comfort in most southern Australian climatic zones.

Let me give you an example — if your house has some good-sized northern windows which let in a fair amount of the warming winter sun it is likely that the room would *overheat* just after lunchtime because the stud and plasterboard walls could not absorb the excess heat, nor could they re-radiate any *significant* heat back into the room at night when the outside temperature falls around sunset. *(See curve 2 below.)* Consequently, there would most likely be a large daily fluctuation in comfort conditions.

If, on the other hand, brick or other high-density internal walls were in the room, they would absorb the excess solar heat during the day and radiate it back into the room at night — smoothing out the temperature variations to a more comfortable level during day and night. *See curve 3 below.*

Time and internal temperatures

The graph at the bottom of this page shows that *time* is an important factor if we are to use internal mass effectively (particularly with curve **3**). It shows that heat absorbed by dense materials such as brick, concrete, stone, and tiles during the daytime from *free* heat gained from the windows can be re-radiated back into the room after sunset when the internal temperature of the house falls below the absorbed temperature of the mass materials.

You may not sense this radiation, but it is there, and will be *helping to delay* the moment when the fossil-fuelled heater needs to be turned on to maintain your comfort.

There is a relationship between the *amount* of mass, the *temperature* of radiant and convected heat in the room (from the sun), the *time* it has available to absorb that heat, and other factors such as ventilation, and the amount and type of of insulation, etc. This is a complicated relationship, beyond the scope of this book.

As I am mainly concerned with *retrofitting* existing houses in this book, you usually have to start with a less-than-ideal structure around you, and see how you can modify it to provide more comfort by using natural solar energy in preference to expensive, polluting, imported fossil-fuelled energy.

Although a high mass ceiling would be most effective, little *useful* mass can be safely or easily added to current lightweight ceiling structures — so I will concentrate on how mass can be *added* to walls and floors, which are a little more manageable in a practical sense.

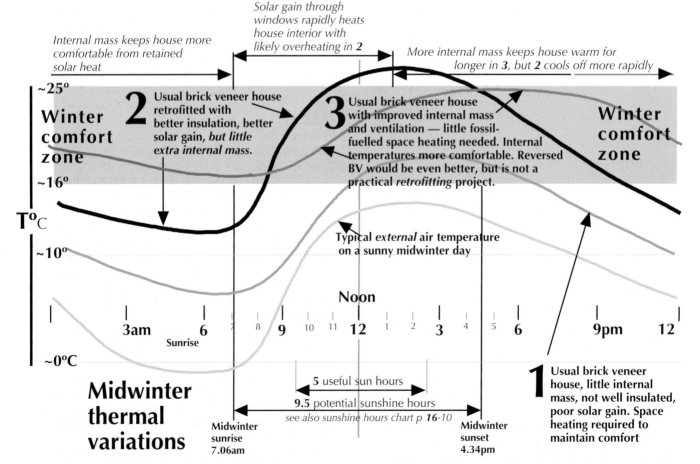

8-2.1   **Daily thermal behaviour of usual BV house (1) compared to two retrofitted cool-climate houses (2 and 3) in midwinter.** *Temperature curves are indicative only.*

How mass can help — *if it's in the right place*

External Walls

The usual wall in existing domestic construction is the brick-veneer wall, in which the brick skin is on the outside.

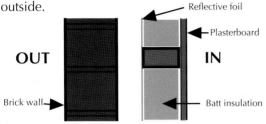

OUT   IN

High mass   Low mass

8-3.1 **Traditional brick-veneer wall of the latter half of the 20th C**

This wall construction came about largely because it enabled the builders to save time and money in construction. Its only thermal advantage to the owners over the old 11″ brick cavity wall (in the Canberra climate) was because 9–5 work patterns were often coupled with space heating such as wood fires, stoves, or oil or electric heaters being turned on in the evening (all fossil-fuelled).

This living pattern in an insulated brick-veneer house gave a quicker warm-up response when the heaters were turned on in the early evening — in comparison to 11″ brick cavity walls, which soaked up most of the artificial heat, to the detriment of internal comfort for the occupants.

However, in *solar* houses (new or retrofitted), which use the sun's penetration through larger windows as a heating source, the brick-veneer walls, with their low-mass internal walls (stud and plasterboard) are at a distinct *dis*advantage — they cannot absorb all the incoming heat in the walls and ceiling, and tend to overheat the air, to the discomfort of the occupants.

To put this simply: *solar houses which can gain most of their internal heat from the sun (particularly with reflectors — p **6**-2) need more internal mass to absorb the heat during the day for use at night when the external temperature falls (see diagram **8**-2.1).*

For this reason, a *reversed* brick-veneer wall (brick on the inside and insulation on the outside) will provide better thermal comfort. However, it is unrealistic to expect owners to change the external walls, so what can be done to increase the internal mass?

We need to look separately at the ceilings, walls, and floors of rooms, which have a significant input of solar heat through windows.

Ceilings

As the warm air tends to accumulate in the upper section of the room, the ceiling would be a logical place to add extra mass; but, unfortunately, the usual type of construction is inadequate to support any significant extra weight.

Surprisingly, plasterboard does have a high specific heat value (*due to its density*), but is too thin to be of significant usefulness. Even if a second layer were to be applied, the small gain would not be worth the effort. Its papery skin acts as an insulator, reducing thermal conductivity between the plaster layers, thus limiting its potential for absorbing and radiating heat.

A new material is now available in Australia, a phase-change material encapsulated in a plastic blanket, 430mm wide, which can be used as extra lightweight mass within stud walls, or laid directly on top of a plasterboard ceiling, under the bulk insulation. Details of BioPCM are available at <**www.phasechange.com.au**>.

Walls

Adding extra mass to internal walls is a little bit safer than adding it to ceilings, but will only give value for effort if the wall and the room receives direct sunlight for a reasonable time during sunlight hours. Unfortunately, most answers are messy, expensive, or possibly unsafe, so there is not much incentive.

There is one possible answer — a phase-change (high thermal capacity) plasterboard invented in Germany called *Smartboard*, but it is difficult and expensive to get in Australia. CSR in Sydney make plasterboard but, although many enquiries have been made, they don't seem inclined to make Smartboard, as they cannot be convinced there is a market for it! It has the heat capacity of 90mm of concrete, takes up very little space in the room (15mm), and would not be too difficult to apply. It is, practically, the only real answer to adding mass onto stud walls based on timber-framed floors, as the extra weight *could* be problematical — some extra support underneath may be called for, but that need not be too difficult if there is reasonable access space (*see also section on Trombe walls p **8**-4). Professional advice should be sought.

If, however, internal stud walls are built on a *concrete slab*, there is a possibility that adding a single-brick or block wall onto the solar (warmer) side of an internal wall could be an effective way of achieving extra mass. It could be a dry brick wall (no mortar), which is not so messy to construct, or it could be glued, but in either case should be tied back to the stud wall with metal ties for stability.

One *less messy* way is to build a dry brick wall in front of an existing stud and plasterboard wall, and take the opportunity at the same time of adding insulating batts between the plasterboard and the new wall. It will also need tying back to the wall.

A more inconvenient way of adding more mass would be to take the plasterboard sheets off the studs *on the warmer side*, stack old bricks into the stud cavities, and replace the plasterboard with 25mm compressed fibre-cement board as above. However, the discontinuity between the fibre-cement board and the bricks would be a barrier to conductivity and would reduce its efficiency.

Only rooms which receive solar gain during the day will benefit from this extra mass and, to be really effective, the areas of extra mass should be up to 6x the window area. Adding extra mass to rooms on the cooler side of the house would be of little value and a waste of money — unless reflectors as described on p **6**-2 have also been installed, in which case extra mass *would* be valuable.

In all cases, an engineer's advice should be sought, and you should have the original plans of the house.

See p **8**-5 and p **8**-6 for various other options.

Trombe-Michel walls

The Trombe-Michel heat-retaining wall

The principle of the Trombe-Michel wall (named after the inventors Trombe and Michel) has been around since the 1950s and has been used in various forms.

It is a means of storing the sun's heat inside the room by means of its high thermal capacity, due to its mass.

It can be made of any dense, heavy material such as bricks, concrete blocks, water-filled containers, even damp sand in suitable containers.

Water is by far the most efficient, having the highest specific heat or capacity to store heat. Its fluidity enables it to absorb heat on the side exposed to the sun which then sets up a convection current in the container ensuring that the heat is transferred to the whole of the contained water.

When the sun goes down and the internal temperature begins to fall, the absorber becomes a radiator, and the stored heat radiates *and* convects into the room.

Its main advantage is in providing heat storing mass in a room which has little existing mass – in particular a room with a suspended timber floor such as shown in the diagram below, where the incoming heat from the window would only serve to heat up the air in the room, with little ability to store it for the evening.

If the floor is a concrete slab with a hard integral covering such as tiles, bricks, slate etc. laid in mortar, **there would be no need for a Trombe wall** as the sun's heat would be absorbed by the floor and the view would be retained.

Other than using second-hand radiators from Revolve, I don't know of any commercially suitable water containers *as shown in the diagram below*. But if you understand the principle of the Trombe wall, it only requires your imagination and a bit of hunting.

Concrete-slab floors

Although I have indicated that there is no need for a Trombe-type wall with a hard-surfaced slab floor, there is a case for these to co-exist when you have a wall-to-wall carpet or parquet on concrete.

The carpet/parquet effectively prevents the slab from absorbing the sun's direct heat, so a Trombe system will certainly add absorptive mass to the room.

There is no *thermal* reason why the carpet under the Trombe wall would need to be removed, but the weight of the wall would leave permanent crush marks on the carpet underneath.

Bear in mind the stability of a Trombe wall if you construct it directly on the carpet. Some form of stabilisation may be needed at cross walls or in the centre where the curtains meet. Building on the parquet should not present any stability problems.

Factors to bear in mind are:

1 Will the wall be a permanent fixture or will you need to dismantle it if you wish to sell the house?

2 Cutting back the carpet would entail further expense and necessarily make the wall a permanent feature.

3 It would not be wise to build the wall on the carpet as if you decide to pull it down it may be difficult or impossible to eliminate any crush marks.

4 If the other walls in the room are masonry, building a Trombe wall will only add a small proportional benefit.

5 If the other walls are stud and plasterboard, the Trombe wall should make a noticeable contribution to daytime and evening comfort.

A disadvantage is that a Trombe wall of an effective height will restrict the view from a sitting position.

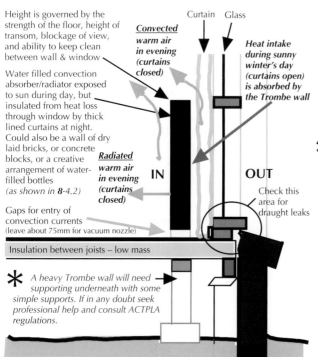

8-4.1   **One way of capturing and storing the sun's heat for use during the evening in a timber floored house.**

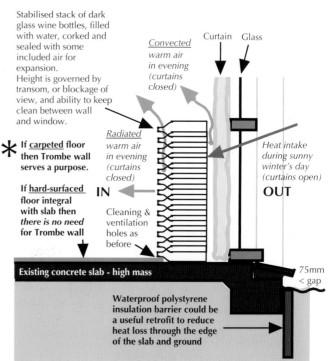

8-4.2   **One way of capturing and storing the sun's heat for use during the evening in a house with a concrete slab floor and carpeted surface.**

Timber floors – *options for increasing mass in sunlit rooms*
(applicable to ground floor or upper suspended floors)

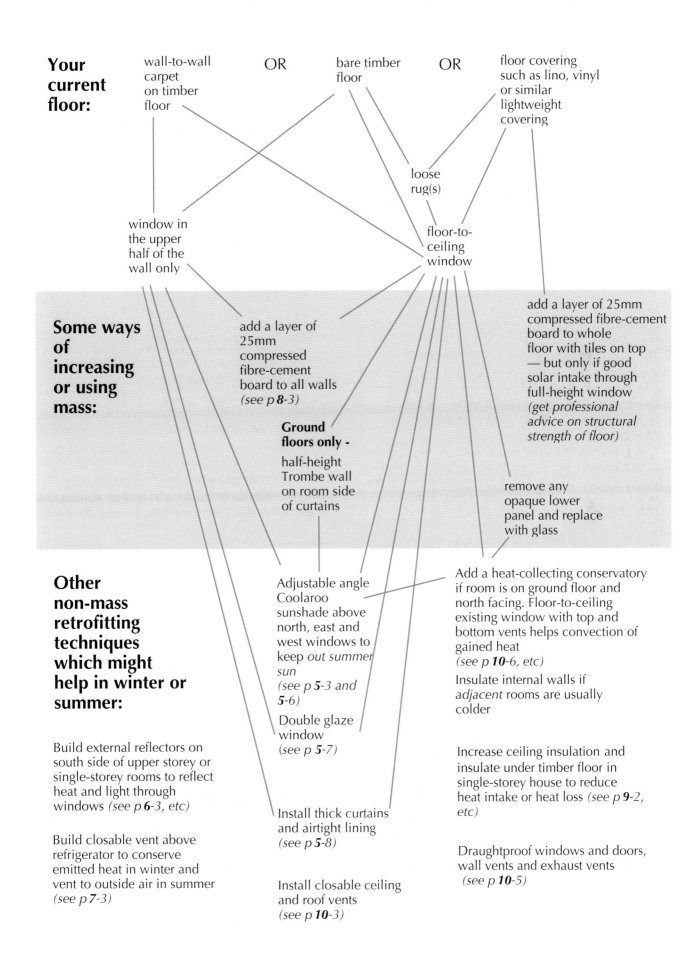

Your current floor:

wall-to-wall carpet on timber floor

OR

bare timber floor

OR

floor covering such as lino, vinyl or similar lightweight covering

loose rug(s)

window in the upper half of the wall only

floor-to-ceiling window

Some ways of increasing or using mass:

add a layer of 25mm compressed fibre-cement board to all walls *(see p 8-3)*

add a layer of 25mm compressed fibre-cement board to whole floor with tiles on top — but only if good solar intake through full-height window *(get professional advice on structural strength of floor)*

Ground floors only -

half-height Trombe wall on room side of curtains

remove any opaque lower panel and replace with glass

Other non-mass retrofitting techniques which might help in winter or summer:

Adjustable angle Coolaroo sunshade above north, east and west windows to keep *out summer sun* *(see p 5-3 and 5-6)*

Double glaze window *(see p 5-7)*

Add a heat-collecting conservatory if room is on ground floor and north facing. Floor-to-ceiling existing window with top and bottom vents helps convection of gained heat *(see p 10-6, etc)*

Insulate internal walls if *adjacent* rooms are usually colder

Build external reflectors on south side of upper storey or single-storey rooms to reflect heat and light through windows *(see p 6-3, etc)*

Build closable vent above refrigerator to conserve emitted heat in winter and vent to outside air in summer *(see p 7-3)*

Install thick curtains and airtight lining *(see p 5-8)*

Install closable ceiling and roof vents *(see p 10-3)*

Increase ceiling insulation and insulate under timber floor in single-storey house to reduce heat intake or heat loss *(see p 9-2, etc)*

Draughtproof windows and doors, wall vents and exhaust vents *(see p 10-5)*

Concrete floors – *options for increasing mass in sunlit rooms*
(applicable to concrete slab on ground or upper suspended floors)

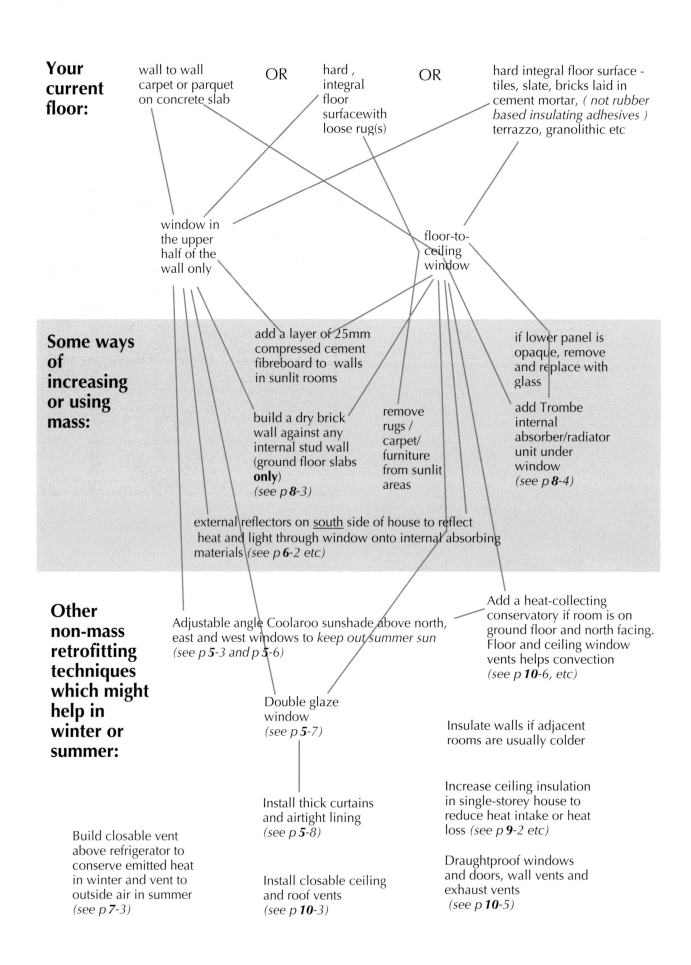

Your current floor:

wall to wall carpet or parquet on concrete slab

OR

hard , integral floor surfacewith loose rug(s)

OR

hard integral floor surface - tiles, slate, bricks laid in cement mortar, (*not rubber based insulating adhesives*) terrazzo, granolithic etc

window in the upper half of the wall only

floor-to-ceiling window

Some ways of increasing or using mass:

add a layer of 25mm compressed cement fibreboard to walls in sunlit rooms

build a dry brick wall against any internal stud wall (ground floor slabs **only**) *(see p 8-3)*

remove rugs / carpet/ furniture from sunlit areas

if lower panel is opaque, remove and replace with glass

add Trombe internal absorber/radiator unit under window *(see p 8-4)*

external reflectors on <u>south</u> side of house to reflect heat and light through window onto internal absorbing materials *(see p 6-2 etc)*

Other non-mass retrofitting techniques which might help in winter or summer:

Adjustable angle Coolaroo sunshade above north, east and west windows to *keep out summer sun* *(see p 5-3 and p 5-6)*

Add a heat-collecting conservatory if room is on ground floor and north facing. Floor and ceiling window vents helps convection *(see p 10-6, etc)*

Double glaze window *(see p 5-7)*

Insulate walls if adjacent rooms are usually colder

Install thick curtains and airtight lining *(see p 5-8)*

Increase ceiling insulation in single-storey house to reduce heat intake or heat loss *(see p 9-2 etc)*

Build closable vent above refrigerator to conserve emitted heat in winter and vent to outside air in summer *(see p 7-3)*

Install closable ceiling and roof vents *(see p 10-3)*

Draughtproof windows and doors, wall vents and exhaust vents *(see p 10-5)*

9

Insulation and internal comfort

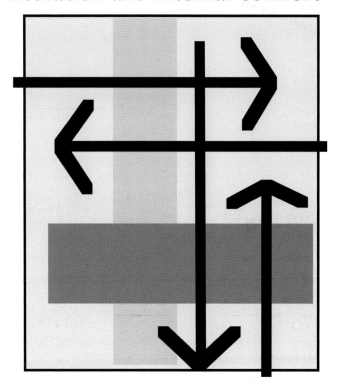

9-2   **Insulation**

9-3   **Insulation and ventilation**

9-4   **Insulation of timber and concrete
       floors**

Insulation

Insulation plays a major role in protecting us internally from the extremes of external heat in summer or the loss of expensive internal heat in winter.

The science of insulation has developed rapidly in the last few decades, yet even today there are many houses being built with inadequate barriers against heat transmission — both into and out of the house.

Before this period there would be millions of buildings with poor or non-existent insulation which are now extravagant users of heat obtained mainly from fossil fuels — electricity, oil, natural gas and firewood — all of which pollute our atmosphere and will become increasingly scarce, expensive to the point of uselessness and, eventually, unobtainable.

Until science and technology find us more suitable alternative sources of cheap heat — such as solar or hydrogen — it is essential that we take every possible step to *conserve* what we do have, to delay the day of reckoning. Hence, for me, the writing of this book.

Insulating new houses is relatively easy — and we now have mandatory minimum insulation levels, but retrofitting insulation into some of the older existing houses is a little more difficult, requiring a little understanding of the science of thermal movements and new methods of application which have only been developed in the last few decades.

It is not the purpose of this book to be a textbook on the science of insulation, but to show practical ways of making existing homes more comfortable for the minimum amount of money.

The ACT region has the reputation of being a cold place to live in, yet houses are still being built which are similar to those of the Sydney coastal region, which has a warmer climate. This is not good design.

The most common form of domestic construction around Canberra is the single-storey, brick-veneer house with a tiled roof, stripped down by competition to the bare essentials of keeping out the weather, but paying little regard to the dual role of keeping us warm in winter and cool in summer. Houses as built today by developers are the equivalent of the model T Ford of 100 years ago. They are not good value for money.

The combined roof and ceiling structure is a most important barrier in preventing heat loss and heat gain, but many *existing* houses have little or no ceiling insulation, and probably no sarking or reflective foil under the tiles.

Retrofitting this area of the house will return good benefits for the money invested.

In most pitched-roofed houses the placing of additional insulation over the ceiling does not present any great problem. It can be a DIY operation to keep costs down, but unless you are particularly agile and enthusiastic it is best left to the professional installer.

Which type of insulation should be used?
The best possible principle to understand is that 'still' air in small pockets will resist the movement of heat (up or down), so any insulating material which is bulky and very light in weight will give you the best results. Fibreglass or polyester batts, rockwool, treated paper, and natural wool are probably the best available today.

How much insulation?
How much you add will partially depend on how much is there already. Often you will find a token layer, perhaps about 50mm of some vague, grey fluffy material, which hopefully is not asbestos. If in doubt, get it tested through the ACT Health Protection Service, and act on their advice.

The recommended minimum bulk insulation for the Canberra region is R4 (the higher the figure the more effective), but if you have the money a bit extra would be a good investment, as the labour charge of putting in, say, R6 instead of R4 is the same.

However, twice as much insulation is not twice as effective. My feeling is that, if you have some existing insulation already in place — perhaps R1 or R2 — extra R4 batts would give a good return on investment.

The existing insulation probably lies between the ceiling joists or the trusses, and the new batts could lie over the joists, or the horizontal lower member of the trusses, thus creating 'still' air pockets between the two types. This improves the R value by reducing convective heat transfer — at little increase in cost.

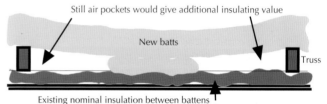
Still air pockets would give additional insulating value
New batts
Truss
Existing nominal insulation between battens

9-2.1 **Combining old and new insulation over the ceiling**

Reflective insulation
Reflective foil is not very efficient in a horizontal position such as over the ceiling as it relies on reflecting radiant heat, both down and up.

While its shiny surface looks good when you install it, if it is installed shiny side up it will soon be covered by a layer of dust which seriously reduces its reflective capability. If it is installed shiny side down on top of the bulk insulation it will not work because it needs an air space under it.

In addition it offers negligible resistance to upward- or downward-convected heat, so this type of insulation is not recommended for this situation.

It is better used as a reflective sarking layer under the roof coverings — tiles, metal decking, etc. Most roofs built in the last few decades have reflective sarking, its main function being to reduce the amount of solar heat emitted to the interior. This might have been fine when minimum insulation was placed over the ceiling, but it is my belief that the roofing is there mainly to keep the rain out, and has only a very small role to play in keeping the house warm or cool.

If your existing roof has no sarking at all, hardly any benefit will be gained by adding double-sided reflective foil to the underside of the roofing battens — more benefit would be gained from this amount of money by putting extra bulk insulation over the ceiling. There is no point in regarding the roof space as part of the habitable volume of the house. The only *cost-effective* barrier to heat loss or gain is the horizontal ceiling insulation.

Insulation and ventilation

Why don't we learn from history?

Modern technology has tended to make us forget our history. Dr Flynn of the Inland designed his naturally ventilated and evaporatively cooled house in Alice Springs in the very early part of the 1900s, drawing in cool air at the basement level and exhausting it at ridge level during the hot summers.

This was a real contribution to the science of natural ventilation, and it should be used today. Summer heat which has penetrated into the house through walls and floors can work in tandem with denser cool air from the outside garden to induce natural upward air movement through the ceiling and ridge vents.

I have now come to believe that the entire roof space inside a pitched roof should be regarded as being part of the external atmosphere in order to assist the vertical ventilation from the rooms below through the roof space out through a large vent in the highest point — the ridge. The diagram below illustrates this principle, which can be applied to almost every existing house with a pitched roof, and should serve to indicate how inter-connected the various aspects of house design are *(see details p 10-3)*.

The combined measures of natural ventilation and ceiling insulation that we have taken in the Mawson house have resulted in our internal room temperature not rising above 26° in a succession of hot days — without any air conditioning.

Air conditioning in cool temperate areas is really not necessary, and if these simple modifications were applied to all existing houses a summer surge in electricity consumption could be prevented.

Regarding the roof space as external space brings into question the need for a sarking layer immediately under the waterproof roofing. Certainly it has a role to play when under a *tiled* roof — to catch and drain any blown water drops down to the gutter. However, a properly laid metal roof over ~25° pitch should not require any such waterproof layer. Below ~20°, condensation could collect and drip down to the ceiling.

In previous decades, when ceiling insulation techniques were not as good as they are now, the roof space was warmer in winter and the warm, moist air would condense on the underside of the metal roof, requiring a sarking layer to convey it to the gutter.

If, however, the air temperatures above and below the metal roofing are similar, condensation would not occur and there would be no need for sarking or any form of insulation. This would be a saving in new construction, but does not help us much when dealing with the need to retrofit existing structures.

Whatever is there already is doing no harm, and there is no merit in pulling it out.

Wall insulation

Approximately 25% of internal heat can escape through external walls. So, if you intend to make the ceiling more efficient, the walls should be considered also. Retrofitting wall insulation (usually blown in) requires professional equipment. One hundred per cent covering of the wall area is not guaranteed; nevertheless it is still worth doing.

Consult a professional insulation installer.

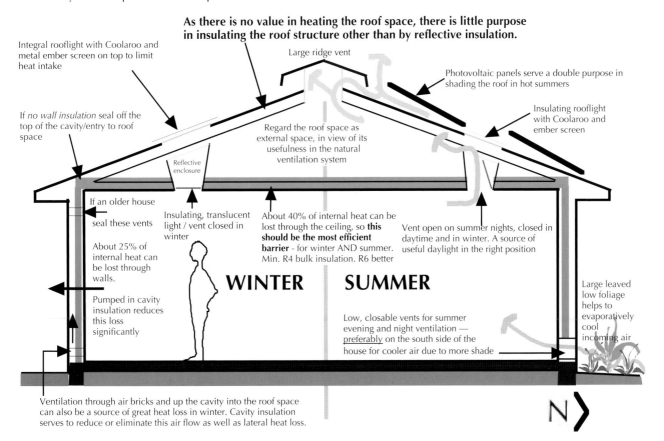

As there is no value in heating the roof space, there is little purpose in insulating the roof structure other than by reflective insulation.

Integral rooflight with Coolaroo and metal ember screen on top to limit heat intake

Large ridge vent

Photovoltaic panels serve a double purpose in shading the roof in hot summers

If *no wall insulation* seal off the top of the cavity/entry to roof space

Regard the roof space as external space, in view of its usefulness in the natural ventilation system

Insulating rooflight with Coolaroo and ember screen

Reflective enclosure

If an older house seal these vents

About 25% of internal heat can be lost through walls.

Pumped in cavity insulation reduces this loss significantly

Insulating, translucent light / vent closed in winter

About 40% of internal heat can be lost through the ceiling, so **this should be the most efficient barrier** - for winter AND summer. Min. R4 bulk insulation. R6 better

WINTER   **SUMMER**

Vent open on summer nights, closed in daytime and in winter. A source of useful daylight in the right position

Large leaved low foliage helps to evaporatively cool incoming air

Low, closable vents for summer evening and night ventilation — preferably on the south side of the house for cooler air due to more shade

Ventilation through air bricks and up the cavity into the roof space can also be a source of great heat loss in winter. Cavity insulation serves to reduce or eliminate this air flow as well as lateral heat loss.

N

9-3.1 The rediscovery of the value of roof ventilation and the growing use of large arrays of photovoltaic panels and hot-water absorbers should cause us to re-assess the need for roof insulation and its location. Most of the above techniques can be retrofitted.

Insulation of timber and concrete floors

Insulation of wooden floors

If your house is more than 20 years old it is likely to have a timber-framed floor of brick piers, bearers and joists with polished tongue-and-groove floorboards.

Not only does this sort of floor have very low mass value, in terms of absorbing any gained heat through the windows, it is also a source of direct heat loss to the cold ventilating air under the floor by radiation and conduction — and, as if that is not bad enough, major cold air infiltration through the shrinkage cracks which inevitably develop between each board and under the skirting board or quad *(see also p **10**-5 on heat losses and draughtproofing).*

These two sources of heat loss could be minimised by the installation of R2 insulating batts pushed into the space between the joists and held in place by perforated reflective sarking (shiny side down) stapled to the underside of the joists. This enables any condensed water vapour on the upper side of the sarking to escape through the holes. Alternatively, *double-sided,* perforated reflective foil *on its own* would be moderately effective (better than nothing).

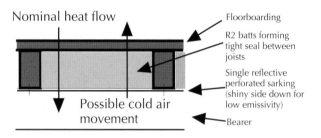

9-4.1   **Part section of traditional timber floor construction showing retrofitted application of insulation and low emissivity barrier**

It has been said that applying insulation in this way may contribute to a build-up of moisture under the floorboards due to condensation of the warm air travelling *down* through the gaps. Australian research on this is sparse, but the law of *convection* indicates that any air flow would be up rather than down (due to temperature differentials), and that any heat loss by *conduction* or *radiation* through the boarding would not be accompanied by a transfer of moisture.

Any warm water vapour from inside the house should theoretically condense on the colder sarking, and the holes would enable it to escape and evaporate to the air in the underfloor area.

In this climatic zone there should be minimal risk in applying the insulation between the joists to *reduce* the downward heat transfers, and in sealing the underside of the joists with a nominally airtight barrier, making a substantial contribution to personal comfort inside the house.

There are still persistent fears about 'dry rot' or *merulius lachrymans*, a throwback to our English heritage where the fungus flourished in unventilated, damp, underfloor spaces. I have not heard of a case in the drier Australian climate; but, if there is, it must have a very low incidence.

If anyone has information on any negative effects of this technique in Australia, please let me know.

Insulation of concrete slabs on ground

It has taken many years for the housing industry to appreciate the value of concrete slabs on the ground, but it still has not accepted the research findings indicating the amount of heat lost through the external edges exposed to the external cold air and moist soil, and how edge insulation can minimise these losses.

If you have an existing modern house on a concrete slab, the application of an insulating cover can be carried out by a lot of digging and placing of waterproof insulation. Most likely the edge of your concrete slab looks something like this:

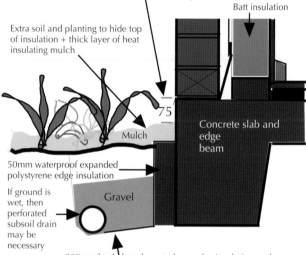

9-4.2   **Perimeter insulation to reduce heat loss from the exposed edge of a concrete slab on ground**

Waterlogged insulation has a reduced efficiency, so care should be taken to ensure it is waterproof grade. In addition, if a location could be regarded as wet, it would be wise to protect your investment by laying a perimeter subsoil drain in gravel to carry the water away to a sump for safe disposal or use in a drier area of the garden.

As this edge-insulation technique is relatively new to Australia, there is little experience about its resistance to termite attack. If the area you live in is regarded as as being termite-infested, it would be wise to contact a local pest exterminator to seek advice on how to termite-proof this edge insulation.

While the Canberra region is not at such high risk as further north, termites are active here. Climate change may well increase this risk. It could be worthwhile sprinkling some boric (or boracic) acid powder around as a deterrent. It is regarded as being environmentally benign.

There are other methods of deterring termites, such as non-toxic, fine granite screenings, stainless steel wire mesh, and impregnated termite moisture barrier film which can be formed around trenches and pipes.

10

Ventilation and internal comfort

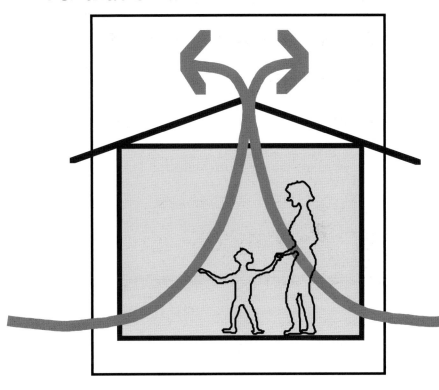

10-2   Using natural, free ventilation

10-3   Ridge and ceiling ventilation system

10-4   Ridge and ceiling ventilation system

10-5   Heat losses and draughtproofing

10-6   Conservatories as heat sources

10-7   Conservatories

Using natural, free ventilation in summer

In an effort to minimise pollution from fossil fuels, it is very appropriate to ask why so many people are installing air conditioners in their homes, when Nature will do it for *free*, given a little encouragement.

Natural ventilation is all based on the simple physical principle that warm air will always tend to rise vertically because of its own buoyancy. It happens without any sound, costs nothing to run and does not pollute the atmosphere — a really sustainable solution to internal summer discomfort.

This is a principle that has been known for many centuries, yet we have been so seduced by the wonders of electricity and our ability to fix every discomfort by simply flicking a switch that we have forgotten that there is a pollution price to pay in the long run.

When electricity is *converted* to work done — for example, electric motors, air conditioners, television, computers, etc — it creates heat which collectively contributes even more to global warming. The canyons of New York are said to be some 10° warmer than usual in summer, partly because of all the air conditioners discharging their collected heat into the external public space. Several cities in the USA have experienced severe overloading of the electricity distribution system, with resultant blackouts.

This situation is now happening around Australia.

An effective cooling system can be created in almost any existing house without using electricity — *so long as we use the natural tendency of hot air to move vertically rather than expect it to move horizontally through windows and doors, against its natural inclination.* This is easily achieved by installing closable ceiling vents in selected positions in the house coupled with a large ridge vent, as shown in the diagram below and operated as described on p **10**-4.

Cooling incoming air

On hot days the external air temperature is usually beyond our comfort level, so it is advisable to close all doors and windows to minimise hot air entry and close all curtains to minimise heat *radiation* from surrounding external buildings, walls, etc, which can be quite substantial (albedo effect).

However, there are at least three ways of obtaining cooler air from the south side of the house — all in conjunction with ceiling and ridge vents to induce vertical ventilation:

1 By using the existing underfloor vents on the *south* wall and closing off the northern vents. This air will be cooled by coming into contact with the surface of the cool soil under the floor.

2 By making an evaporative cooler on the outside wall, moist cool air can be ducted into the house (moist air in the underfloor space will encourage termites).

3 By burying large UPVC or glazed terracotta pipes in the cool soil below the vents, with screened inlets above soil level at each end, vertically ventilated air will be induced, and cooled on its way through. Internal ducting would not be needed unless the duct passed through the wall and was buried in the underfloor soil to obtain more transfer of coolness.

By installing a *vertical* ventilation system it is possible to keep out all or most of the hot external air, enable the cooler air from the southern side of the house to enter and, in the process, enable accumulated hot air in the roof space to escape. The real benefit comes by using the vertical ventilation system to operate throughout the cooler night to remove any residual heat from the house structure so that it has a lower temperature starting point for another hot day.

*How to do it? See pp **10**-3 and **10**-4.*

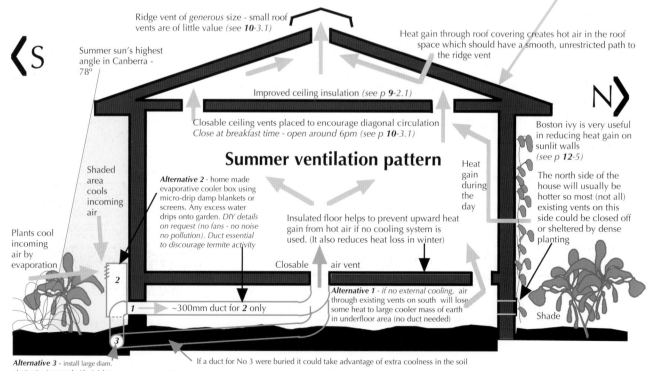

Ridge vent of *generous* size - small roof vents are of little value *(see **10**-3.1)*

Heat gain through roof covering creates hot air in the roof space which should have a smooth, unrestricted path to the ridge vent

‹S

Summer sun's highest angle in Canberra - 78°

N›

Improved ceiling insulation *(see p **9**-2.1)*

Closable ceiling vents placed to encourage diagonal circulation
*Close at breakfast time - open around 6pm (see p **10**-3.1)*

Boston ivy is very useful in reducing heat gain on sunlit walls
*(see p **12**-5)*

Summer ventilation pattern

Heat gain during the day

The north side of the house will usually be hotter so most (not all) existing vents on this side could be closed off or sheltered by dense planting

Shaded area cools incoming air

Alternative 2 - home made evaporative cooler box using micro-drip damp blankets or screens. Any excess water drips onto garden. *DIY details on request (no fans - no noise no pollution). Duct essential to discourage termite activity*

Insulated floor helps to prevent upward heat gain from hot air if no cooling system is used. (It also reduces heat loss in winter)

Plants cool incoming air by evaporation

2

Closable   air vent

Alternative 1 - if no external cooling, air through existing vents on south will lose some heat to large cooler mass of earth in underfloor area (no duct needed)

Shade

1   ~300mm duct for **2** only

3

Alternative 3 - install large diam. plastic pipe in ground with air inlets either end to supply *ground cooled* air to underfloor duct - the longer the better

If a duct for No 3 were buried it could take advantage of extra coolness in the soil

10-2.1 **Diagrammatic section through a traditional timber-floored house showing three alternative ways of cooling the incoming air in summer *without the need for energy-consumptive air-conditioning equipment or fans***

Ridge and ceiling ventilation system

Ceiling vents

These are controllable openings in the ceiling which serve a triple purpose: to enable any accumulation of hot air near the ceiling to escape to the outside air, thus enabling cooler air from the outside to replace the hot air in the room; to cool down the house structure overnight, ready for another hot day; and to provide daylight to dark spaces in the house.

The vents in the Mawson house *(details below)* are operated by a somewhat Heath Robinson system of fishing line, screw-eyes and a ring pull in a convenient location for operation when required. There is no need for hinges, which are rather difficult to place in what are usually confined spaces.

These ceiling vents are essentially a summer device, being sealed tight in winter. The closable panel is a translucent panel of polycarbonate Twinwall which acts as an insulator to reduce any heat loss. Under this panel is a flywire frame, and both are loose and easily removable for cleaning.

Location does not seem to be too critical, although it is best to pick a place which would benefit from some extra daylight, which is often in the centre of the house in a corridor. Ensure that it is possible to locate a skylight in the roof covering above the ceiling hole.

Make sure that the vent is visually placed in relation to walls and other ceiling features — lights, etc. Its size is not very critical, and can vary from a minimum of, say, 300mm square to up to 1m x 500mm. Its size will be determined more by the ceiling timberwork and appearance and — rather importantly — your ability to get your head and shoulders through it to see what you are doing than by any desire for a specific size!

Cutting ceiling vents in a plasterboard/batten ceiling is not a difficult operation for the average handyperson, but it does need patience and accuracy in locating the hole to suit the batten placement.

This requires access to the roof space above where you would like the vent to be in order to measure the space available between battens. After this, most work can be done from underneath, which is more convenient.

An easy way to locate a hole to avoid battens is to pick your approximate spot for the vent and drill a small hole roughly in the centre of where you want it to be.

Push a brightly coloured knitting needle or straight piece of wire up into the roof space through any insulation, so that you can see it in the roof space.

Having got this reference point, it is easy to measure where the battens are and transfer the sizes onto the ceiling underneath to enable accurate cutting with a sabre saw or padsaw. *(You'll need a nose mask.)*

Battens can be cut through — in moderation — as the rest of the plasterboard fixings can usually cope.

Roof lights and heat ingress

Because the roof space will be fully ventilated it is not critical that sun shading be placed on the outside to reduce heat intake. There is also no real need for expensive rooflight frames or domelights, nor for the ventilating variety which become more expensive.

Rooflights can be as simple as a DIY acrylic or polycarbonate insert of the same metal profile, or glass or acrylic tiles which are similar in form to the terracotta tiles. It is surprising how much light penetrates through a very small opening.

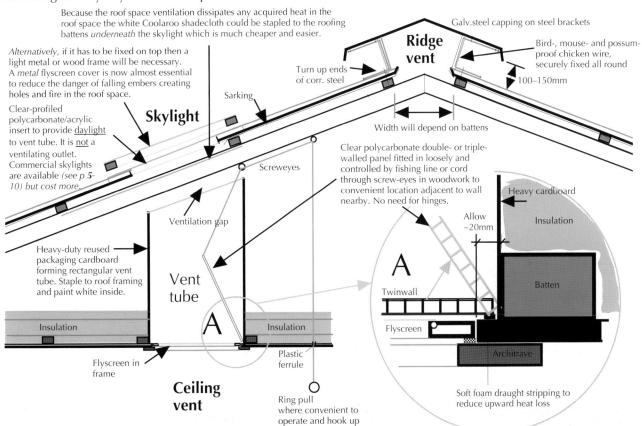

Because the roof space ventilation dissipates any acquired heat in the roof space the white Coolaroo shadecloth could be stapled to the roofing battens *underneath* the skylight which is much cheaper and easier.

Alternatively, if it has to be fixed on top then a light metal or wood frame will be necessary. A *metal* flyscreen cover is now almost essential to reduce the danger of falling embers creating holes and fire in the roof space.

Clear-profiled polycarbonate/acrylic insert to provide <u>daylight</u> to vent tube. It is <u>not</u> a ventilating outlet. Commercial skylights are available (see p 5-10) but cost more.

Skylight

Sarking

Turn up ends of corr. steel

Ridge vent

Galv.steel capping on steel brackets

Bird-, mouse- and possum-proof chicken wire, securely fixed all round

100–150mm

Width will depend on battens

Clear polycarbonate double- or triple-walled panel fitted in loosely and controlled by fishing line or cord through screw-eyes in woodwork to convenient location adjacent to wall nearby. No need for hinges.

Screweyes

Ventilation gap

Heavy-duty reused packaging cardboard forming rectangular vent tube. Staple to roof framing and paint white inside.

Vent tube

A

Insulation

Insulation

Flyscreen in frame

Plastic ferrule

Ceiling vent

Ring pull where convenient to operate and hook up

Heavy cardboard

Allow ~20mm

Insulation

A

Batten

Twinwall

Flyscreen

Architrave

Soft foam draught stripping to reduce upward heat loss

10-3.1 Details showing functional relationships between skylight, ceiling vent and ridge vent to exhaust hot air from rooms below and to provide daylight in dark areas

Ridge and ceiling ventilation *(cont.)*

Ridge vent — the key to natural cooling

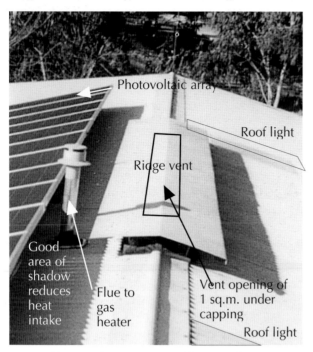

10-4.1 **Ridge vent: the secret to natural house cooling in summer. Also note very effective summer shade from photovoltaic panels.**

The ridge vent capping is long and low, and integrates well with the form of the roof. It is important, particularly on a low-pitched roof such as this, to stop-end or turn up the corrugated iron valleys at the top to stop wind-blown rain from entering the roof space.

Details *(see 10-3.1)* are for a corrugated steel roof, but the concept would work equally well with minor modifications for any other type of roofing.

As we have worked on the principle that the roof space is an external space, we did not make a closable flap in the ridge vent. On occasional hot windy days in summer we have noticed a warm downdraft under an open ceiling vent, but it should have been closed anyway during a hot day. Putting a closable flap in the ridge vent was a more complicated exercise and, on balance, we don't feel it is a necessary item.

There is a simple routine for the few hot days we sometimes experience in Canberra — keep everything open in the early morning until the outside temperature becomes the same as the internal temperature — about 9am — then close all doors, windows and ceiling vents, and close the curtains to *keep out the radiant heat and maintain the stored coolness.* This is where the natural daylight ceiling panels and the rooflights *(see photo above)* play their part in maintaining adequate lighting levels in the house.

At sundown, when the external temperature falls to the same as the internal temperature, we open everything up again to purge the house of any small amount of heat that may have filtered through. We keep the house open all through the night, so that it can cool down in readiness for another hot day.

By following this routine during hot summers, the Mawson house temperature has not risen above 26°, which we find quite acceptable — *without any noise, electricity or pollution*.

Conclusions

The system has worked very well over the last five years and the summer comfort range in the house — *without any air conditioning*— has been between 14° min. and 26° max.

These comfortable extremes are not just the result of the natural ventilation system. It is a combined result.

The Coolaroo sunshades are major contributors in keeping the hot sun off the east and north windows, as is the Boston Ivy on the eastern wall.

The photovoltaic panels also cover and shade *(see photo)* approximately 50% of the northern roof area.

In addition, the vine canopies and the deciduous trees on the northern side of the house ensure that the air around that side of the house remains as cool as possible, ready for when we open up the house around 6pm to let this cool air in to push the warmer indoor air out through the ridge vent.

In total, the house is now very comfortable in summer and, even with the curtains closed on a hot day to minimise the albedo radiation-effect, the daylight vents ensure that the interior is not dark.

It is becoming quite clear that there should be no real need for any air-conditioning system in any house in the south-east corner of Australia.

In fact, the presence of any air-conditioning system on the outside of a house is a good indicator that the house is not well-designed for the climate.

With climate-warming changes ahead of us, there is sure to be a big demand from house-owners for air-conditioning systems to be installed. The extra load on our power-generating facilities may well imitate the disastrous power failures experienced in California around the turn of the century.

If only we could convince people that nature can work for us, we could reduce atmospheric pollution — instead of placing implicit faith in polluting technology as the only solution. The switch on the wall has become far too convenient.

Other thoughts

I have often considered the advantage to be gained by taking further advantage of the sun's energy by installing a solar chimney.

The vent on the Mawson house (see above photo) has worked well enough, but it does not use the direct heat of the sun. If a taller, dark-coloured vent were installed the convected effect could perhaps be much improved. Consider this possibility:

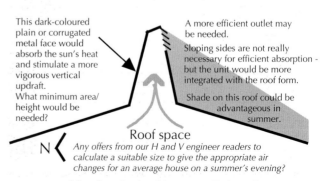

This dark-coloured plain or corrugated metal face would absorb the sun's heat and stimulate a more vigorous vertical updraft.
What minimum area/height would be needed?

A more efficient outlet may be needed.

Sloping sides are not really necessary for efficient absorption - but the unit would be more integrated with the roof form.

Shade on this roof could be advantageous in summer.

Roof space

N *Any offers from our H and V engineer readers to calculate a suitable size to give the appropriate air changes for an average house on a summer's evening?*

10-4.2 **Possible solar-stimulated house ventilation exhaust**

Heat losses and draughtproofing

Gaps

A very high percentage of internal heat is lost in winter because of gaps around doors, windows, vents, chimneys, exhaust fans, skirtings and wooden floors and other outlets, particularly in older houses.

Every leak of expensively warmed air to the outside is lost money, and every leak of cold air into the room has to be heated again. So every air movement — in or out — is a heat loss!

Every loss makes the global warming situation that bit worse, as most of our heating is fossil-fuel-based — natural gas, electricity or firewood — which means that it is putting CO_2 and other gases into the atmosphere, as well as using an increasingly scarce resource.

The easiest way of finding air movements is to use incense sticks: the thin plume of smoke is a very sensitive and visual indicator.

There are many sealing strips which can be used to close the gaps around doors and window sashes, and it is well worthwhile installing these. Chimneys in older houses and kitchen exhaust fans can be a big source of leakage, with not only warm air going up, but occasionally cold air coming down to replace the warm air leakage somewhere else. It is worth checking with an incense stick to assess the direction and velocity of the flow. Either way, it is bad news.

A simple way to eliminate the flow through the kitchen exhaust fan, if you are not using it on a daily basis, is to put a piece of paper or plastic film over the filter. *But don't forget it is there!* If you ever need a new fan buy one which has self-closing flaps.

It was common practice in old Victorian houses to stuff crumpled newspapers into the flue just above the fireplace — simple and reasonably effective *as long as you remember it is there* when you light the fire.

If you have decided to install ceiling vents (*see p* **10**-3.1), the translucent panel should seat itself on a soft draught strip similar to those around the doors.

Wooden floors

Another source of leakage in older-style houses is immediately under the skirting board where the timber joists and bearers may have shrunk away from the skirting, leaving a gap. Even though it may only be a 3mm gap it would add up to the equivalent of a

hole in the floor of 230mm x 230mm (about 9" x 9"), allowing cold air into the average living room. In mid-winter such a hole would be enough to neutralise any convective heating system in the room.

As if this isn't bad enough, there is often air leakage in the joints between the floorboards. Shrinkage of each board takes place over the years leaving small gaps which allow the cold air under the floor to blow up into the living space. In an average living room with a boarded floor a small gap of only half a millimetre between each board would add up to a hole 365mm x 365mm (1'2" x 1'2"). Add this to the skirting gap, and we get a hole some 432mm x 432mm (1'5" x 1'5"), which would almost turn the room into a refrigerator.

The draughts in such a room would be very diffuse and barely noticeable except for the fact that the heater has to be on for many hours to maintain warm conditions. The air leakage is usually being amply supplied by the numerous air vents in the brick or timber walls below floor level — probably a throwback from our English heritage when dry rot was very much feared in the damp English climate.

Closing the gaps in the floor could be achieved by a liberal coating of timber sealer.

Underfloor vents in external walls

These are a hangover from our English heritage, and are not really appropriate in dry areas such as the ACT region. They not only allow cold air into our living spaces, but hot air in summer.

Most of these air vents could be sealed up, leaving perhaps four vents — one in each corner of the house.

Leakage around the access door and holes in the mortar joints should also be looked at.

The next step — if you have sufficient access room under the floor — would be to add some insulating batts between the floor joists (*see diagram p* **9**-4.1)

If the incense-stick test indicates there is still air leakage around the floorboard joints or skirtings, all the joints should be caulked with a colour-matched elastic filler. These retrofit measures should make a big difference to your comfort and your heating bills.

Ceiling and wall vents

Although I doubt if you would find any in Canberra, the central ceiling feature of Victorian or Edwardian rooms in Sydney and Melbourne was a very decorative circular plaster moulding, with several holes to allow the combustion gases from the gas lighting fumes to escape. There is no such need now.

These are also leakage points, and could be filled with plaster or caulking.

Plaster or metal wall vents near the ceiling were usually obligatory under the building regulations until a decade or so ago. It is doubtful if they serve any useful function at all. These could also be sealed off, as they are undoubtedly a source of heat loss by ventilating to the external wall cavity.

The installation of operable ceiling vents/lights as described on pp **10**-2 and **10**-3 should cater for summer ventilation in a more functional way.

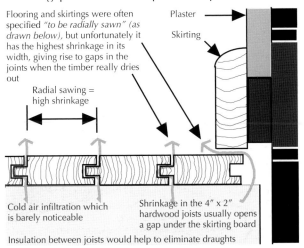

Flooring and skirtings were often specified *"to be radially sawn"* (as drawn below), but unfortunately it has the highest shrinkage in its width, giving rise to gaps in the joints when the timber really dries out

Radial sawing = high shrinkage

Plaster

Skirting

Cold air infiltration which is barely noticeable

Shrinkage in the 4" x 2" hardwood joists usually opens a gap under the skirting board

Insulation between joists would help to eliminate draughts

10-5.1 **Even small shrinkage gaps between floorboards and under skirtings could mean a large volume of cold air entering the room**

Conservatories as heat sources

A fully glazed, attached conservatory on the northern side of the house can be a most efficient collector and circulator of useful heat in winter — *providing* certain precautions are taken against summer overheating.

First, the basic principles. Ordinary glass is really a most remarkable material — it admits the short-wave heat radiation from the sun, which then heats up any dense material such as concrete, tiles, stone, bricks, etc. that it shines upon inside the house.

Having absorbed sufficient heat during the sunlit hours, these dense materials then emit long-wave radiation *which cannot pass back through the glass*.

This simple principle is the reason why gardeners' greenhouses are so warm when the outside temperature is cold — a principle we can use to advantage to warm our houses, *without noise and with no running cost*.

Conservatories also work on another principle — that *passive houses require active occupants* — which will soon become obvious.

There are several standard kit conservatories on the market now, but none that I have found are really designed to meet the requirements of a *house-heating* system, being merely glazed additions to a house for semi-outdoor living without any functional integration with the house itself.

This is a pity, because an attached conservatory could be much more useful in *heating the rest of the house*.

A simple test applied to a well-designed conservatory with the appropriate vents, top and bottom, is usually very convincing: put a lighted incense stick with its plume of smoke near the upper outlet into the house, and observe its direction and velocity.

Put the incense stick near the lower window and you will see a reverse smoke direction. These natural air movements are illustrated in the diagram below.

My first conservatory, built in the 1970s, worked very well, and was usually a very pleasant 10° warmer than the house in winter — even in cloudy weather.

Take the following list of requirements along to a supplier and ask them to modify their stock model — or hopefully they will read this and put a better version on the market. Please let me know if they do.

A conservatory such as shown below can usually be added to an existing house, *but the following eight principles must be adhered to, if you wish it to heat the house effectively (bold letters in text refer to diagram below):*

1 It must be on the northern side of the house, otherwise its efficiency as a heat collector will be much reduced.

2 It must be of an appropriate length relative to the house area to be heated; depth is not so critical except for living requirements.

3 It must have closable vents/windows of a sufficient area near the house ceiling (**a**) and closable vents/windows of the same area near the house floor level (**b**) in order to enable the warmed air to circulate around the house by convection.

4 It must have sufficient closable vents/windows in the lower part of the external conservatory wall for cooling ventilation in summer (**c**).

5 It must have generous operable vents in the top area of the conservatory (**d**) to exhaust the hot air to outside in summer through roof vent (**e**).

6 It must have some adjustable, translucent shading system (**f**) above or below the conservatory roof to exclude the heat, but permit daylight for growing plants, or

7 It must have only a small amount of *effective mass* inside the conservatory to enable the air to be heated for circulation around the house.

8 The occupier must understand the principles on which the conservatory works and act appropriately if the system is to be effective.

It could, of course, be completely automated to act independently of human intervention. But that would take away some of the healthy activity, and would not be in harmony with the principles of sustainability which are now evolving — *of understanding nature and acting in concert with it.* These principles are discussed in more detail in the following pages.

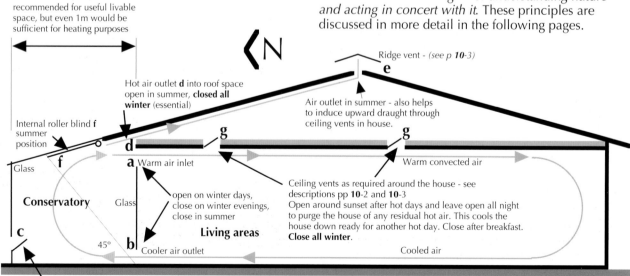

10-6.1 Basic requirements for the efficient functioning of an attached conservatory/house-heating system

Conservatories – *the working principles*

Principle 1 *(from previous page)*
Place the conservatory on the northern side of the house for optimum efficiency. Anywhere between 30° east to 30° west will be fine, but the western half is preferable as the afternoon intake from the sun has less time to dissipate the acquired heat before the cool of the evening sets in. However, if the house faces east or north it will heat up that much earlier in the morning: 15° = 1 hour of solar movement.

The northern side also allows the low-angle sun to penetrate into the house through the existing windows for maximum benefit *(see diagram p **5**-2.1).*

Principle 2
The collecting area (the area exposed to the sun) should bear some relationship to the area you expect to heat. There does not appear to be any research on this aspect; but a small depth, even only 1m, may be quite adequate for air heating, provided the conservatory is the same length as the house. However, other factors, such as cost and *usefulness* of the area, have to be considered. It would be reasonable to assume that the length of an added conservatory would produce beneficial results for that length of the house, but a lot might depend on the movements of people in the house — activities that disturb the flow of air and push it around. It is a somewhat empirical science, and more research needs to be done.

Principle 3
The positions of the opening vents between the conservatory and the house should be as near to the ceiling and to the floor as possible, to provide least resistance to the rather delicate convected air flow that is established by the differential temperatures.

Top and bottom vent areas should be roughly equal, and should not be less than half the length of the conservatory — about 300 to 400mm high. The top vents should preferably be bottom-hung, opening in; and the bottom vents should be top-hung, opening out, to minimise resistance to air flow.

Existing doors which are not full-height and normal half-height windows do not work effectively, as they either concentrate or interrupt the induced air flow which is slow moving and easily disturbed.

One advantage of having the top hopper opening into the living space is that it interferes with the closing of curtains, reminding you that on closing the curtains at night you have to close the vents (**a**) and (**b**) also! *(See diagram **10**-7.1 opposite.)*

Principle 4
A rule of thumb is noted in the American *Solar Greenhouse Book* (see p **16**-4) of having at least 1/6 the floor area of the conservatory as inlet vents (**c**) for summer cooling.

These vents should not be right down at floor level, but raised about 300–400mm above so as not to chill any plants growing in soil pockets below the vents.

These cooling vents work in association with the summer outlet vents (**d**) at the highest point of the conservatory, establishing a diagonal cross-ventilation pattern. Lower and upper vents (**a**) and (**b**) should be near the end walls so as to minimise pockets of still air, but just avoiding the opened curtains.

Principle 5
There *must* be operable vents at the highest point in the conservatory to exhaust the hot air that will try to accumulate in summer. This is vital if overheating in the conservatory is to be avoided, and can be achieved in two ways.

Commercial conservatories usually have top vents, but make sure there are enough of them and that they are at the highest point. These should be about 1/5 the floor area, because there is a greater volume of hot air to exhaust than there is of cooler air coming in from the lower external vents *(see diagram **10**-7.1 below).*

Unfortunately these opening vents usually preclude the placing of effective sun shading above or below the glass, as both are needed at the same time. This method of venting is not preferred.

A more efficient way is to vent into the roof space, providing there is a ridge vent of appropriate size installed. This has the advantage of ventilating the roof space and reducing the amount of heat being transmitted to the ceiling insulation in summer.

A greenhouse of at least half the length of the house would be needed to obtain good benefit from these ventilating techniques.

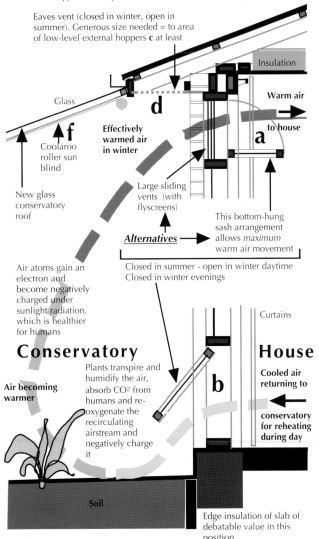

Eaves vent (closed in winter, open in summer). Generous size needed = to area of low-level external hoppers **c** at least

Insulation

Glass

d

Warm air

Effectively warmed air in winter

to house

a

Coolaroo roller sun blind

f

New glass conservatory roof

Large sliding vents (with flyscreens)

This bottom-hung sash arrangement allows *maximum* warm air movement

Alternatives

Closed in summer - open in winter daytime
Closed in winter evenings

Air atoms gain an electron and become negatively charged under sunlight radiation, which is healthier for humans

Curtains

Conservatory

Plants transpire and humidify the air, absorb CO_2 from humans and re-oxygenate the recirculating airstream and negatively charge it

b

House

Cooled air returning to

conservatory for reheating during day

Air becoming warmer

Air becoming warmer

Soil

Edge insulation of slab of debatable value in this position

10-7.1 **Winter ventilation movements in a retrofitted conservatory to a brick-veneer house** *(refer to **10**-6.1 for notation of detailed construction elements)*

Conservatories *(cont.)*

Principle 6

Ventilation of the conservatory is essential for removal of accumulated hot air in summer, while the direct penetration of desirable, low-angle winter sunshine through the conservatory to the living area behind also needs some kind of control. These control systems can be conflicting in operation, so careful design is needed in the conservatory roof area if you are to achieve good results with minimum effort.

The Coolaroo shading system described on p **5**-3 is, in theory, still appropriate here, but is not very practical in operation, bearing in mind that it has to be operated above a glass roof which is difficult (and dangerous) to reach and operate, so it is not shown here.

External shading of any kind would conflict with the usual hopper-type vent at the top of the roof glazing, so the alternative of venting through the eaves with a ridge vent becomes essential with this type of shading.

The shade area does not need to cover the entire conservatory roof — only enough to cover the window sill of the living room wall from mid-September to mid-April. This requires a cut-off angle of about 45° from the window sill *(see diagram below)*.

The important thing to remember if growing plants are present in the conservatory is that most require light in order to maintain their vitality, so shading is only really necessary for the *living room*, rather than all of the conservatory.

Internal roller-blind shading under the glass roof using 90% Coolaroo is probably the best solution, even though the sun's radiation is <u>inside</u> the glass, meaning that the internal air temperature will rise. However, if the eaves vent/ridge vent system is operating, this small disadvantage is not seen to be any problem.

One aspect which I regard as very important is the way in which the Coolaroo shadecloth permits the transmission of *daylight* so that the interior of the house does not become too dark, as with the more opaque canvas blinds and awnings.

Also, as mentioned in the section on sunshades, the quality of light under the white Coolaroo sunshades is really extremely pleasant — and useful *(see photo p **5**-3.3)*.

Daylight coming from overhead has a very definite quality that horizontal light from a window in a wall does not have, and the arrangement shown below has been tested over several years. The space proved to be very useful all the year round for relaxing, reading and gardening with an extended growing season.

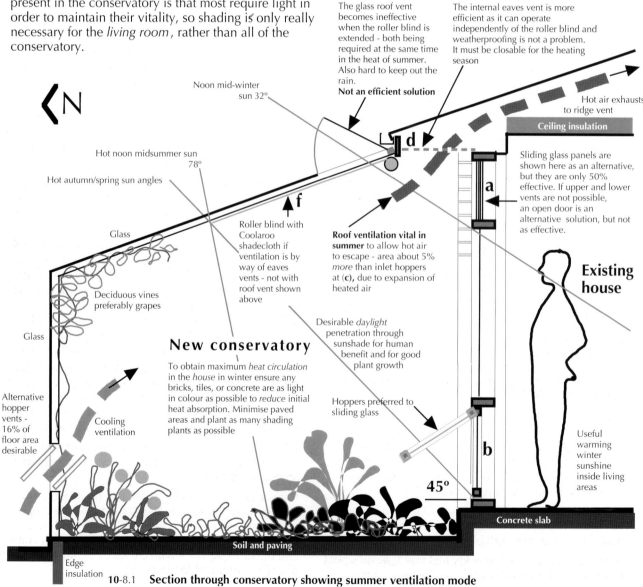

Alternative venting openings — vital for summer.

The glass roof vent becomes ineffective when the roller blind is extended - both being required at the same time in the heat of summer. Also hard to keep out the rain.
Not an efficient solution

The internal eaves vent is more efficient as it can operate independently of the roller blind and weatherproofing is not a problem. It must be closable for the heating season

Hot air exhausts to ridge vent

Ceiling insulation

Noon mid-winter sun 32°

Hot noon midsummer sun 78°

Hot autumn/spring sun angles

Glass

f

Roller blind with Coolaroo shadecloth if ventilation is by way of eaves vents - not with roof vent shown above

d

a

Sliding glass panels are shown here as an alternative, but they are only 50% effective. If upper and lower vents are not possible, an open door is an alternative solution, but not as effective.

Roof ventilation vital in summer to allow hot air to escape - area about 5% *more* than inlet hoppers at **(c)**, due to expansion of heated air

Existing house

Glass

Deciduous vines preferably grapes

Glass

New conservatory

To obtain maximum *heat circulation* in the *house* in winter ensure any bricks, tiles, or concrete are as light in colour as possible to *reduce* initial heat absorption. Minimise paved areas and plant as many shading plants as possible

Desirable *daylight* penetration through sunshade for human benefit and for good plant growth

Alternative hopper vents - 16% of floor area desirable

Cooling ventilation

Hoppers preferred to sliding glass

b

Useful warming winter sunshine inside living areas

45°

Concrete slab

Soil and paving

Edge insulation

10-8.1   **Section through conservatory showing summer ventilation mode**

Principle 7

The usefulness of thermal mass inside the house applies only minimally to conservatories. A properly vented (and controlled) conservatory as described here acts more as a daytime heat *collector and convector* than as a thermally smoothed living space. It is the engine room of a natural heating system.

Perhaps this can be explained by considering two extremes:

1 A conservatory with **minimal mass***, glass on three sides and light-coloured surfaces* would heat up the contained *air* very quickly under the sun's radiation, and this collected heat would enable the convection current to be established as quickly as possible to the colder regions of the house — to warm up its air and its structure, and return as cooler air to the conservatory for reheating.

The conservatory is continually converting the sun's radiant heat into heated air for circulation by a natural process which does not require any fans or use of electrical energy.

If the sky clouded over in the afternoon (as often happens) and the heat intake diminished, at least there would have been some benefit to the living areas of the house from the morning's circulation.

2 On the other hand, a conservatory with **maximum mass***, brick walls at both ends, dark slate floor and a brick external wall to the existing house* would waste a lot of the early sunshine hours, *absorbing* the incoming heat, rather than heating up the air for convective circulation. *This time-delay does not initially benefit the living part of the house.*

As with the first example, if the sky clouded over in the afternoon the morning's absorption would mainly benefit the conservatory, convecting little into the house. Some of this stored heat might be persuaded to convect into the house in the early evening by leaving the vents and the curtains open — but normally the owner would be wanting to *close* them to conserve whatever heat the house had acquired during the day. This would be conflicting.

At least the warmer conservatory would reduce the heat loss from the house during the evening and night, and carry some of its store of heat into the cold hours of early morning — so some benefit would be gained.

Little published research has been done on the dynamics of this situation; but we feel sure, from empirical experience, that a low-mass conservatory structure would give the best convective results for the benefit of the house.

Principle 8

Like many of the purchases we make these days, it pays to read the instructions and become familiar with how to make the thing function; and, in this case, the underlying physical principles of a functional conservatory also need to be understood.

Just as we learn to drive our car and respond to various stimuli, so we need to learn to 'sense' our house to obtain comfortable conditions.

In **late spring***,* you will quickly feel that the sun's heat has become undesirable and it is time to change

over to summer mode — usually around mid-September in the Canberra region.

Shade the glass roof as much as is needed, open the conservatory eaves vents (**d**) *(see diagram p **10**-6.1)* to exhaust any hot air, and open the hopper vents (**c**) at the bottom of the outside conservatory wall. Close the upper and lower vents in the living space (**a**) and (**b**). This conserves the residual *coolness* in the house.

If the living areas in the house have accumulated some unwanted heat by evening time in summer, open the vents (**c**), (**d**) and (**h**) to exhaust the hot air to the roof space and the ridge vent (**e**). Close vents (**a**), (**b**) and (**h**) in daytime.

Leave all these vents open during the night to purge the house as much as possible and to attract the cool ground air into the house so as to have as cool a start as possible if another hot day is forecast.

In **mid-autumn** (when the hot days have gone), retract the roller blind (**f**) to allow maximum solar access, close the external conservatory vents (**c**), open the top and bottom house vents (**a**) and (**b**) at breakfast time to allow convection circulation to start, and close again at night when the sun has gone down. Close the curtains at night to conserve gained heat.

You would find it very helpful to buy an indoor/outdoor digital thermometer to develop a sense of your comfort range and to guide your opening and closing of vents. The outdoor sensor could be placed in the conservatory at the indoor lower vent level (**b**) — but *not* where the sun can shine on it! — and the LCD display which registers indoor temperature could be on your desk for ease of reference.

If the conservatory is large enough for a pond, the water, with its high specific heat, would make a good absorber, *but only if* you wish to increase the mass. Otherwise it is a disadvantage.

Rainwater could feed the pond, and you could grow watercress and circulate the water with a hydroponics system for a soil-less and low-water-consumptive way of growing your vegetables.

A little-known fact is that of ionisation of the air in the conservatory. Without going too much into the physics of how the sun's radiation affects the attachment of electrons to air atoms inside the conservatory, it does create negative ions which, we are led to believe, are healthier for us than positive ions. These then get circulated around the house to replace the staler air, which returns to the conservatory for re-ionisation.

An attached, integrated conservatory is a marvellous mechanism for collecting and circulating warm air, and works well in the cooler ACT region — once you have learned to drive it. It sounds complicated, but is really easy once you understand the theory behind it.

It has the warmth to extend the growing season for all your vegetables, and it makes a pleasant eating area among all the greenery.

It is not just an extra living space to be added onto your existing house; it is a very functional heating control system for the house and a delightful spot for those rare moments when you can relax with a coffee and the newspaper — with excellent lighting and a very pleasant, comfortable temperature.

Conservatories – *alternative extensions*

A glazed living space or a heating machine?

In adding a glazed enclosure or conservatory onto an existing house it is important to be clear about your expectations and to understand the effects of *time, mass* and *colour* in such an addition.

There are four likely types of existing ACT houses:

1 Existing brick exterior with slab floor

If you have a brick exterior to your house (often dark in colour), the sun's heat will be absorbed by the brickwork mass in the *early* part of the winter's day. As the house will be low on the ground you will have two extension options: **a**, extend the slab, which will add more mass and initially absorb the heat from the sun in the first part of the morning, leaving little heat to set up a warming convection current for the house.

There are only about four hours of useful warming sun in winter, which could be a critical factor if you are expecting the conservatory to warm your house. To make matters worse, the warmed mass will give up its heat in the late afternoon, setting up its convection current too late to have much effect upon warming the house — around 5pm you will very likely be wanting to close the curtains in the living area and close the wall vents at the same time. This process is *out of step* with the basic principle of our natural heating system.

It has one advantage, however: it will reduce the heat loss through the connecting wall because the conservatory will be quite warm until around 7pm.

In this situation it is important that you reduce the heat absorption of the brick wall and the new floor by making them as light in colour as possible. The sun's heat will then be reflected (rather than absorbed), and will heat the air rather than the mass, setting up the convective current much earlier in the day — *which is what you need if you wish to heat the house.*

Alternative **b** would be to have an earth floor with lots of plants which would minimise the absorption of solar radiation by their transpiration. A small amount of brick paving would be OK to give some living space amid the greenery. *This is a more efficient arrangement if you want the conservatory to heat the house by convection.*

2 Existing brick exterior with suspended wooden floor

This may well require an extended wooden floor for your new conservatory, which is good in that its lack of mass will help the convection current get started early in the day. To avoid losing the gained solar heat through the suspended wooden floor it is important to insulate it underneath *(see pp 9-4.1 and 9-4.2)*. Paint any existing brickwork white or a very light colour as described in **1** above.

3 Existing timber external wall on slab floor

Paint the existing wall a light colour and use very light tiles on the new slab — or have an earth floor as in **1**.

4 Existing timber external wall with wooden floor

As **3** and insulate the floor as in **2**.

In all cases the principles of summer relief venting *must* be carried out as well as the adjustable sunshading below the glazed roof (see p **10**-8.1).

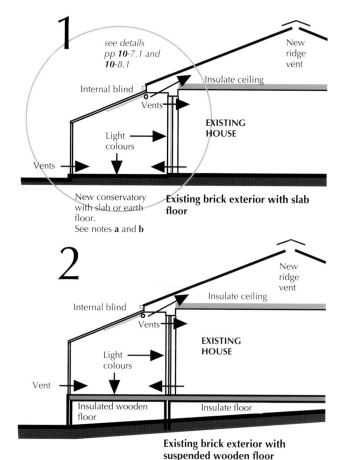

Existing brick exterior with slab floor

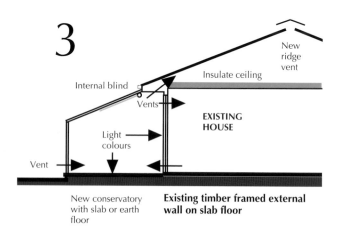

Existing brick exterior with suspended wooden floor

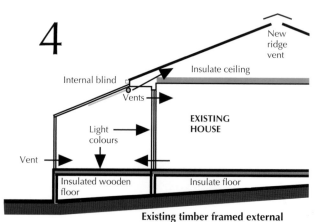

Existing timber framed external wall on slab floor

Existing timber framed external wall with wooden floor

10-10.1 **Different extension possibilities to suit the existing house**

11

Rationalising water usage

What use is money in the bank if there's not a drop

to

drink

11-2 **Our profligate usage of water**

11-3 **Reducing our water consumption**

11-4 **Modifying our water-using equipment**

11-5 **Rainfall**

11-6 **The arguments for and against tanks**

11-7 **How much rainwater can we collect?**

11-8 **Where can we place tanks?**

11-9 **Sizes and location of tanks**

11-10 **Option 1** – *tank input/output graph*

11-11 **Option 1** – *tank flow analysis*

11-12 **Option 1** – *the physical possibility*

11-13 **Options 2 and 3**

11-14 **Comparative analysis of Options 1, 2, and 3**

11-15 **So what is the best value?**

11-16 **Gutter guards, diverters, and filter bags**

11-17 **Low-cost variable toilet-flushing mechanism**

11-18 **Re-using domestic greywater**

11-19 **Direct and subsoil disposal of greywater**

11-20 **Re-using kitchen greywater**

11-22 **On-site subsoil drainage of greywater**

11-23 **Making suitable connections to existing greywater outlets**

Our profligate use of water

What we have become used to

Urban societies around the world have grown up with water, sewerage and stormwater systems developed in Victorian times to suit the circumstances of those days.

They undoubtedly served us well in the 19th and 20th centuries, reducing disease and giving us a high degree of convenience — if you will pardon the pun.

We now take water quality and quantity and the disposal of our wastes for granted. due to the skill and diligence of the engineers employed by our local authorities.

However, increasing population, air pollution and our consumer society, our inappropriate use of land, and our destruction of tree cover are now affecting our climate through global warming — evidenced by the increasing severity of droughts, floods, dust and topsoil storms, cyclones, etc.

All this is putting increasing pressure on our man-made systems. The time has arrived for a review of how we use water and how we dispose of our wastes.

This is a huge problem, well beyond the aim of this book, but there are modifications that each of us can make to our houses which could very well save our local authorities from having to build extremely expensive new dams — which, of course, will increase our rates and taxes.

What can we do?

Firstly, we must clarify what the problem *really* is as it affects our existing houses, so that we can optimise any solution and keep its cost to an acceptable minimum — otherwise, to be realistic, it won't get done at all.

Our mains water is purified and treated to make it suitable for human ingestion, yet only around 1% or 2% is used for this purpose. The result is that about 98% of our water is much too good for washing ourselves, our clothes, our dishes and our car, flushing toilets, and watering the garden, etc.

This *pure* water is used as a transport agent through the sewers for our toilet and other wastes. Until every house and living unit treats its own wastes on-site (highly unlikely) we must continue with this system.

The collected rainwater from all our roofs is piped away to the stormwater system, ending up in the surrounding seas. Those of us who live in urban areas make little or no use of this valuable resource. This is enormously wasteful and very unsustainable.

As with most other sustainability issues, time is now a critical factor and corrective measures cannot be put off indefinitely.

Individuals can collectively make great changes and we all have some responsibility to do our bit.

Three changes could have a significant effect:

1 Every individual could reduce his or her total usage of drinkable mains water.

2 Every existing urban house could find ways of using its rainwater as effectively as possible.

3 Every existing urban house could find ways of re-using some or all of its grey water.

Each of these three retrofitting measures will be dealt with in following sections of the book. But, first, it is important that each household understands the various components of its current level of water consumption — and what it is costing at the moment.

The figures are naturally very variable, depending on individual preferences, how we share water usage as with clothes and dishwashing machines, car washing, etc, but it will at least give you a guide to help in making your own assessments and to see where you can save both water and money.

If you need wider guidance in assessing your usage, read Allan Windust's very detailed book *Waterwise House and Garden* (see p **16**-4).

It is easiest to assess usage on an individual daily basis, as it allows you to extrapolate your figures to any size of family, garden or number of cars.

Current daily water usage for one person

Usage point	Estimates of what we have become used to	Reader's usage estimates
Washbasin	Cleaning teeth, washing hands and face under running tap, or using warm/hot water in bowl requiring cold run-off say 3 x 3L = **9** L	
Shower (no bath in use)	Deluge type of shower head and long showers say 20 L/min x 5mins./day = **100** L	
Bath	Bath once per week say 140 L (+ daily showers shown below) (daily equiv.) = **20** L	
Toilets	Single flush of about 9L in many existing houses. Say 8 flushes/day = **72** L If dual flush 6/3 cistern, this could be = **27**L	

Shared usage for family of ~three

Kitchen sink (no dishwasher)	~ 3 washups of 8L + cleaning vegs. + drinks + cooking + misc. uses, say 30 L for family of 3 = /pers/day= **10** L	
Dishwasher (*alternative* to sink washups only)	1 full cycle wash of 39L + cleaning vegs. + drinks, + cooking + misc. uses at sink, say 45 L for family of 3 = /pers/day = **15** L	
Clothes washing machines	Consume between 38 and 192 L / wash of *potable hot and cold* water = ~115L average for 1 or a small family of 3 - say 2 uses per week = 230 L / week /3 persons/7 days = /pers/day = **11** L	
External garden taps	Hosing, sprinklers on lawns, flower beds, washing car, say 1500 L /wk average over year, for family house of 3 = /pers/day = **71** L	
Tub	Perhaps occasional use for handwashing of delicate items. Say 1 use /week of ~ 20L for 3 people = /pers/day = **1** L	

11-2.1   These estimates would give us a variation of approximately 294 (washing up)– 300 L /pers./day (using dishwasher) giving annual consumption figures of :

1 person = **107,310–109,500 L/yr**
2 persons = **214,620–219,000 L/yr**
3 persons = **321,930–328,500 L/yr**
4 persons = **429,240–438,000 L/yr**
5 persons = **536,550–547,500 L/yr**

Note: It must be appreciated that these estimates could vary considerably depending upon personal usage, wastage due to dripping taps, etc, but they do serve to give an order of consumption which can be used for comparison with rainfall collection figures and what we might reasonably aim at as a more sustainable situation — *see following pages.*

Reducing our water consumption

Change the big ones first

If we group similar current water usages together in a pie chart we can get a better visualisation of the major consumption pattern:

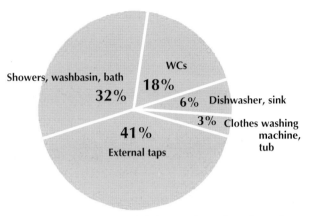

11-3.1 **How we are currently using our domestic mains water**

The major uses of **garden, personal washing and WCs** use approximately **91**% of our total *potable* water consumption, *all of which is too good for those purposes.*

If we wish to significantly reduce our use of this expensive water then obviously these three areas should be the first ones to look at.

The aspects we should consider **as a matter of urgency** must be:

1 *Our extravagant use of water: determining what is reasonable usage, then changing our habits and needs.*
The garden is the greatest consumer of our super-pure water, and lawn areas are without doubt the most significant. A life-cycle analysis of well-maintained lawns show that they really are an expensive and consumptive luxury in domestic gardens *(see p 12-6).*

Washing cars at home, hosing down driveways and paths, and excessive lawn watering running down the gutter should be matters of personal embarrassment.

Showers, toilets and baths are the most consumptive of our regular uses indoors, and with a little bit of discipline the amount of mains water used could be reduced very significantly by behavioural change.

2 *The efficiency of the various pieces of equipment we use: shower heads, dishwashers, clothes washers, WCs, garden irrigation sprays, drippers, etc.*
For example, changing the shower heads to AAA rating is probably the easiest, quickest and cheapest way of making a useful change — other items need more discussion.

Obviously, no one is going to immediately throw out their dishwasher or clothes washing machine just because they are not regarded as the most economical in water use. But the *way* in which they are used can be reconsidered — *right now!*

Buying a new machine should be a last resort and could well be counter-productive when the total energy and resources embodied in the product are considered.

3 *The possibility of using other sources of water in place of mains water.*

Having looked at *and acted upon* **1** and **2** above, we could investigate the effectiveness of using other sources of water, such as rainwater, greywater and perhaps, if pushed, borewater *(see pp **11**-5 and **11**-18).*

Climate change implications

The recent drought in Australia has made us all much more conscious of our looming shortage of water. To our credit as a thinking community, we have already reduced our consumption in Canberra very significantly.

Long-range weather forecasts indicate that global warming and resultant changes in climate should cause us to *continue* to be water conscious.

All the more reason, then, that we should be making some assessment of what minimum water use we can reasonably achieve — both immediately and as a long-term goal — remembering that global time is ticking away.

Consider the following estimates which could be put into effect immediately by changing our behaviour:

Analysis of daily water usage by one person *if we really tried to change our behaviour*

Estimates of what we *could* become used to:

Washbasin	Cleaning teeth, refreshing hands and face under small dribble of cold water, shutting off when not using. Minimise or eliminate use of soap. Use electric razor if you can, instead of lather and razor .... < 1 L
Shower (no bath in use)	Install AAA shower heads (9L/min) and limit showering time to 2 minutes. Minimise soaping ....**18** L (some AAA shower heads can be modified to 6L/min.)
Bath	Nil. Eliminate bath usage. Use shower instead. -
Toilet	Install dual flush (6/3) WCs, (or modified cistern mechanism), ... **28** L

Shared daily usage for three people

Kitchen sink (no dishwasher)	2-3 washups/day of 6L + cleaning vegs. under a dribble of water + drinks + sparing misc. uses ie. save cold run off water in bucket to water plants ....24 L /3 = ... **8** L
Dishwasher (*alternative* to sink washups only)	Don't use the dishwasher at all as even one use exceeds daily use of the sink. Use sink as above. -
Clothes washing machines	Cold washes are now regarded as just as effective as hot but only saves electricity rather than water. ~115L/ wash as previously. Assume need for 2 *cold* washes /week = ~224 L / week / 3 people / 7days with grey water on garden................ **11** L
External garden taps	Reduce usage, no sprinklers, no lawn, no car washing, but hand held hosing on dry areas. Keep small bucket for cold run-off in sink for garden areas which receive no rain + WM effluent-mains water.....**20** L
Tub	Use could almost be eliminated *Too small to be included in calculation.*

11-3.2 **What we could save by behaviour modification**

The total daily usage for one person could be reduced to about **86** L largely *by behaviour modification*, which represents a very significant 70% saving over what we have become accustomed to. The following *reduced* annual consumptions for various sizes of families can now be compared with the previous estimate of *usual* usage:

Reduced consumption	Usual *(from p **11**-2.1)*
1 person = **31,390** L / year	**107,310** minimum
2 persons = 62,780	214,620
3 persons = 94,170	321,930
4 persons = 125,560	429,240
5 persons = 156,950	536,550

Modifying our water-using equipment

There are several books and booklets available which detail the physical and behavioural modifications which the average water consumer can put into effect, so this section will only cover aspects which I have experimented with or which I feel have not been covered in other books.

Toilets
There are now available various toilet units which give alternative flushes of 3 and 6 litres, but I have found from my enquiries that the shops are only interested in selling you a bowl *and* a cistern, maintaining that a 3/6 cistern on its own does not adequately flush a normal bowl. This is somewhat biased advice, as I have modified our cistern flushing mechanism to give smaller flushes with the same bowl, which works 95% of the time.

Our Caroma cisterns had a push button on top which, by lever action, initiated a *fixed* flush of about 9L.

By taking out the mechanism and installing a home made lift-up button, which simply lifts the bottom rubber washer off its seat, we can now obtain quite adequate flushes to clear the bowl with **1.8** and **3.9** litres — say **2/4** instead of the **3/6**. A competent handyperson could manage this, but alternatively, bend down the float arm to reduce the volume of one full flush — or put a 1L plastic bottle in the cistern.

Potential savings could be:

Usage with 9 L flushes per year =   **26,280L** (usual)

Usage with 3/6 L flushes per year =   **9855L** (38% less)

Usage with lift-up flushes per year = **6023L** (77% less)

Saving = ~ 20,000 L/pers/year over normal toilets.

Showers
These are the big consumers — but one of the easiest to remedy! There are now several types of shower head on the market, rated AAA by the Water Services Association of Australia. They are easily fixed onto the projecting arm with a spanner and a bit of white plumber's tape. But *do not overtighten*, otherwise you run the risk of cracking a soldered joint behind the tiles — which would be quite expensive to repair.

An AAA showerhead should give an **8–9** L/ minute shower, compared to the more usual 15–20 L/min — which represents a saving of ~8760 L/yr for a daily 3 min. shower, not to mention the saving in *hot* water.

However, by placing a restricting washer in the connection joint you could save even more and still have a good shower. A rigid plastic or metal washer 17mm diameter with a 2.5mm centre hole will reduce the flow down to ~**4.6**L/min at Canberra pressure.

Even more savings can be made by behaviour modification, such as limiting your shower to *one minute* — yes, it can be done — or by not washing your hair so often, or even by not using soap, which enables the natural skin oils to be retained to protect the skin. Challenge yourself —a shower in 4.6L!

With indications of drier weather and an increasing population, long, hot showers will be an undoubted luxury and may come to be regarded as *unthinking, selfish indulgence at the community's expense. Your own tank water system is quickly becoming an obvious necessity.*

Taps
The most satisfactory way of reducing water usage is by *cultivating the sensitivity of the human hand* — there is usually no need for a tap to be running full-bore at about 15-20L/min.

A smooth dribble about 3mm thick is about 150 mL/min. *(1/100th of full bore)* and has quite a remarkable and sufficient wetting action. It is extremely easy to *refresh* hands and face in 50mL, and to brush and rinse teeth in even less.

Aerators and spray nozzles on washbasin taps *look* as though they are saving water, but they actually do little other than give you a good feeling.

For the kitchen-sink centre-swivel outlet there is a useful screw-on swivel adaptor which allows full-bore or spray, the latter being useful for scrubbing potatoes. But again, the same result can be achieved by reducing the flow! Try a restricting washer.

Washing machines
If you are in the market for a new machine, consider a front loader rather than a top loader if you are water conscious, and be guided by the star rating system. Otherwise, avoid warm-water washes to save both energy and water.

Dishwashers
Unnecessary water guzzlers that consume energy and resources from birth to death. Instead, use the sink with 6–8L of water and one squirt of phosphate/sodium-free detergent *(they are available)*; have a companiable social discussion over the washing up, which imparts a warm, fuzzy feeling; and, of course, feel good as the grey water spreads all over the dry spots of the garden *(see p 11-18).*

Garden equipment
Adjustable drippers placed just under the mulch, gravity-fed from water tanks, must be the ultimate watering system — computer-controlled if you must, or otherwise by a clockwork timer (don't leave them out in the frosty weather, as they stop functioning). Oscillating sprays are probably the ultimate guzzlers, but do install a timer — as we can all be forgetful when it comes to turning them off manually! Better still, dispense with your extremely consumptive lawns.

Washing the car
Cars are designed these days to stay out in the weather, so why not leave yours out in the rain to wash itself? We *never* wash our car, and it looks acceptably clean.

If you really must, take it through a car wash that recycles its wash-water.

Hosing the concrete driveway
Incredible as it may seem, some people *still* do this.

Why not sweep the leaves into tidy piles and put them in the compost bin — and benefit from a bit of exercise?

Modifying equipment is only a small part of the solution — the *real* answer is changing our *mindset* toward more conserving patterns of behaviour and, dare I say it, *limiting our population growth.*

The stark alternative of an *expanding* city having no water just does not bear thinking about. Money in the bank will be of absolutely no value if there is no water in the dams.

Rainfall – *the forgotten resource*

Why don't we use it in our towns and cities?

The previous pages indicate that something like a 70% saving in the use of drinkable mains water can be made largely by changing our habits and installing items like water-saving shower heads, all of which is fairly easy and can be done cheaply and quickly.

To make even more significant savings — which must be done if we are to make a real impact on the water shortage problem — we must turn to the two resources we have left. Both of them, unfortunately, require the spending of money and some altruistic commitment arising from a social conscience.

This further step is even more necessary for those who *can* do it because there are many in our society who can't - those who rent or live in apartments (eg. no gardens or no roofs) and there are also people who are apathetic and just can't be bothered.

The two sources of water the average house owner has freely available are **rainwater** from the roof and **greywater** from showers, washing machines, washbasins and kitchen sinks. We will deal with rainwater first.

Before we rush in to solutions however, we should understand the background to rainwater harvesting:

1 Rain falls on all domestic roofs which is then piped away *unused* into the stormwater system, This is wasteful, unsustainable and utter madness.
2 This rainwater is, in most cases, fit to drink.
3 It is a free resource, and offers the potential for reducing our continuing living costs.
4 The population of Australia continues to grow and many local authorities are now having difficulty in providing the quantity and the quality of drinking water we have become used to.
5 We have become very wasteful in our use of water and the knowledge that we are in control of our own collected water should engender a more careful and responsible attitude toward its use.
6 Town (mains) water is treated to a high degree of purity to enable us to drink it safely, yet only a tiny percentage (perhaps about 2%) of what we consume is actually ingested.

7 About 98% of the water we use is too good for most of our purposes and this quality costs us all money through our water rates.
8 Mains water in most towns contains fluoride and chlorine which many people do not like, or to which they are medically sensitive.
9 Mains water in Canberra is usually at a high pressure, causing noisy water hammer (and some damage) which increases the potential for tap washers to leak and waste water. The use of rainwater with a lower-pressure pump system can usually alleviate these problems.
10 The cost of water has been underpriced for many years and will inevitably rise, particularly if our local authorities are forced to build another dam. Recurrent savings on future water costs would help to amortise any outlay, particularly if all members of the household practise a careful use pattern.

The table below gives some idea of the range of rainfall that the southern cities in Australia have received in *past* years:

	Minimum rainfall mm /month	Median	Maximum rainfall mm /month
Adelaide	17 - January	38	60 - July
Canberra	29 - June	44	58 - November
Hobart	30 - June	42	55 - December
Melbourne	48 - February	56	65 - October
Perth	10 - January	87	165 - June
Sydney	60 - September	91	123 - June

Monthly rainfall extremes for southern Australian cities
Source: Bureau of Meteorology 2001

However, the future *could* be very different.

A 2001 CSIRO paper, 'Climate Change, Impacts for Australia', indicates there is likely to be a bias toward *reduced* rainfall in the 35° latitude belt we are concerned with:

	2030	2070
South East Australia	**-10%** to +5%	**-35%** to +10%
South West Australia	**-20%** to +5%	**-60%** to +10%

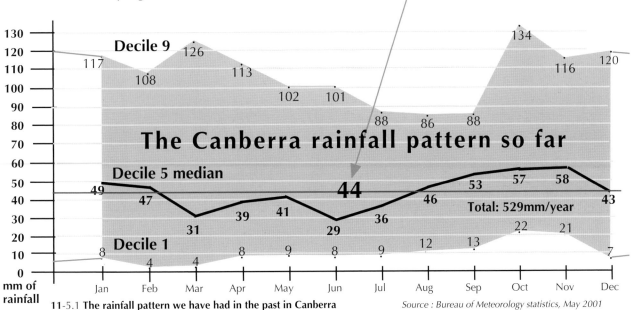

11-5.1 **The rainfall pattern we have had in the past in Canberra**

Source : Bureau of Meteorology statistics, May 2001

The arguments for and against tanks

Before getting too carried away with the idea of being self-sufficient in water it would be a good idea to just sit down and objectively weigh up the advantages and disadvantages — as far as is possible.

The decision is not an easy one to make, and for most of us it is a lot of money to spend — mainly for the social good. Even though you may not necessarily have all the facts at this stage, evaluating your own household needs should stimulate a number of queries which need answering.

The following analysis may help you to appreciate some of the pros and cons.

Photo by courtesy of Bushmans Group Pty Ltd

FOR

1   Rainwater is a freely available, if erratic, source of clean water, which could help reduce your water bills.

2   The cost of mains water is very cheap at the moment, but must inevitably increase in the coming years.

3   CSIRO predictions indicate that rainfall will almost certainly be lower in future, because of climate change and population growth, so individual collection should be maximised.

4   Rainwater is free of the chemicals added to mains water — usually chlorine, fluoride and magnesium.

5   If enough people install decent-sized tanks, it is possible that a new, expensive dam could be avoided, or at least postponed.

6   Installing water tanks could become a large local industry, creating a lot of employment.

7   Tanks could reduce the use of drinkable mains water for such 'non-drinkable' tasks as carwashing, WCs, garden watering and clothes washing.

8   Tanks installed by most suburban householders could help to delay price increases of mains water for socially disadvantaged residents.

9   A new dam would use a lot of fossil fuels, create atmospheric pollution, use a lot of finite resources in new infrastructure — pipelines, pumps, filters, roads, buildings, etc — and would be destructive of the ecology of the area.

10 If adopting a total system (see Option 1, p **11-10**), the internal house plumbing already exists, reducing the overall cost.

The broader picture
I assume that a new Canberra dam with infrastructure would cost around $150 million, and a reasonably useful tank system to a house would cost, say $4500.

This means that about 33,300 homes could be equipped with a water tank for the cost of one dam.

At say 2.5* persons/house x 33,300 houses = ~83,250 people at about 80,000 L/year (reduced consumption), 6,660,000 kL could be saved every year in Canberra by the use of water tanks for the cost of one dam. How much water could a new dam supply per year? (*ACT population projections 2002–32. The population in 2032 is predicted as 2.2/house. ACT government.)

AGAINST

1   The capital cost of installing a reasonably useful domestic tank system could be between $4000–$6000.

2   Electricity would be needed for the pump.

3   Tanks are large and would need careful placement to avoid inconvenience.

4   Tank systems require attention and some maintenance for satisfactory service.

5   A mains reserve system will be needed to avoid failure in a dry period, so mains connection will still be necessary.

6   Amortisation would take several years as the return on investment would be very low — it being largely an altruistic gesture by an individual to society.

7   Rainwater can accelerate corrosion in copper plumbing (although it is slow acting and will take several years; there are ways of countering this action)

8   Those requiring fluoridation would need to take alternative action.

9   Tanks and new plumbing lock up resources of copper plastics and steel for many years (but are eventually recyclable or re-usable, unless they have rusted away)

10 Socially disadvantaged members of society will probably not be able to afford a tank installation, and those living in flats or apartments are unlikely to be able to participate anyway.

11 Rainwater usage will initially delay the outflow of roofwater and stormwater into the Murray-Darling catchment, but should be OK afterwards.

12 Some people don't like the appearance of tanks, perhaps remembring old, rusty, corrugated tanks. Coloured plastic tanks are a vast improvement.

This rough evaluation of the advantages and disadvantages of installing tanks may or may not encourage you to consider such a move. No doubt others with more information have done their sums based on a more holistic life-cycle analysis, and should share their conclusions with the general public.

The real questions are: should we continue to rely on local governments to supply all our water or should those who are able aim at a good measure of self-sufficiency? Should local governments offer better incentives to install tanks in all houses? How big can we allow our cities to grow without mandatory water self-sufficiency in existing and new housing?

It is hoped that the information on the following pages will help to clarify your minds on this rather complex issue.

How much rainwater can we collect?

Our roofs are already made to collect rainwater.
Why don't we take advantage of this?

Fortunately, as our atmospheric pollution level is still very low compared with Europe and the USA, our roofwater is usually suitable for drinking and we have the possibility of collecting a large part or even all of our water needs from our roofs.

Most suitable roofing materials are galvanised or Colorbond steel. Some people feel that more porous surfaces such as terracotta or cement tiles could harbour fungi or bacteria, but there does not seem to be any evidence to prove this claim.

Painted roofs could be suspect, and enquiries should be made from paint companies as to possible toxicity.

How much rainwater can we expect to collect?
The ready reckoner *(see below)* should help you to get some rough idea of what you might collect based upon previous statistics — but don't forget the CSIRO predictions mentioned before.

Two further corrections should also be made for evaporation and diverter losses.

Rain falling on a roof material which has been warmed by the sun will vaporise the rain to some extent, reducing the amount collected. This is a dynamic loss compared to the static evaporation statistics from still water given by the Bureau of Meteorology (BOM), so their relevance is perhaps questionable in our calculations.

Such figures as are available seem to be around 5–10% of the initial precipitation. The higher figure could be used for summer and the lower one in winter because of differences in temperatures.

The other loss is from the diverter, which is used to keep the collected water as clean as possible *(see p **11**-16)*

Losses which need considering
Assuming a statistical rainfall of 6mm every 3.5 days *(derived from BOM median figures),* on one of the Mawson roof areas of 74m^2 = **444** L

less a CSIRO prediction of reduced rainfall in the coming decades — let's say 5% = **422** L

less 10% **summer** evaporation = **380**L

less 37 L *per shower of rain* for the diverter loss *(from p**11**-16)* =**343** L input into the tank

which = a **loss of 101** L = **23%** of the rainfall figure.

The same calculation for **winter,** with say 2% evaporation, could result in a loss of **15%**.

A heavier fall in summer of say 30mm could result in a loss of **11%**.

In the absence of more refined calculations, perhaps we should adopt a **loss factor of about 20%** from the BOM statistical figures as shown in the table below.

This is on the higher side of the 11-23% loss range because most of Canberra's rain statistically comes in the summer months, which has greater evaporation.

The diverter size of 37 L quoted above comes from the discussion on diverters on p **11**-11 and is suitable for *one* northern area of the Mawson roof of 74m^2. As there are two main collection areas to the Mawson house, there will be a diverter to each tank.

The diverter 'loss' should not be seen as wasted if it is allowed to percolate slowly into the garden by way of drippers. It would be 'wasted' if it was put straight into the stormwater tie, which is disconnected during installation of the tank.

As Rod Wade points out in his book *Sustainable Water from Rain Harvesting* (see p **16**-4), the bigger the diverter volume the clearer the water in the tank. It is a fine balancing act between quantity and quality.

Roof areas in sq.m. *(measured horizontally)*

		10	20	30	40	50	60	70	80	90	100
Rainfall	10	100	200	300	400	500	600	700	800	900	1000
		LITRES PER MONTH based on BOM statistics - deduct losses as described above									
in mm	20	200	400	600	800	1000	1200	1400	1600	1800	2000
per	30	300	600	900	1200	1500	1800	2100	2400	2700	3000
month	40	400	800	1200	1600	2000	2400	2800	3200	3600	4000
Canberra @	50	500	1000	1500	2000	2500	3000	3500	4000	4500	5000
530mm/year =	60	600	1200	1800	2400	3000	3600	4200	4800	5400	6000
44mm/month (median)	70	700	1400	2100	2800	3500	4200	4900	5600	6300	7000
	80	800	1600	2400	3200	4000	4800	5600	6400	7200	8000
	90	900	1800	2700	3600	4500	5400	6300	7200	8100	9000
	100	1000	2000	3000	4000	5000	6000	7000	8000	9000	10000
	110	1100	2200	3300	4400	5500	6600	7700	8800	9900	11000
	120	1200	2400	3600	4800	6000	7200	8400	9600	10800	12000
	130	1300	2600	3900	5200	6500	7800	9100	10400	11700	13000
	140	1400	2800	4200	5600	7000	8400	9800	12000	12600	14000
	150	1500	3000	4500	6000	7500	9000	10500	12800	13500	15000
	160	1600	3200	4800	6400	8000	9600	11200	13600	14400	16000

11-7.1   **Calculated monthly rainfalls in litres on various roof areas** *(no allowance for losses as above)*

Where can we place tanks?

What possible locations do we have?

Before you get involved in locating tanks you will need to know what types, sizes and prices of water tanks are available. Look under 'Water Tanks' in your Yellow Pages directory and collect whatever catalogues you can, so that you will be able to get a better 'fit' between what you need and what you can get.

Before you can make a decision on how *big* a tank you can place around the house you will need to know where the *potential* locations are and the space limitations of each. Access paths, fences, doors, steps, downpipes, etc will all place limiting factors on tank locations. A scale plan of the house will enable you to select the best sites that fit within all the constraints *(see below). It is worth spending time on this aspect.*

Most appliances are usually on the southern side of the house (bathrooms, laundries), and as this is also the shady side of the house the smaller pipe runs and the coolness are a happy coincidence. Concentrate on this area in looking for potential tank positions.

Look for blank external wall spaces at least 2m wide which are near a downpipe under a southern eaves, and note the maximum projection from the wall that you could tolerate. If you have a larger wall length available, this will give you the freedom of extending your storage capacity, should you need to.

If a large tank is going to be needed you will almost certainly be looking at circular drum tanks. These take up more garden space, location difficulties arise, and aesthetics begin to play a more determining role in the decision — but they are cheaper on a cost/litre basis.

Flat, tall, wall tanks are aesthetically preferable as they become part of the existing architecture more easily — but they tend to be more expensive on a cost/litre basis.

There is a limited range of tanks available that are suitable for placing flat against the wall and which *are also tall* to utilise the height available under the eaves.

Gravity feed or pump?

It would be nice to think that we could supply all our internal appliances (washing machine, dishwasher, WCs and showers) by gravity, thus avoiding the need for the use of electricity. But this is not practicable with a low-level tank placed under the eaves, due to the low head of pressure then available.

An automatic, 240v pressure-activated pump will be needed to give sufficient pressure and volume to high outlets such as showers, sinks and washbasins.

There could be a little bit of intermittent motor noise with this type of pump, so place it away from bedrooms and particularly close neighbours — it could be irritating.

Use of a pressure pump is a critical issue as it could be a deciding factor on whether or not a rainwater system is possible at all. There are covers available which will reduce this noise level; there are also virtually noiseless submersible pumps as a last resort, but they are more expensive. There will also need to be an external power point near the pump.

Rainwater supply points

The Mawson house has four roof areas which can supply rainwater *(based on BOM stats, less 20%:*

A 18.91 m2 supplying about 8018 L/year - DP 4

B 74.13 m2 ....31,431 L/year - DP 3

C 18.91 m2.......................... 8018   - DP 5

D 74.13 m2 31,431   - DP 1

totalling   **78,898** L/year

which should theoretically be sufficient for two people on a reduced-usage basis of **62,780** L/year *(from p 11-3.2),*leaving a surplus for the garden.

However, roof areas **A** and **C** are not *easily* connected to a main storage tank more suited to the main roof areas **B** and **D,** so it seems more reasonable to concentrate on collecting the two larger amounts from **B** and **D,** amounting to 2 x 31,431 L = **62,862** L, leaving the west-end roof in reserve for garden watering later on. Not perfect, but it will make an effective contribution to the water conservation problem.

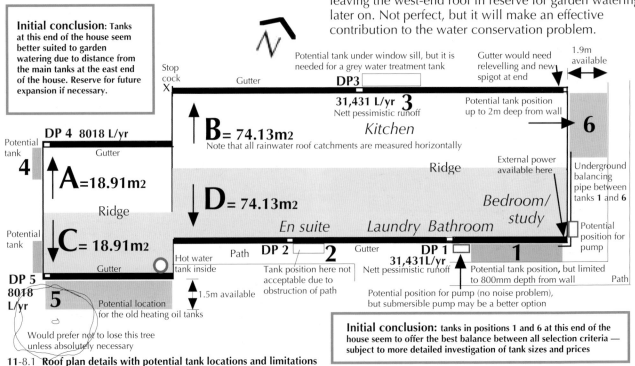

11-8.1 **Roof plan details with potential tank locations and limitations**

Size and location of tanks

Location will determine size

Existing gutter falls, position of downpipes, space available and window and door locations will be strong determinants on the most appropriate locations for tanks. The situation shown below has a simple answer, but others are not so simple.

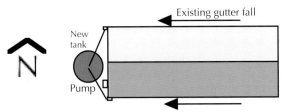

11-9.1   This could be quite feasible, providing gutter levels and tank inlet were at compatible heights to ensure good flows.

When every drop becomes precious and our rather small gutters cannot handle sudden downpours, the distance to a tank becomes critical. If the length of gutter feeding a tank is greater than, say, 10m, or too shallow, or in the wrong direction, it may be wiser to put in two (or even more) smaller tanks.

They will then be able to absorb a big rush of water from a storm, with a small underground balancing pipe — say, 25mm diameter — between the two tanks to even up the total quantity between them at a slower rate.

This way there is less likelihood of a gutter overflow and wastage (see **11**-9.2 below).

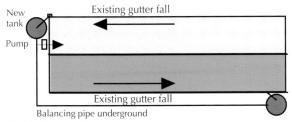

11-9.2   Two smaller tanks may be necessary to take a surge of stormwater, with a balancing pipe between. Alternatively, the southern gutter could be re-levelled to put both tanks at the western end of the house.

A further factor which must be taken into account in retrofitting is that hipped roofs with several separate collecting surfaces and a number of downpipes will also determine how many tanks you may need to have — each one connected to the others to contribute to the total capacity needed.

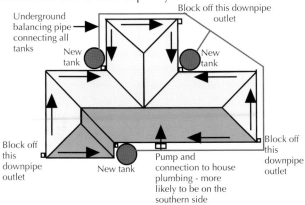

11-9.3   A more complex hipped roof may well require three tanks to take the surge of rainwater, possibly of differing capacities to suit the collected roof areas. Pump and supply pipe to house could be at any point on the balancing pipe to suit connection to internal plumbing, noise factor, etc.

What is an economic size which suits all these variables? *(using the Mawson house as an example)*

A commonly used formula is:

Daily consumption per person x number of people in the house x average number of days between rain periods = total storage capacity of tank(s).

A reduced consumption was calculated on p **11**-3.1 as **86** L/pers/day x **2** people in household. However, as we sometimes have one or two guests for a few days, this figure could perhaps be increased to ~**2.1**.

Number of days *between* rain periods (based on BOM statistics of min.6.5 and max.11.1 rain days/m (*average* 8.8). Assuming 9 days all coming at once, (31- 9) = ~**22** dry days/month, so **86** x **2.1** x **22** = rain input of **3973** L every month.

If we adopt a precautionary principle and allow for CSIRO future predictions *(see p 11-5)*, diverter losses, evaporation, etc — and, of course, we can have dry spells of several weeks which might get *worse* — let's assume **30** days without rain in lieu of 22.

So, using the above formula, 86 L/pers/day x **2.1** persons x **30** days

= 5418 L   **tank capacity for one month's safe usage.**

Cross checking to normal occupancy (86 L/pers/m x 2 people x 31 days) = **5332 L/m <u>consumption</u>**, so it should be OK.

The plan of the Mawson house *(see p **11**-11.2)* shows that there is room at the NE corner for a 4500 L tank and for a further 1600 L tank on the southern side linked together with an underground balancing pipe, giving a total of **6100** L storage capacity *(erring on the safe side)*.

Let's cross check again with a different formula: **consumption** + **15**% to allow for losses etc = **3973** L/m + 15% = **4569**L — so we should be on the safe side with a tank capacity of 6100 L. *But where does the 15% come from? Is it an inspired guess?*

On this latter formula, <u>3600</u> + 1600 L tanks = **5200 L** might be satisfactory. But as the difference in tank cost between 5200 L and 6100 L would only save $50 (with all other costs remaining the same), it could be false economy ($50 is a very cheap safety factor).

Don't forget also that our consumption figure is based on a reduced usage basis of grey water on the garden, no lawns, no car washing, short showers and low-use toilets. If you don't practise these water-conserving measures, you will either run out of water occasionally or you will need a larger tank/roof.

The potential rain input for the main areas **B** and **D** of the Mawson house = **5238** L/m average.

Theoretically, with a **6100** L tank capacity, this input of **5238** L/m would be 180 L /m below our consumption *if* we have a dry spell of about 30 days.

Do we take the risk? The difference is close — the figures are very rubbery, there are many assumptions, and a good number of peripheral factors to be considered. As an exact balance is impossible to achieve, and we still have space left for extra tanks, I feel it is worth the risk. This is a very inexact 'science' so fairly generous allowances would be appropriate.

Option 1 – a preliminary analysis of Mawson rainwater collection and consumption to satisfy full house supply

This chart is a visual attempt to simplify the monthly and annual collection inputs and the fairly constant outputs for a two person household operating a voluntarily reduced consumption of mains water, so that possible 'waste' from overflow and likely reliances on inputs of mains water can be minimised.

From the inputs *(collection, in grey)* and outputs *(consumption, in black)* shown below, the future tank capacity can be more accurately estimated *(see chart 11-11)* and varied to show its effect on quantities of overflow and required mains input to ensure continuity of supply to household.

Annual *median* runoff from main roof (area B and D) @ 530mm/yr =78,430 L/yr
less evaporation, diverter losses,
lower rainfall prediction, total 20%.................. = 62,742 L/yr (5228 L/m)
Consumption for all uses (reduced level) estimated................ = 62,780 L/yr (5231 L/m)
coincidental similarity

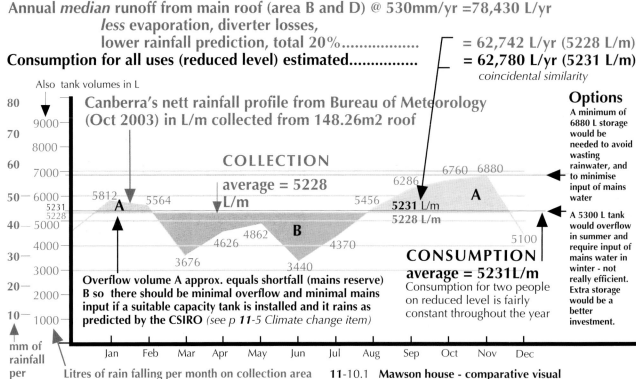

Options
A minimum of 6880 L storage would be needed to avoid wasting rainwater, and to minimise input of mains water

A 5300 L tank would overflow in summer and require input of mains water in winter - not really efficient. Extra storage would be a better investment.

11-10.1   **Mawson house - comparative visual analysis of rainwater inputs and consumption outputs for a 2 person household in Mawson, based on a reduced consumption**

Litres of rain falling per month on collection area of 148.26 m2 of roof, allowing for 20% losses for evaporation, diverters and climate change
1mm = 120 L on Mawson roof - areas B + D

Conclusions from graph:
As collection matches consumption so closely *(quite coincidental)*, then a tank size of approximately **5300 L** would give an *uncontrolled* overflow (**A**) in summer, but a shortfall in winter (**B**), the latter provided for by mains reserve. While the overflow would be absorbed in the subsoil around the tank locations it *lacks control over where and how the overflow is used* which is not an efficient way of using it.

The basic aim of installing tanks is to reduce the household use of *mains* water, so a tank large enough to **conserve** the **excess** summer rainfall **A** and to reduce the input of the mains water **B** should be aimed at.

This could roughly equate to the Oct/Nov rainfall of ~ 6800 L/m, = a tank of, say,7000 L.

This size of tank would provide extra storage to minimise or eliminate overflow so that it could be controlled and *used more effectively* from the tank by the owner on areas of the garden which *need* watering.

If not used on the garden (we mainly use grey water instead) this extra stored water could provide a carry-over reserve(if full) to reduce the need for using mains water during the drier winter months.The extra storage would also be available for firefighting during summer.

A more detailed water flow analysis showing *carry-over* residue quantities is shown on p **11**-11 which confirms this assessment.

Practical conclusion
Space available around the Mawson house is a major determinant and when available commercial tank sizes are factored in it would seem that 1/5600 L Tankmasta PE tank at the NE corner with 1/1600 L PE Plastank on the southern wall would be appropriate. Space is then available for some expansion if necessary *(see comment below and location plan on p **11**-12).*

Chart *11-14* compares this Option 1 with other water saving measures to assess their relative values to the individual owner *and to society as a whole* - which is now of major significance.

Future use changes
It is important to bear in mind that the Mawson household operates on a reduced level of consumption by 2 people. Should the house change hands to a family of 3 or 4 people the consumption could rise to 94,170 L/yr or 125,560 L/yr, based on a reduced level of consumption *(from p **11**-3).* Would it be be worth installing a tank capacity above 7200 L as a selling factor? *There is little value in putting in extra large tanks if the collected rainfall is insufficient to fill them.*

There must be a balancing limit, and careful monitoring of tank water levels in the 7200 L system would indicate what potential would exist for expansion.

Option 1 – Flow analysis of selected tank for full house supply

Using the preliminary estimate of ~7000 L required storage from p 11-10 this flow analysis gives a more detailed visual picture of monthly rainfall collection and consumption showing the dynamic effects of overflow, shortfall and carry-over residues.
The black rectangle visualises the actual tank volume with graphed monthy inputs and outputs.It assists confirmation (or otherwise) of the earlier tank size decision reached on p 11-10 using the same figures in another way
(note that the rainfall input profile is the same in both graphs):

Useful rainwater =
62,636 less mains
supplement 4100=
58,536 L/year =
~93% of total
reduced
consumption of
62,780 (2 people)

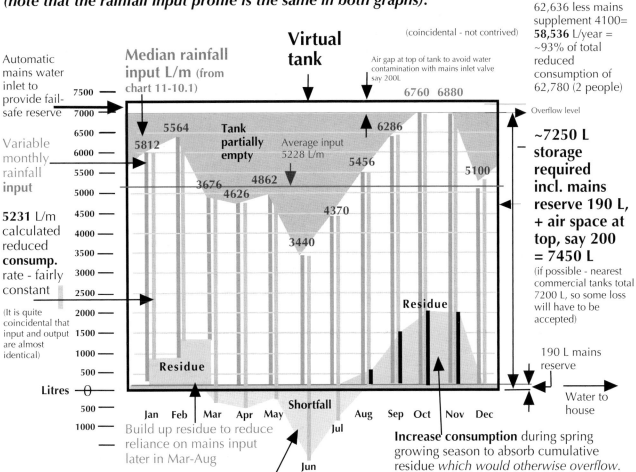

Automatic mains water inlet to provide fail-safe reserve

Median rainfall input L/m (from chart 11-10.1)

Virtual tank

(coincidental - not contrived)

Air gap at top of tank to avoid water contamination with mains inlet valve say 200L

Variable monthly rainfall input

5231 L/m calculated reduced **consump.** rate - fairly constant

(It is quite coincidental that input and output are almost identical)

Tank partially empty

Average input 5228 L/m

Residue

Shortfall

Residue

Overflow level

~7250 L storage required incl. mains reserve 190 L, + air space at top, say 200 = 7450 L
(if possible - nearest commercial tanks total 7200 L, so some loss will have to be accepted)

190 L mains reserve

Water to house

Build up residue to reduce reliance on mains input later in Mar-Aug

Increase consumption during spring growing season to absorb cumulative residue *which would otherwise overflow.*

This increase could be used to water the garden Aug - Nov. allowing more controlled and efficient use of a smaller tank.
An automatic watering system would perhaps be useful for this purpose to counter human forgetfulness, working in conjunction with an electronic water level device.

MAINS RESERVE INPUT 4100L total

Based on monthly usage of 5231 L/m there should be an estimated reserve usage of ~**4100 L mains** water during the colder months of the year when rainfall is lowest - shown by graph of monthly inputs.
This is a factor over which we have no control
Tank size of 7200 L (red line) needed to eliminate overflow and minimise mains input = 1- 5600 L Tankmasta + 1- 1600 L Plastank Slimline

= **7200** L total storage capacity

This gives the following advantages :
1 Minimises input of mains reserve water (~ 4100L)
2 Eliminates *uncontrolled* overflow
3 Accommodates some summer residues (carry over) Jan-March
4 Summer residue helps to reduce winter shortfall
5 A smaller and cheaper tank can be used by storing and consuming
      the summer overflow in a *controlled* way, enabling the residues
      to build up in Jan / Feb as a good bushfire precaution,
6 Makes more efficient use of the tank - less empty space
      in winter months

Extension of storage capacity
There is still room on the south wall for another 1600 L tank and a 5600 L tank on the east wall as a fall-back position should the consumption needs rise (eg. more people regularly living in the house, should it change ownership).
However, the rainfall may not be adequate to make full and efficient use of the extra capacity. (Refer back to CSIRO predictions - p 11-5) Monitoring of inflow and outflow during the initial period of use, together with rainfall statistics would enable a more accurate assessment of the need for extension and its value relative to expenditure.

Stop Press note (April 2004): The recent introduction of the Aquasource system which controls tank water and mains water without any possibility of contamination is a welcome innovation. It obviates the need for the mains reserve allowed for in the above estimates and in effect increases the volume available for rainwater and reduces the amount of overflow. A brilliant Australian invention.

11-11.1   **Mawson house - comparative visual analysis of reduced consumption of 62,780L/yr, using 7200 L tank capacity**

Option 1 – the physical possibility

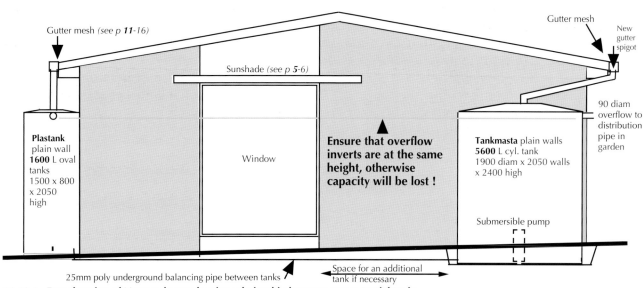

Gutter mesh (see p **11**-16)

Sunshade (see p **5**-6)

Window

▲
Ensure that overflow inverts are at the same height, otherwise capacity will be lost !

Gutter mesh

New gutter spigot

90 diam overflow to distribution pipe in garden

Plastank plain wall **1600** L oval tanks 1500 x 800 x 2050 high

Tankmasta plain walls **5600** L cyl. tank 1900 diam x 2050 walls x 2400 high

Submersible pump

25mm poly underground balancing pipe between tanks ⁄

Space for an additional tank if necessary

11-12.1   **East elevation of Mawson house showing relationship between two potential tanks**

Designing an integrated water supply system can be fraught with problems so it is vital that every element should be seen as part of the total system to see how it all works together and to identify potential problems.

Missing a vital factor will inevitably trip you up sooner or later and if you have already expended money then it could become a very expensive remedial exercise.

It pays to do your homework to ensure the project runs smoothly and effectively!

Possible bugs : ensuring that gutter falls are correct; adequate pipe falls from gutter to tank to allow for surge; suitable tank height; overflow heights of multiple tanks coinciding; pressure pump at a suitable height so that it remains primed when water level in the tanks is low (or install a submersible); ensuring that you have a suitable connection to the house plumbing so that you can avoid expensive internal work - and many others.

Talk to a 'green' plumber.

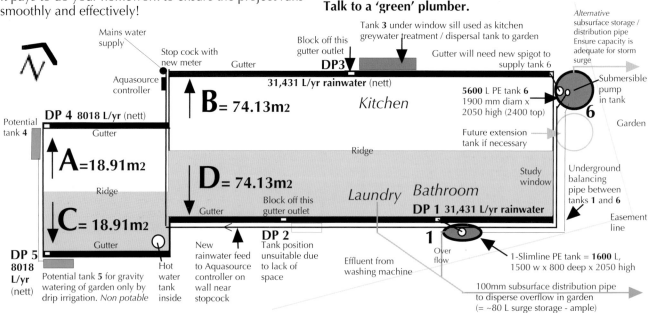

Mains water supply

Stop cock with new meter

Gutter

Block off this gutter outlet

DP3 ▼

Tank **3** under window sill used as kitchen greywater treatment / dispersal tank to garden

Gutter will need new spigot to supply tank 6

Alternative subsurface storage / distribution pipe Ensure capacity is adequate for storm surge

Aquasource controller

31,431 L/yr rainwater (nett)

B= 74.13m2

Kitchen

5600 L PE tank **6** 1900 mm diam x 2050 high (2400 top)

Submersible pump in tank

6

Garden

DP 4 8018 L/yr (nett)

Potential tank **4**

Gutter

A=18.91m2

Ridge

Future extension tank if necessary

Ridge

D= 74.13m2

Laundry   *Bathroom*

Study window

Underground balancing pipe between tanks 1 and 6

C= 18.91m2

Gutter

Block off this gutter outlet

Gutter

DP 1 31,431 L/yr rainwater

Easement line

DP 5 **8018** **L/yr** (nett)

Potential tank **5** for gravity watering of garden only by drip irrigation. *Non potable*

Hot water tank inside

New rainwater feed to Aquasource controller on wall near stopcock

DP 2 Tank position unsuitable due to lack of space

Effluent from washing machine

Over flow

1

1-Slimline PE tank = **1600** L, 1500 w x 800 deep x 2050 high

100mm subsurface distribution pipe to disperse overflow in garden (= ~80 L surge storage - ample)

11-12.2   **Mawson house plan showing most suitable tank positions, with extension positions if found to be necessary**

From p **11**-9 calculations, together with the input /output graphs on p **11**-10 and 11 we now have a tank **6** (5600L) + tank **1**(1600L) giving us a linked capacity of **7200** L with room for expansion.

This gives a theoretically reasonable balance of all factors which should significantly reduce overflow and use of mains water. A major consideration by our regulating authorities is that rainwater and mains water should not be in contact at any time to avoid contamination. The Aquasource (Rainbird) controlling system, manages this without requiring a need for a reserve of mains water in the tanks.

The Aquasource controller is placed on the wall above the stopcock and is set to *preferentially* use rainwater. In the event of the tanks running dry the mains supply is then utilised.

If tank overflow should occur, it should preferably be piped into a subsoil storage / distributing system which will water the garden and help to maintain ground water levels. The submersible pump is completely quiet. The current drought (2006) has emptied our tanks and we are now on the mains, but a good shower will automatically put us back onto tank water and the mains chlorine smell will disappear.

Options 2 and 3

Option 2: a system to supply *toilets, washing machine and garden* from rainwater with mains reserve

This is another option open to those wishing to save water.

It does not aim to supply all domestic needs and because of this it cannot utilise the house's existing plumbing system. It must necessarily rely on a separate plumbing installation to supply the toilets the washing machine and external taps so that there is no possibility of contamination of the normal water supply from the tank supply. *Option 1 used all the existing plumbing.*

The analysis is not presented here but the conclusions are as follows:

Conclusions

Using only area **D** of the Mawson roof, collection closely matched consumption with an *uncontrolled* overflow during the warmer months and a shortfall in winter.

A tank of about 2500–3000 L should theoretically meet the reduced needs, but does not use water efficiently, due to excessive overflow wastage and extra input of mains reserve water.

There is also one important difference between the two systems: Option 2 requires some duplicate plumbing, and this higher total installation cost of about $4200 gives a much lower individual value *(see comparative chart p **11**-14)*. This is not as economical in time, resources or money.

While Option 2 theoretically serves some useful purpose it begs the question of what to do with the rainwater from roof area **B** which is still connected to the stormwater system, contributing nothing to our water conservation ideal.

Taking our total household consumption of 62,780 L/year, this option would only save about 28,460 L, which is equal to about 45% of the total.

This system does not fully utilise the resources available and does not satisfy our social need to conserve as much mains water as possible.

To utilise roof area **B** would require more tanks purely for the purpose of watering the garden areas, adding to the cost without doing anything toward lowering the heavy water-demands of showers, washbasins and sinks.

This imbalance shows up clearly in the comparative analysis set out in **11**-14.1, showing that it does not represent good value for money.

Option 3: a system to supply *drinking water only*, and/or to facilitate a small amount of *garden watering*

Its contribution to the main aim of saving mains water would be relatively small and there would likely be an imbalance between the rainfall available and the small tank capacity, resulting in a lot of overflow which could, in a rainstorm, be too much for the garden to absorb.

If used for drinking water you would have to be very fastidious about water quality — no chlorine, no fluoride, etc, and the amount saved — say 3650 L/year — would be literally a small drop in the bucket.

As with Option 2 it would contribute little to the primary aim of saving mains water. See relative savings below.

Slightly better value would be achieved by using the water on the garden, but in reality it still would not make much impact of the total conservation problem.

Again, the garden watering system would have to rely on drippers, as there would be little head of water to give a suitable hose pressure. Installing a small pump would resolve that one, but it is all extra expense.

Relative savings

The following savings might make it easier to assess the likely *relative* reduction of the use of mains water *(see p **11**-3)*:

Option **1 - 57,136**L/yr =   **91**% reduction in use of mains water

Option **2 - 28,464** L/yr =   **46**%   "   "

Option **3 -   3650** L/yr =   **6**%   "   "

A more detailed comparative analysis is shown on p **11**-14.

Value to the householder — or to society?

In writing this it has become clear that there is very little incentive for the average suburban householder to invest a few thousand dollars in a system with such little financial return. The ACT government's financial incentives do very little to encourage the average householder, and shows that it is not taking the situation at all seriously.

However, the recurring droughts and CSIRO's predictions that these are likely to become more severe in the not-too-distant future seem to indicate that we need to distinguish between value to *society* compared to a more economic rationalist's view of value to the *householder*.

It seems to depend upon your own level of social commitment — how far are you prepared to go with your personal expenditure to help society?

Only you can answer that.

My own view is that our governments should publish the comparative costs of building future dams as against the cost of subsidising individual householders to 'do the right thing'. They should open up the debate on the advantages and disadvantages of taking either course — or, indeeed, combinations of the two.

It would make interesting reading.

Comparative analysis of Options 1, 2 and 3

This chart aims to quantify the relative values of these water-conserving systems to the *householder* and to *society*

These figures are based on a **reduced** consumption for two people as described on p **11**-3. If consumption remains at normal, unsustainable levels, the case for conservation of water is even stronger.	Option **1** p 11-10 **All domestic water uses on reduced basis (7200 L tank)**	Option **2** p11- 13 **WCs, washing machine & some garden drippers (3200 L tank)**	Option **3** p11-13 **Drinking or garden water tank only (1000 L tank)**	**4** Other system of choice
a Anticipated saving of mains water in kL (collected rainwater)	62.86kL	28.46kl	3.6kl	
b % saving based on total nett available roof collection (roof area in m2 x med. rainfall/year) -20%	(Mawson = roof area of 186m2 x 530mm/year = 98.62kL/year gross rainfall less 20% = **78.9**kL/year nett available for use from areas B and D) Water saving = **80%**	saving = **36%**	saving = **4.5%**	
c Anticipated annual $ value of savings @ 75c/kL	$47.25	$21.35	$2.7	
d Approximate **DIY** cost of installation	$3400 (no internal plumbing modifications needed)	$3300 (some new separate internal plumbing needed)	$400	
	These DIY estimates are included purely to give a rough guide as to the possible savings by DIY			
e Approximate **commercial** cost of installation	$4500 (no internal plumbing modifications needed)	$4500 (some new separate internal plumbing needed)	$1000 These figures are conservative — they may well be more, depending on circumstances	
f Altruistic/satisfaction cost index to **householder** : $\frac{\text{Mains water saved (kL/yr)}}{\text{Comm. cost to h'holder(k\$)}}$ $\frac{a}{e}$	13.96 (highest = best)	6.32	3.6	
g Value to **society** mains water saved (kL/yr) a	62.86 (highest = best)	28.46	3.6	
h **Final combined index** and visual indicator of value to householder + value to society (highest = best) **f + g = h**				

2h is only half the value to society as a whole compared to **1h** — *yet the cost is similar*

3h makes little impact on the problem of conserving water and may not justify use of resources

11-14.1 **Comparative value chart of three water conservation measures**

Conclusions

1f represents an indicator of satisfaction/cost to an individual householder in doing the right thing on behalf of society. *The value of that option to **society**, however, is very significant (1g), particularly if we compare it to the catastrophe of a city without water.*

The final results of **2h** and **3h** are of significantly lower value to the householder and to society, making their outlay of money and resources of questionable value. The actual cost of the mains water saved has little or no bearing on the ultimate useful value. The **real** value of installing systems **2** and **3** depends largely on the severity of the drought in the ACT region and how many systems are installed to make the total significant. If we reach the point where *'every drop counts'*, perhaps there will be merit in installing such small systems. All systems require a high degree of altruism on the part of the householder, as the return on investment is not good unless the cost of water increases markedly (as it may well do), or the government decides to subsidise tank installations more generously (this is really essential).

The bottom line seems to be that a tank system which aims to supply the whole house would seem to be the best value for individual householders *and* for society, *providing* the tank(s) are sized to minimise or eliminate overflow and minimise use of mains reserve water. The reader must appreciate that these figures are necessarily 'rubbery' — but they are broad indicators.

So what is the best value — *for the environment and for you?*

Consumption/conservation — a mindset challenge

The last decade or so has woken most of us up to the fact that we have a water problem in Australia and an urgent individual responsibility to do something about our profligate attitude to water use. Manufacturers have responded well, and a much wider variety of tanks and water-saving devices are now available — but what are the most effective ways to live with less?

Cost is often raised as a possible disincentive to excessive water use, but there is no question that we have all taken it for granted that cheap, drinkable water will *always* flow out of the tap, and the idea that we can simply raise the cost of water to reduce consumption is wishful thinking. *To do so would also unfairly affect those who can least afford it.*

Conserving an increasingly scarce resource by regulation will have to be accepted because it is more socially equitable and it makes people feel that the rules apply to everybody in a fair manner. The harder part of the solution, however, is to change *individual behaviour*, which requires effective community education.

It is not difficult to use less water in many of our water-consuming activities. Water is probably the greatest wetting agent ever, in that a little goes a very long way — have you ever considered that most times when we 'wash' our hands and face using soap and a full flow of water from the tap, we are simply *refreshing* our skin rather than actually *cleaning* it?

Try this instead: turn the tap on to a mere dribble not more than a 3mm stream, use no soap, and wet your hands and face. You can do that with *less than an eggcupful of water* — less water, less soap, less time, less pollution. The result is still refreshing, and you haven't stripped the beneficial natural oils from your skin. Take that attitude into the shower and challenge yourself to a 4-litre, 2-minute shower with no soap!

The WC could be much less consumptive — ours have been 3/1L rather than 6/3L for several years simply by a bit of DIY change to the cistern mechanism *(see p 11-17)* — and it could be filled with partially treated greywater by using a filter, collecting sump, and a pump.

In the kitchen, the dishwashing machine is the most consumptive user of water and energy (and, if we are really honest with ourselves, the least needed), with the electric hot-water jug being the next worst offender in the pollution stakes, as people almost invariably boil more water than they actually need.

Before any retrofitting decisions are made, you should learn the requirements of your local council, as they will have a good knowledge of conditions in your area. Next, obtain a copy of the comprehensive annual *Rainwater Consumer Guide*, published by the Rainwater Harvesting Association of Australia, from your local environment shop, and get their advice on local 'green' plumbers who understand the need to conserve water and how to do the right thing.
<**www.arid.asn.au**>

The *Rainwater Consumer Guide* gives a good analysis of the types of tanks and fittings available to you, ranging from the new galvanised-iron models to the latest bladder tanks (which can make good use of the space under wooden floors or external decks) to the more expensive underground tanks (which also have the advantage of keeping the water cool).

The analysis on p **11**-14 indicates that from a *personal* and a *social* point of view it is better to buy as big a system as you can afford, or at least allow for expansion — bearing in mind that CSIRO has told us *(p 11-5)* that rainfall in this south-east region of Australia is likely to reduce rather than increase.

However, space around our houses in the suburbs is reducing quite substantially as land prices rise, so this tends to squeeze water tanks underground, which is logical but more expensive — and often impossible as a retrofitted answer.

Above-ground *cylindrical* tanks are generally the lowest cost per litre stored, but to maximise storage takes up a lot of what open space is available, so the slimmer tanks come into their own because they can fit under the eaves in the narrow spaces left between houses and fences.

Space and cost are thus becoming the critical factors in determining the volume of stored water you can afford to buy — not exactly a rational way to buy an increasingly valuable life-supporting resource. This may well be the first noticeable screw to be tightened by global warming.

Manufacturers have quickly responded to the challenge by raising the quality of tanks, compared with the old image of the rusty galvanised-iron country tank, and health concerns are coming to the fore with food-quality inner linings, mosquito-proof openings, filters, pumps, and a variety of sizes and colours, making selection much easier and more convenient.

Greywater recycling, disposal, and reuse can also achieve much more in reducing the domestic consumption of water, and is dealt with in the next section, but a word of warning — humans beings tend to be forgetful and lazy about maintenance, and where health is concerned the technical solution has to be simple and easy — otherwise it just doesn't get done.

Above all, do your homework about the *urgent* need for water conservation; understand the need for retaining water as high up the water system (on your land) for as long as possible, and for selecting the most appropriate washing powders and liquids — and find out about their long-term effects on the soils and plants around your house. This may well be the most critical aspect of water conservation, so precisely stated in the very old epithet, *'Don't foul your nest'.*

Gutter guards, diverters and filter bags

Gutter guards

The January firestorm in Canberra made most householders realise how their gutters were clogged up with many years of rubbish which had dried out to a tinder dry collection of leaves, twigs etc - all good compostible stuff, but disastrous in a bush fire.

If we are to collect good quality drinking water then some screening of the gutters is necessary to keep out this rubbish.

The problem has been recognised in the last decade and a few products have come on the market which claim to solve the matter.

It is worth looking at the criteria by which we judge a good gutter guard in a *retrofit* situation :

1   It should let the rainwater through to the gutter, with max. openings of 6mm to keep out as much leaf and twig litter as possible.

2   It should not melt under bushfire embers, support combustion, or electrolytic corrosion.

3   It should not allow litter to collect above the gutter and should enable it to blow away with minimum wind pressure.

4   It should not be visually obvious from most usual viewpoints around the house. It should preferably match the colour of the roofing material - but this is not critical if it cannot be seen.

5   It should be easily fixable by the average handyperson to an existing gutter with the minimum of tools from a ladder position against the gutter, preferably without having to climb onto the roof.

6   It should be suitable for application to tiled or metal clad roofs with stability when press fitted to awkward situations,

7   It should last at least 20 years,

8   It should be mosquito proof if possible (difficult).

9   It should not be too difficult to occasionally lift the front edge of the gutter screen for gutter cleaning *when a ladder is leaning against it.*

If you are having your gutters covered in this way, ensure that your contractor meets these requirements.

There are now several gutter guard systems available - and new gutter types such as Smart Gutter which are more suited to new housing, unless you have to replace your gutters.

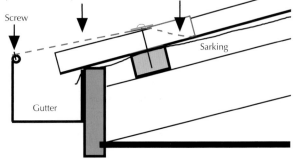

Gutter guard secured by first row of roofing screws with cut galvanised perforated metal strips. Note that it should ideally be sloping down toward gutter to minimise collection of leaves, twigs, tennis balls etc., but low pitched roofs may make it difficult to achieve the ideal.

11-16.1 Application of mesh to metal deck roofing

Diverters

Diverters are installed essentially to keep leaves and decomposed gunk out of the tank, but I am beginning to question the need for these, particularly in areas such as Canberra where the rainfall pattern is usually short, sharp showers fairly well distributed throughout the year - compared to more monsoonal patterns where it all comes at once.

In bushfire areas a gutter guard is now essential and with the addition of a filter bag in the tank entry then I feel there is no need for a diverter as well especially as it 'wastes' about 20 - 50 litres of precious water *at every shower.*

This topic is dealt with very fully in Rod Wade's excellent handbook " *Sustainable Water from Rain Harvesting"* - a handbook full of useful information (*see p16-4 for contact details*). He gives a method of calculating diverter size and using that for *one* area of the Mawson roof of 74m^2 would result in a diverter volume of 37 L, so I would lose 74L at every shower.

Other opinions state that the first flush of water does little more than moisten the **dried** residue in the gutter, filling up the diverter and that it is the **second or continuing** flush which carries the softened residue into the tank - tending to nullify the value of a diverter.

Both our tanks have a removable,10microns filter bag which need cleaning occasionally and the water has remained clean. This is the best approach.

11-16.2 A DIY solution, using cut strips of galvanised perforated metal fixed by the existing roofing screws and small self-tapping screws at the gutter's rolled edge. The top edge is dressed down into the corrugations and has worked well. It is a neat and relatively inexpensive solution which cannot be seen from the ground. Its a bit hard on the knees though !

This method of keeping leaves and twigs out of the water harvesting system is a good compromise.

While the top edge does collect a few heavy leaves I have not found any large build up of litter which would constitute a bush fire hazard.

Its invisibility, low cost, DIY nature works well, with the filter bags in the tanks catching the small stuff.

Bird poo doesn't seem to have affected us in any way.

Low-cost variable toilet-flushing mechanism

Reducing the flush

Several biological treatment systems are now emerging which promise to revolutionise the disposal of human waste, but they will not solve the enormous problem of literally millions of existing toilets in Australia consuming unnecessarily large volumes of scarce and increasingly valuable water.

The introduction of the 3/6L dual-flushing system some years ago went some way to improving this problem, but it still seems to be a lot of water and a complicated and expensive mechanism. Using 3L of potable water to flush away a pee is still extravagant — and quite unnecessary.

If we are to resolve this problem quickly, we need a simple, cheap, retrofit solution, adaptable to most existing cisterns. One elegant device available in hardware stores is a cylindrical blue weight, 'Cistern weight' (about $10–15), which is easily added to most (but not all) mechanisms inside the cistern.

It functions by flushing only when the button is pressed, and it is claimed to save 20kL/year/house.

Over the last ten years, we have been experimenting with ways of manually varying the water volume to suit the need — a pee not needing as much as a poo. The mechanical linkages inside our two cisterns were clever but complicated (and would seem to be unnecessarily expensive to produce), so we felt that a simple lift-and-drop system could surely be adequate, simple, and less costly to make initially.

We modified our two cisterns, and they have worked well for the last few years. And although a pee flush (if actually used) could be reduced to even less than a litre, a poo flush still needed about 5L due to the pans being older, with the larger water area. Modern pans now have 30% less water area, which increases the

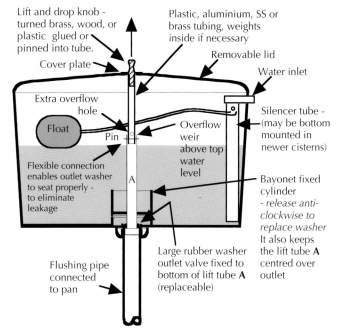

11-17.1 Nominal section of variable-flow flushing mechanism showing single lift tube in centre with large washer at bottom — simple and very effective

velocity of flow and creates a more thorough, economical cleansing action. This combination of manual flush and more efficient pans has worked extremely well, with a poo flush now only needing 3L (measured inside cistern).

The table below shows the significant reductions achievable — a saving of 89% (over the original single-flush cisterns) for a household of two retired people who rely on 7600L rainwater tanks for 52% of our consumption — even during the drought in 2006. This has helped us to reduce our water usage to about 80L per person per day (2008).

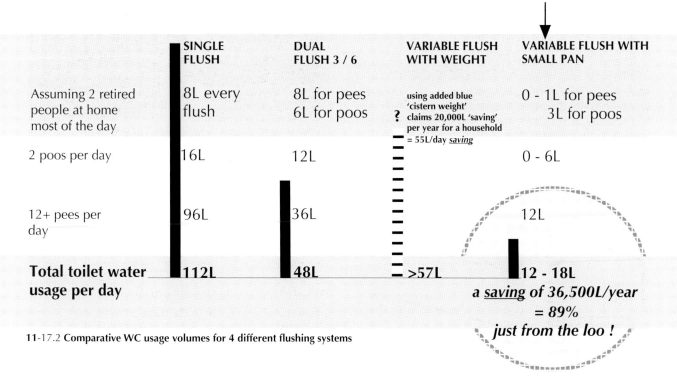

	SINGLE FLUSH	DUAL FLUSH 3 / 6	VARIABLE FLUSH WITH WEIGHT	VARIABLE FLUSH WITH SMALL PAN
Assuming 2 retired people at home most of the day	8L every flush	8L for pees 6L for poos	? using added blue 'cistern weight' claims 20,000L 'saving' per year for a household = 55L/day *saving*	0 - 1L for pees 3L for poos
2 poos per day	16L	12L		0 - 6L
12+ pees per day	96L	36L		12L
Total toilet water usage per day	**112L**	**48L**	**>57L**	**12 - 18L**
				a *saving* of 36,500L/year = 89% just from the loo !

11-17.2 Comparative WC usage volumes for 4 different flushing systems

Re-using domestic greywater

By retaining, treating and re-using grey water we can reduce our consumption of clean mains water.

Grey water is the term for all bath, shower, wash-basin, kitchen and laundry-tub waste water, including clothes-washing and dishwashing machines.

It is increasingly being regarded as a valuable resource rather than waste, containing items of nutritious value to soil organisms. However, it must be treated with caution as it usually contains soaps, detergents, bleaches, etc including sodium, which can cause problems with soil structure.

While phosphates are undesirable in our waterways where they cause algae to grow, they are essential nutrients for growing plants. Current opinion seems to be that, if present in filtered grey water for use on the garden, they should be acceptable. Phosphorus must be regarded as a diminishing, non-renewable resource.

Houses built on a concrete slab are probably the most difficult to modif, depending on surrounding ground levels. Houses with timber floors built higher off the ground usually make it easier to re-direct the grey water sources to a useful end on site, providing it stays on site and does not offend the neighbours.

Specialist contractors are now in business to build grey water filtration systems such as reed beds, oxygenation and other biological systems to produce an outflow which can end up providing subsoil watering of your vegetable garden.

The essential word is CAUTION: consult your local authority, which may or may not have its regulations in operation. The ACT recently published theirs.

At the time of writing there are new systems for treating waste water being commercialised with increasing frequency. It would seem that we are all in a period of experimentation which will, I hope, lead us to some clearer understanding of what works and what doesn't.

All that can be shown here is what *seems to be working*. Time will no doubt reveal the strengths and weaknesses of the various methods. and the science will become better understood.

Some of the systems which are now available in Australia for the treatment of grey water are:

Reed bed purification pond (see photo and diagram)

Clivus Multrum Pre-filter system, both of which are suited to modification of existing grey water systems, including kitchen-sink waste water.

Greywater Saver will recycle grey water from the laundry in concrete-slab houses, and from baths, basins and showers in houses with timber floors.

A *Greywater System* has recently come on the market in the ACT which will treat bathroom and laundry water from timber-floored houses only.

Perpetual Water have also entered the field of treating domestic waste water.

Reed beds

The imaginative use of rocks, rushes, reeds and other water plants with symbiotic wildlife can make a useful and attractive water-purification system, supplying increasingly scarce water to the garden. It does, however, take up a fair bit of space.

A grease trap interceptor is necessary to remove undesirable fats and greases before entering the system, but it does need cleaning out occasionally.

Preferred fall of the land to assist the flow of the filtration system

Seven days travel from beginning to end keeping grey water away from surrounding soil allows macrophytes and bacteria to remove pathogens and excess nutrients

Rocks

GT

Grey water effluent from house - from shower, bath, washbasins, sink and laundry tub, clothes-washing and dishwashing machines

Reeds

Reeds

Waterfalls to assist oxygenation

Water lilies, bullrushes, irises, reeds etc.

Settlement pond

To sub-surface garden irrigation system

11-18.2 **Elements of a reed bed system**

11-18.1 **Settlement pond of a reed bed filtration system in Duffy, ACT** *(At the home of Gösta and Pauline Lynga, taken the day before it was all destroyed by the Canberra firestorm of 18 Jan 2003)*

The combination of plants, bacteria, algae and sunlight breaks down the chemicals in the water, converting ammonia to nitrites and then to nitrates and nitrogen. Specific plants can be used to absorb heavy metals while others can be used to destroy pathogens. Seek professional advice.

Larger settlement ponds could support small invertebrates and fish which eat mosquito larvae.

Advice on appropriate species should be sought from the Australia New Guinea Fish Association. <http://www.angfa-nsw.org/index.html>

Microbats could also be encouraged into your garden to eat mosquitos —up to 400 in one night. <http://www.wires.org.au/animals/bats.htm>

Direct and subsoil disposal of greywater

If you are unable to install a full reed bed system to safely dispose of your grey water there are other ways in which you can contribute to the environmental problem of saving and/or re-using grey water.

A word of caution is necessary about the safe use of grey water directly onto the garden. I can do no better here than to refer you to pp 38–40 of Allan Windust's book *(see p 16-4)*.

Clothes-washing machine effluent

Quite a lot of relatively clean water is put into the drainage system from washing machines, and this is easily diverted into the garden by means of flexible plastic hoses, now available in hardware shops.

Most machines have a hooked outlet which clips over the edge of the laundry tub or into a hole which leads into the trap underneath and this can be utilised.

The simplest way is to buy a flexible plastic hose and push-fit it onto the end of the hooked outlet, coiling the long hose in the tub when not in use. Black hose will stand up to the ultraviolet better than white.

When starting the washing machine, take the long hose outside and put it in a suitable place in the garden which needs watering. This location should be varied with every wash. It worked well for us as a temporary measure, but was somewhat inconvenient.

A better method, which has now been done in the Mawson house, is to drill a hole through the external wall and connect the internal hose in a more permanent way to a rigid plastic or stainless steel tube cemented into the external brick skin. Externally, a rigid plastic connecton has now been made to a sump in the ground *(see photo below)* which contains a fine removable filter to remove any lint, etc that may otherwise clog up the subsoil percolation pipe.

This is much more convenient and details are shown in the drawing **11**-23.2 sump **B**.

A better, but more difficult method, would have been to connect into the existing outlet pipe in a similar way as in sump **A**.

11-19.1 **Washing machine outlet now piped directly into sump B with filter before entering subsoil percolation pipe. (Garden is just being rehabilitated!)**

As to the washing machine itself, there is no real environmental advantage in replacing it if it is still washing adequately. The embodied energy cost would probably be a distinct negative.

If it does go wrong and can be repaired, this is preferable to buying a new one in many cases. If it is too uneconomical to repair, consult *CHOICE* evaluations on the latest equipment available, and compare carefully the continuing consumption figures of water and electrical energy.
(Back issues of CHOICE magazines are usually available in public libraries.)

Detergents

The use of detergent washing powders in washing machines needs careful consideration. Check to see if you can find one which has the minimum sodium content, as this could have a deleterious long-term effect on soil. *ReNew* magazine has done some checking on the constituents of detergents, and published a very informative list of detergents with their relative levels of phosphorus and sodium, in issue 81, Oct/Dec 2002. *(See p 16-4 for contact details.)*

Liquid detergents would appear to be less harmful than powders.

Dishwashing machine/sink effluent

Despite what all the commercial blurb says, domestic dishwashers are **not** environmentally friendly.

Firstly, there is a large amount of *embodied* energy in their materials, manufacture, transportation and installation (and disposal). Every use takes about 11–36 litres of water and about 1.5–2.1 kWh of electrical energy to drive the pump and heat the water; and their effluent is usually discharged into the sewer, requiring more energy for treatment downstream.

The use of powder detergents in dishwashing machines can put large amounts of phosphorus (an increasingly scarce and *non-renewable* resource) and sodium into the sewer system which, if not extracted, eventually ends up in our waterways with potential deterioration of the environment.

This practice is not sustainable.

When we moved into the Mawson house in 1991, we gave the dishwasher away, preferring to rely on the less consumptive double-bowl stainless steel sink. We washed up in one and kept a 4L plastic bowl with a handle in the smaller bowl for run-off water.

When finished, we ladled the used water — using a 2L icecream tub — into the bucket, and carried it out to the garden. It is full of nutritious, compostible bits which are very good for the garden. Because we are vegetrians, the fat content is very low.

We use one squirt of biodegradable detergent — *Homebrand* or *Bushland* — which the tests *(above)* have shown to contain very low levels of phosphorus and sodium.

We used to put about 18 litres onto the garden every day, which saved having to use clean mains water.

The system worked well for a few years, but I felt there had to be a better way. This eventually resulted in the aerobic tank system *(see pp 11-20 and 11-21)*, which incorporated a large planter box under the kitchen window — a visual delight and a delightful disguise for the more mundane sewage works underneath. It has been working well since December 2002.

The wash-up

While the clothes-washing machine has been a tremendous device in relieving humans of a tedious and back-breaking task, I doubt the same can really be said for the dishwashing machine.

It would be interesting to weigh up all the many factors for and against these two devices which are so similar in general function, yet so different in their social, physical and environmental impacts.

Re-using kitchen greywater

Disposal of kitchen greywater seems to be generally regarded as being difficult because of the use of detergents and the fats and food solids which are discharged down the sink outlet. Discussions with two microbiologists indicated that the use of aerobic bacteria and a sparing use of detergent low in phosphorus and sodium should adequately convert the sink effluent into a liquid which can be safely dispersed by drippers into an external garden.

This proved to be the case in the Mk 1 model described in previous editions of this book and it worked satisfactorily for a few years, except for the fact that the filter was too small, needing frequent emptying into the compost heap. So I built a Mk 2 version which, from the outside, looks exactly the same *(see photo 11-20.2)*.

The Mk2 has two removable tanks, one above the other, each of a capacity which can accommodate up to two sinksful (about 14L) of initial effluent. The upper tank contains a large filter area of galvanised perforated metal which collects the food scraps and can be removed for cleaning. It also serves the purpose of enabling the liquid to cool down to be within the 'comfort range' of the aerobic bacteria. The bacteria can be bought at your local aquarium supplies shop by the name of "Sludgebuster". A tablespoon of this solution down the plughole every month seems to keep the system happy, but this may well be unnecessary as the bacteria seem to reproduce very well, so be guided by experience.

Holes in the bottom of this tank let the cooled and filtered liquid dribble down into the tank below .

The 12mm and 4mm dripper lines then supply adjustable, cleanable drippers to plant positions, and they can be re-arranged if necessary.

When the system was establishing itself (ie. not enough aerobic bacteria relative to water flow), there was a little bit of odour present, but this disappeared when the bacteria colony really established itself after about 3-4 weeks. Since then there has been no problem.

I believe the boxing in of the tanks and the venting system are essential to its satisfactory functioning.

11-20.2 **The geranium disguised grey water treatment tank**

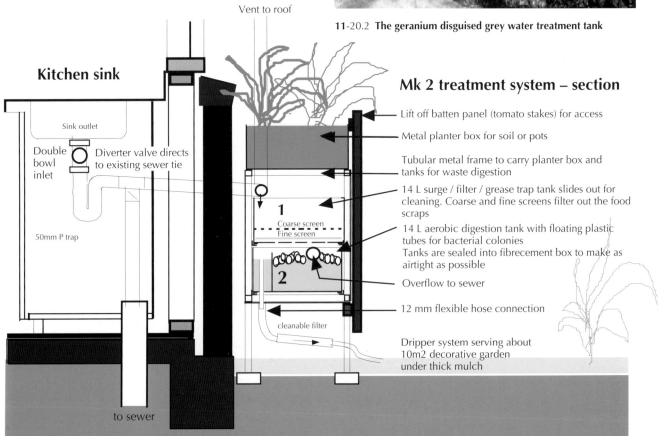

11-20.1 **Section through sink, wall and storage tank to show critical height relationships between sink outlet and upper tank**

Re-using kitchen greywater *(cont.)*

Operating the Mawson greywater system

'Operating' is not the right word, as in practice there has been very little to do. I fully expected to have to clean the filter about every month, but in reality it hasn't been necessary — the aerobic bacteria have disintegrated all food scraps, and the system seems to have reached a state of balance. The advice given to me has been, 'If it ain't broke, don't fix it,' so it has not been touched in over two years. The filters have not clogged up, and it is treating about 30L of warm sink effluent per day.

It is too early to assess the effects of the final effluent on the soil structure — it is an experiment that could take several years. However, our microbiologists' advice is that there should be no problem, as the soil bacteria will convert the greywater for a useful purpose, and its pH of 7.2 is regarded as good.

The two users of the Mawson house are vegetarian, so consequently there is less fat discharged down the sink after washing the dishes.

The detergent we use is Homebrand (Woollies), which was investigated, and from a laboratory analysis is said to contain only very small quantities of sodium and very low phosphorus content, which would be good *if* the effluent was going straight into the sewer (excessive phosphorus causes eutrofication and algae growth in rivers — unless filtered out by the soil).

Phosphorus is, however, a necessary nutrient for plant growth (Australian soils are deficient in phosphorus); but it is also a *non-renewable chemical which will eventually run out globally* — so on balance I think we are doing the right thing.

What has been learned from this experiment?

In principle, the system deserves further development as it has given every indication of suitability for purpose. The *aerobic* bacteria certainly do their work, effectively liquifying all the organic matter in the greywater, *but certain design changes would be advisable*:

1 Increase tanks to about 20L each to cater for the occasional double wash after a party, to avoid overflow, and to allow space for the vigorous growth of the grey, fuzzy bacteria.

2 The outlet pipe should not be less than 20mm in diameter, as the bacterial growth tends to clog up the top edge at water level.

3 All steel surfaces need to be sealed against corrosion — low-toxicity bituminous paint worked well, and greased plastic sliding runners for the tanks gave no trouble in moving the tanks.

4 The tank chamber should be sealed with a 50mm vent pipe to above the gutter level. Open base OK.

5 Easy access for inspection and cleaning of the outlet pipe is necessary.

6 Keep all filters and diverter valves above ground for easy maintenance access.

7 Install a diverter valve under the sink so that the system can be disconnected for maintenance.

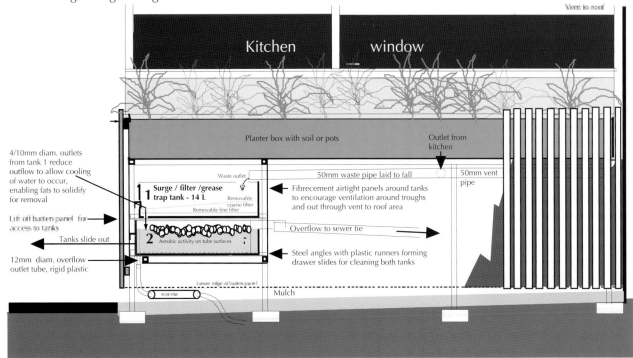

Mk 2 treatment system - sectional elevation

Note: the tubular framework is largely to hold up the weight of the planter box which is an aesthetic delight when seen from the window when washing up — we have no dishwasher, nor do we need one. The greywater system is a relatively minor part of the structure, and a smaller system design could be quite appropriate without the planter.

11-21.1 Long section through sink, how the greywater from the kitchen sink is treated before entering the dripper system in the garden

On-site subsoil drainage of greywater

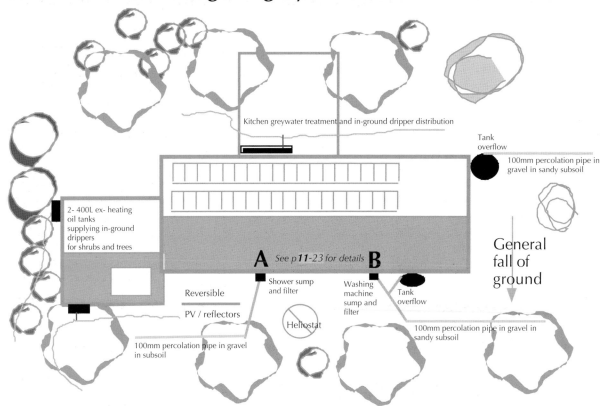

Kitchen greywater treatment and in-ground dripper distribution

Tank overflow

100mm percolation pipe in gravel in sandy subsoil

2- 400L ex- heating oil tanks supplying in-ground drippers for shrubs and trees

A   *See p **11**-23 for details*   B

Shower sump and filter

Washing machine sump and filter

Tank overflow

Reversible

PV / reflectors

Heliostat

General fall of ground

100mm percolation pipe in gravel in sandy subsoil

100mm percolation pipe in gravel in subsoil

11-22.1 Site plan showing all sub-soil percolation and dripper lines

Safe disposal of greywater

The location of drainage points, the concrete slab floor, the small site and established trees did not allow for a centralised reed bed purification system at Mawson *(see p **11**-18)*, but a range of plastics drainage sumps is now on the market which make *decentralised* disposal of greywater more feasible.

The RELN range of *recycled*-plastic sumps (pits) made it much easier to provide a disconnection and filter point between outflow pipe and percolation pipe. These are particularly suitable for bathroom and laundry greywaters which need filtering to avoid eventual blocking of the holes in the percolation pipe.

They also allow the various effluents to be spread over a wider area, helping to maintain the ground water levels — a critical factor in the survival of our landscaping in times of drought.

The avoidance of excessive overloading at any one point is very important, and the use of distributing pipes *which also act as surge storage* is valuable.

We have used the black plastic, 100mm diameter, flexible percolation piping which now comes with a fabric covering to keep out fine sand from the surrounding soil. Its flexibility is very helpful in laying and its internal volume can store a large discharge, such as from a washing machine or bath.

A number of aspects need to be considered - levels and locations of outlets around the house, frequency and volumes of discharges, absorptive quality and fall of the ground, existing pipes, trees (root invasion), garden layout and possible discharge of excess water onto neighbour's land.

How long should the percolation piping be?

A simple calculation will help you to determine the length of subsoil piping needed, starting with the maximum anticipated discharge volume and its frequency. The worst case is likely to be the bath with perhaps a single, continuous ~150L discharge. The pipe will hold about 8-10L /lineal metre so about 19m will be needed.

You can get some idea of the porosity of the ground by digging a trial hole, filling it with water and seeing how quickly it soaks away.

Washing machines can discharge around 60L of water over a few cycles of several minutes (once or twice a week) which does not necessarily require a full 60L storage in the subsoil pipe. Test the outflow quantity using a hose and large plastic container before you start digging.
(1L = 10cm x 10cm x 10cm)

It might be important to consider the possibility of the washing machine or bath discharging at the same time into the same pipe or even a coincidental overflow from the water tanks during a storm. These coincidences are unlikely, but are possible — err on the safe side.

Another alternative would be a sump in the ground, lined with bricks or stones and covered with a paving slab. This is a point disposal source, suitable only for porous, sandy soils, not for clay subsoils. Your local authority may be able to give you some guidance from their local knowledge.

There is a downside to this system — the filters need cleaning out occasionally !

Making suitable connections to existing greywater outlets

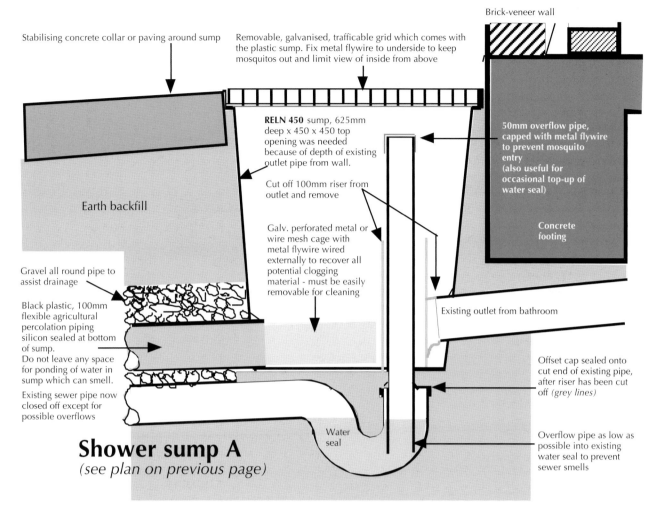

Stabilising concrete collar or paving around sump

Removable, galvanised, trafficable grid which comes with the plastic sump. Fix metal flywire to underside to keep mosquitos out and limit view of inside from above

Brick-veneer wall

RELN 450 sump, 625mm deep x 450 x 450 top opening was needed because of depth of existing outlet pipe from wall.

50mm overflow pipe, capped with metal flywire to prevent mosquito entry
(also useful for occasional top-up of water seal)

Earth backfill

Cut off 100mm riser from outlet and remove

Concrete footing

Galv. perforated metal or wire mesh cage with metal flywire wired externally to recover all potential clogging material - must be easily removable for cleaning

Gravel all round pipe to assist drainage

Black plastic, 100mm flexible agricultural percolation piping silicon sealed at bottom of sump.
Do not leave any space for ponding of water in sump which can smell.

Existing outlet from bathroom

Offset cap sealed onto cut end of existing pipe, after riser has been cut off (grey lines)

Existing sewer pipe now closed off except for possible overflows

Water seal

Shower sump A
(see plan on previous page)

Overflow pipe as low as possible into existing water seal to prevent sewer smells

11-23.1 Section through bathroom sump discharging grey water from bath, shower and basin (not toilet)

Making a sustainable connection

The above drawing shows how the conversion was made between the existing 100mm plastic sewer outlet from the shower and basin and its existing disconnector trap.

The sump is a bit larger than is really necessary, because the outlet through the wall was rather low, requiring the deepest plastic sump available.

The following principles to be observed are:

1 There should be no residual ponding of greywater in the bottom of the sump, so the outlet invert should be as low as practicable *(ponding could attract mosquitos and also start smelling after a few days).*

2 An overflow pipe into the existing trap should be made to relieve any back-up of grey water from from any blockage in the percolation line *(this serves as a refill point to keep the existing trap full, to avoid smells from the old line).*

3 Removable filter on the outlet is necessary to avoid any clogging up of the holes in the percolation pipe *(from hairs and general 'gunge').*

4 As with some other sustainable devices, a degree of 'active occupant' is necessary — cleaning of filters, etc.

A similar sump and filter arrangement was made at **B** *(see plan, p **11-22**)* to take the grey water from the tub and washing machine.
The percolation pipe also receives any possible overflow from the water tank system lower down the line (no need for filter).

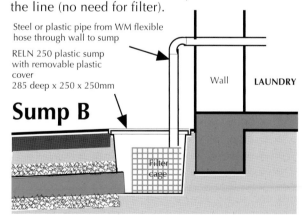

Steel or plastic pipe from WM flexible hose through wall to sump

RELN 250 plastic sump with removable plastic cover
285 deep x 250 x 250mm

Wall **LAUNDRY**

Sump B

Filter cage

11-23.2 Section through laundry sump for washing machine

The removable filter cage is larger in this case to accept the larger volume of water being pumped under pressure from the washing machine.

An entry into the sump similar to detail **A** could have been made, but other factors made detail **B** more convenient at the time.

We are living through a period of great change in everything we have become used to, and we now have to question every belief. But one fundamental premise we have to believe — *and practise*: nature has a growth imperative, but it also dies, decays, recycles its nutrients, and had continued in balance for billions of years until an increasing human population with consumptive desires upset that balance — in 300 years. We have not yet learned that nature has all the answers and will win in the end.

Making a useful landscape

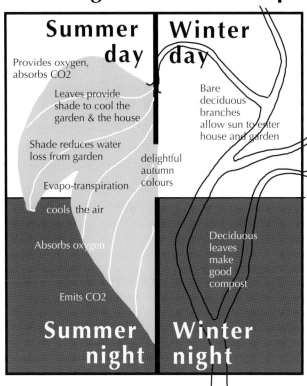

Summer day

Provides oxygen, absorbs CO_2

Leaves provide shade to cool the garden & the house

Shade reduces water loss from garden

Evapo-transpiration cools the air

Absorbs oxygen

Emits CO_2

Summer night

Winter day

Bare deciduous branches allow sun to enter house and garden

delightful autumn colours

Deciduous leaves make good compost

Winter night

12-2   **A solar garden?**

12-3   **Natural automatic shading**

12-4   **Deciduous trees**

12-5   **Deciduous vines and climbers**

12-6   **Lawn alternatives**

12-7   **Holding the roof down**

A solar garden?

All gardens are reliant on sunshine, light and warmth, nutrients and water — all solar in origin. In our quest for a house which relies on natural energies for its comfort, convenience and enjoyment, we have to explore and learn from the house/garden relationship.

The garden can be more than a decorative area surrounding a house. It can be extremely functional, but often it is not — large paved areas and lawns being good examples of negative energy areas.

All plants, from weeds to large trees, have some usefulness to the environment, but the secret of any landscaper's skill is to know *how* they can be *useful* to the overall house/garden symbiosis as well as to provide aesthetic delight.

In the Canberra climatic zone (cool temperate) we are fortunate in having four distinct seasons of growth and dormancy, which we can use to our advantage.

Leaves begin to appear around September/October when the spring temperatures are beginning to warm up; and by the time the warm weather arrives in November/December they are fully formed to shade our houses and to provide evaporative cooling - if we have had the foresight to place the right plant in the right place a few years before.

The wrong plant in the wrong place can be a real problem when wanting to take advantage of the sun — this applies particularly to the positioning of trees.

Trees
The passion for planting tall evergreen casuarinas, eucalypts and conifers around the east, north and west of houses is now proving to be a problem when we want to place solar water-heating absorbers or photovoltaics on our existing roofs *(see photo p3-3.1).*

Great care and foresight are needed in placing such trees — not only from the point of view of shading our own roofs, but from the shading of neighbours' roofs as well. Indeed, there should now be some planning restrictions on the planting of these types of trees.

However, as we are dealing with *retrofitting* situations in this book, it is quite likely that you will have to confront some very difficult decisions arising from the existence of large trees, such as:

1   What do you do about tall evergreens which shade your roof? *Loss of visual amenity; effect on wildlife habitat, atmospheric cleansing, etc.*

2   Do you cut them down? *Expensive — several $100; will you get permission to remove a substantial tree?*

3   What can you do if the trees are on your neighbour's land? *What if they refuse to cut them down?*

4   Do you abandon the idea of a solar hot-water system or a PV system simply because of shading problems?

5   Are there any alternatives? *Perhaps a tracking installation in an unshaded part of the garden?*

These are critical issues which must be evaluated before any further action is taken about modifying the house or installing any solar roof equipment.

(See also p4-3 describing the requirements for an efficient location of solar hot-water absorbers.)

The relationship between houses and trees is a very complex one, involving emotions, aesthetics and simple practicality.

Trees are essential elements in our landscape, playing a vital part in our survival by sequestering the carbon dioxide we breathe out and creating the oxygen we breathe in.

In the process of transpiration they evaporate water vapour from stomata in the leaves, which act just like evaporative coolers on buildings. They cool the surrounding atmosphere, which is useful to us when we open our houses at sundown to purge the house of any collected hot air — *if you have a ridge vent (see p 10-2).*

The shade they provide in summer also keeps the ground and low plants cool as well as the house — assuming they have been placed in the right position.

Their transparency in autumn and winter also serves us well in permitting the desirable warming sun to penetrate into our windows to help warm the interiors.

We cannot do without them, and in this age of solar awareness they serve as natural, automatic sunshades which can provide comfort in winter and in summer.

Our forebears mistakenly tended to regard the sun as their enemy, using big evergreen shade trees, often resulting in very dark houses which were cold in winter *(see photo 3-3.1)*

Delight in summer can be dismay in winter —so we need to find ways of using trees which are useful in all seasons.

Deciduous trees can play a significant role. It is most unfortunate that we have developed a culture that shuns deciduous exotic trees and praises the virtues of Australian native vegetation.

Many of the dominant native trees — the eucalypts and casuarinas — are *evergreen* and usually tall, shading us *in winter* as well as in summer. Mature eucalypts become a semi-transparent tracery of branches under a top canopy of thinning evergreen leaves — the very opposite of what would be most useful to us when considering solar access to our houses.

In analysing all the solar factors, I can only conclude that these tall evergreens are not really suitable trees for closely developed suburban situations.

12-2.1   *Acer negundo* — **Box Elder. A graceful and very useful shade tree, virtually transparent to the low-angle winter sun.**

Natural, automatic shading – *deciduous trees*

Planning a solar garden

Firstly, establish the facts by drawing a scale plan as described on p **3**-3 and **4**-3 showing your garden, house *and adjacent neighbour's trees* on the east, north and west sides of your property *(see **12**-3.1)*

It is particularly important that you establish your boundaries reasonably accurately with significant trees, so that you know who owns them — they may be a problem now or in the future. Remember, trees have a habit of growing, and a sunlit roof today may well be shaded in the near future, making a very expensive array of collectors uneconomic and ineffectual in reducing greenhouse gases and supplying your power.

From your drawing, you will be able to plot likely shading problems from particular tall trees and perhaps conclude that certain trees are unsuitable for your solar needs and may have to be removed. A bit of simple geometry with a protractor will tell you what lengths of shadows you are likely to get at certain times of the day.

However, all is not lost — they could be replaced by more suitable species which, with careful thought, could give you the qualities you are really seeking.

If there is room left on the *northern* side of the house, the judicious placing of deciduous trees, shrubs and vines is an obvious answer, but care should be

taken to choose those which drop their leaves before mid-autumn to allow the sun to penetrate the house when you need it.

A major factor in using planting as a retrofitting tool is to select *vigorous growers* which will give you some useful return within the shortest possible period.

From my 46 years' experience of living in Canberra, I have found that the Box Elder, the grape vine, the summer vine and Boston ivy give excellent solar control and are fast growing as well. They will all give you some pleasure and satisfaction within 3–4 years.

The **Box Elder** is of the maple family and can grow to up to 10m in height. It has soft, green leaves in summer, which give good shade underneath with a delicate translucency; and it drops its golden leaves early in autumn, leaving a fine tracery of twigs which do not obstruct the winter sun too much.

Having a moist type of leaf and sappy wood, it does not support fire as does the eucalypt, and so is suitable for growing reasonably close to the house.

It is a graceful tree, and can develop several trunks if pruned back when young. At 10m high it should not present a problem of shading roof-mounted absorbers if kept at least 5m away from your northern wall.

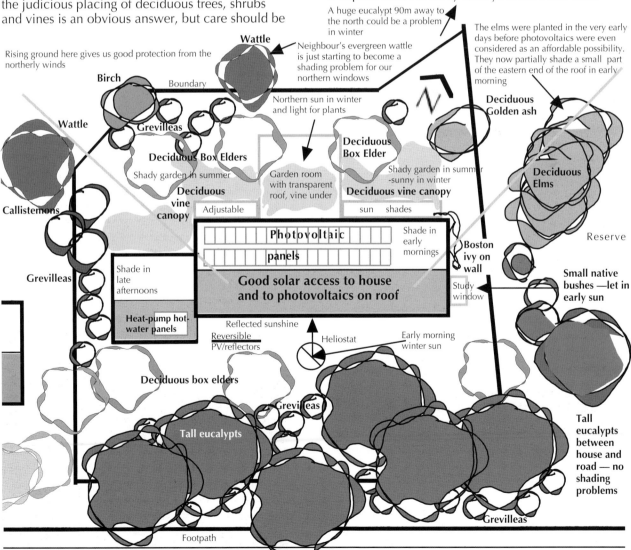

12-3.1   **Plan of Mawson house showing tree types and their solar relationship to the house — indicating three potential shading problems**

Deciduous trees – *how they work for us*

Their usefulness in summer

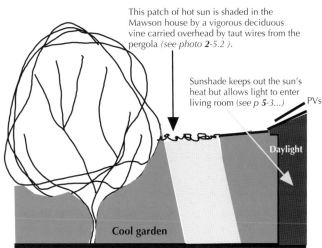

This patch of hot sun is shaded in the Mawson house by a vigorous deciduous vine carried overhead by taut wires from the pergola *(see photo 2-5.2)*.

Sunshade keeps out the sun's heat but allows light to enter living room *(see p 5-3...)*

Daylight

PVs

Cool garden

12-4.1   Desirable shade around noon, midsummer ~ 78°

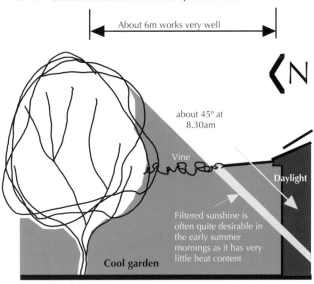

About 6m works very well

⟨N

about 45° at 8.30am

Vine

Daylight

Filtered sunshine is often quite desirable in the early summer mornings as it has very little heat content

Cool garden

12-4.2   Desirable shade around 8.30am, midsummer

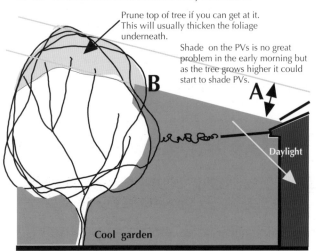

Prune top of tree if you can get at it. This will usually thicken the foliage underneath.

Shade on the PVs is no great problem in the early morning but as the tree grows higher it could start to shade PVs.

B

A

Daylight

Cool garden

12-4.3   Desirable shade early morning, midsummer for the house, but shade at A after breakfast would affect the efficiency of any solar panels on the roof. If the tree is existing, any new solar panels should be installed further up the roof or the tree should be pruned to a lower height. If you are planting a new tree, put it further away from the house — under a line about 10° from the lowest point of any panels as at B. Under this line the sun is only marginally effective in the early morning due to the lower angle of incidence on the panels.

... and in winter

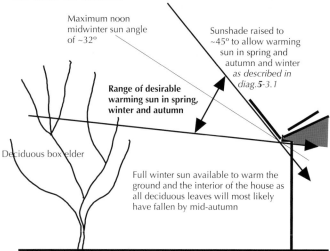

Maximum noon midwinter sun angle of ~32°

Sunshade raised to ~45° to allow warming sun in spring and autumn and winter *as described in diag.5-3.1*

Range of desirable warming sun in spring, winter and autumn

Deciduous box elder

Full winter sun available to warm the ground and the interior of the house as all deciduous leaves will most likely have fallen by mid-autumn

12-4.4   Desirable sun all day, late autumn, winter and early spring

My fondness for Box Elders *(in the face of some critical public comment)* is based largely on their usefulness as natural, automatic solar devices. They are in full leaf by the time the sun becomes hot in mid-spring, and they lose their leaves in mid-autumn when we begin to welcome the sun's warming penetration into the house.

It is a great pity that landscapers and horticulturalists regard this elegant tree as a weed because of its prolific seeding habit — we have never had any problem with unwanted seedlings. They are easy to pull up or to transplant into needed areas. If a weed is the wrong plant in the wrong place, Box Elders can be the right plant in the right place.

Because of their usefulness, they deserve every encouragement.

In addition, they are invariably graceful in their branching form and respond well to severe pruning in their early years to encourage multi-trunking, which keeps the canopy lower and denser. They are a really elegant solution to human needs.

At the risk of offending the 'natives only' brigade, I must confess that many of the indigenous trees and shrubs are, in my experience, nowhere near as useful. They tend, in their mature years, to become leggy with all their leaves on top; and, of course, their evergreen nature makes them useless for solar utilisation.

They need regular tip-pruning to keep the canopy low; but as they get higher they get beyond any reasonable human ability to do that, and grow ever upwards.

The debate seems to hinge around the fact that they attract native birds, and I am all in favour of encouraging this. Perhaps it is a matter of 'horses for courses' — natives around houses in positions where their non-solar characteristics are no problem, but deciduous trees around the sunny sides of our houses.

Could this be a reasonable compromise?

Not being a qualified horticulturalist, I would be most grateful if any reader could alert me to any natives which do not have these solar disadvantages. It would be good to build up a list of trees having useful solar characteristics.

Deciduous vines and climbers

Vines — and coolness

While deciduous trees are extremely useful for the purpose of shading specific areas in summer, they are necessarily 'moving blobs' of shade, causing us to think carefully about where the shade area will be at specific times.

Vines, on the other hand, can be trained into horizontal and even vertical areas of shade which can be quite dense and shady in the hotter months, giving longer and more *constant* areas of shade on the garden below, thus retaining its coolness.

This stored cool air is a critical, symbiotic factor when we come to cool the house down after a torrid summer's day — and it applies just as well to a southern side garden as to a northern side.

The volume of cool air stored in the shady garden can be quite substantial. Around 6pm after the heat of the day we encourage this mass of cool air to enter our house through the sliding doors and low windows which then, by the natural difference in density (cool air being heavier), will push the collected warmer air in the house up through the ceiling vents and out through the ridge vent.

This cools the mass of the house in readiness for another hot day, and makes the use of an air conditioner quite unnecessary in an average house.

These areas of openings should be as large as you can manage to encourage the flow.

The psychology of a shady garden

A significant part of the landscape design at Mawson has been a personal, aesthetic need of mine to be able to walk 'into' a garden rather than 'onto' it.

This overhead vine canopy is now paying handsome dividends in the two courts we have at each end of the northern elevation — they are absolutely delightful in summer and autumn when the leaves turn magenta, and drop their leaves in time to permit the warming sun to enter the windows.

We were given cuttings of the ornamental grape *(Vitis alicante bouchette)* when we moved into the house, but if I was starting again I would put in real grape vines. Both are vigorous growers and will give good shade in about three years.

12-5.1   The eastern court in early autumn when the vine has turned magenta and dropped about half its leaves. This gives some idea of the sense of enclosure — of walking 'into' rather than 'onto' a garden.

Climbers

Deciduous climbers on sunny walls can be a very important part of your climate-control system.

The Mawson house has a blank wall facing approximately east which used to get very hot in summer as it received the sun from sunrise to 1pm.

The room behind this wall used to become very hot in summer; but now that the Boston ivy has established itself on the wall, the room is quite cool.

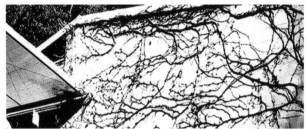

12-5.2   Boston ivy in winter. Good sun penetration which warms the wall, thus reducing heat loss at night.
(Parthenocissus tricuspidata veitchii aka Japanese ivy)

12-5.3   Boston ivy in summer. Virtually 100% sun shading with evapo-transpiration cooling leaf action — a natural air conditioner.

English ivy can damage brickwork, but Boston ivy *does not invade*, using small sucker pads to cling to the surface instead. This is no problem until you have to repaint the wall. Then you have little alternative but to paint the branches of the vine as well — in winter.

This is a drawback, but acceptable to us because of the tremendous benefit of the shading.

Virginia Creeper is not so successful — it does not support itself nor does it shade adequately.

Ground cover

If your windows go down to floor level you will need to grow low-level plants which do not obstruct the entry of the sun at sill level. There are many to choose from and they do not, of course, have to be deciduous. Star jasmine *(Jasmine trachelospermum)* grows about 20cm high, is evergreen, and has lovely white star flowers with a most fragrant perfume, which can be quite delightful in an entry court.

12-5.4   Star Jasmine — low growing and beautifully scented

Lawn alternatives

How useful are our lawns?

The traditional function of lawns has been to provide large walkable and playable areas as an open contrast to shrubs, bushes and trees.

They are delightful in England where ground moisture is adequate to maintain healthy grass, but I feel we must, in a low-rainfall area, question the suitability of such large areas of energy and resource-intensive manicured grass.

Well-maintained lawns are undoubtedly very pleasant areas to have around a house, but how often do we stop to consider the negative environmental aspects of their presence?

The initial establishment of lawn areas involves clearing of the area, levelling, soil importation, fertilising, the growing and bagging of seed, retailing, etc — most of which requires the use of fossil fuels.

The growing, cutting and laying of turf seems to involve even more intensive resource and energy use.

Once established, under constant watering with unnecessarily pure water, we spend hours cutting back what we have laboriously nurtured, with more fertilising, spraying with herbicides and pesticides to control weeds and pests, coring and thatching, rolling, and edge-trimming — all of which creates noise and atmospheric pollution, and uses precious resources, such as phosphate, with enormous amounts of runoff, which further pollute our waterways with algae and eutrofication, and cause death to many aquatic animals and fish from oxygen deprivation.

It has been estimated that the amount of atmospheric pollution created in mowing one domestic lawn with a two-stroke mower would be the same as driving a well maintained car 200km.

Taking all that into consideration. the domestic lawn must be one of the most energy-intensive and polluting areas in the landscape.

Another factor forced our hand at the Mawson house: in establishing a shady deciduous garden for summer coolness on the northern side of the house, we found that the lawn was patchy and never looked good.

A major factor was lack of light in summer months when the garden is cool and shady.

Not being energetic gardeners, we opted to remove all the lawns around our house and replace them with renewable wood chips, laid about 75–100mm thick on layers of newspaper to control any residual growth.

We did not spray harmful chemicals and have had no serious re-growth through the cover.

A lot of environmental negatives were eliminated in one operation — it was the best move we ever made.!

This has worked well for us, and looks good when it has oxidised to a pleasant grey brown. It can be a bit messy around the edges sometimes, and the chips had to be delivered by a large truck — but those are very small prices to pay for the huge environmental benefits of no mowing, no watering, no noise, no atmospheric pollution, no fertilising, no pollution of the waterways and the enormous continuing savings of fossil fuel.

We haven't missed our lawns one little bit, and we've sold the lawnmower.

Why then are we all so dedicated to our highly consumptive lawns in such a low rainfall area? Surely there must be better alternatives for some of these broad, open areas?

There are several plants which cover large areas with low-growing, walkable green. Dichondra and Thyme are often recommended as walkable surfaces, but how often do we see them? Others might be Lippia or Kidney weed.

However, they all need watering and good sun if they are to thrive and look healthy *— which tends to work against our need for a shady garden* with no water input.

The only real answer lies in some form of cover which does not require all these inputs — most commonly nowadays, wood chips of various grades.

The recent fire in Canberra has tended to question the use of chips, but I feel that if the very coarse wood chips are used (not the small flaky chips), the risk is minimised. Hardwood chips would last the longest, compared to softwood, but which are the most renewable? This needs some investigation.

12-6.1 **Coarse wood chips turn an attractive grey-brown, let the water through, don't degrade as quickly as the flaky chips, and cast a lot of shadow which helps to keep it and the underlying soil cool. Children can play on it without any injuries, but the edges can become untidy unless contained.**

I have tried Sedum, and find it covers a large area quite quickly. Its major advantage has been that it is very drought-resistant, having stayed green and moist throughout the drought of 2002–2003 with hardly any watering. It *can* be walked on, but is not a lawn alternative. It is good for steep banks or berms where mowing would be impossible. It casts good shadow, which keeps the ground cool underneath.

12-6.2 **Sedum — soft, succulent and shady ground cover, but not a very walkable surface. Drought resistant and excellent for mounds.**

Holding the roof down

Storms

Global warming is now accepted as being largely caused by human action and the resultant climate changes are now becoming evident. The oceans are warming, the major currents are changing their behaviour and the ice caps are melting.

The warmer seas are causing an increase in the number of cyclonic storms and CSIRO predictions are that they will tend to come further south in Australia, mainly in the coastal regions.

Cyclones have ravaged the northern areas of Australia in the past and Sydney has already experienced severe winds. In almost all cases it is roofs which suffer most damage, and it is *suction* rather than *pressure* that does most of the damage.

Tiled roofs are especially vunerable and very hard to remedy (not discussed here), but metal decked roofs can be strengthened.

Metal sheet roofing

Experience shows that metal roofs act in a more cohesive way, but failures can occur after repetitive stresses on the roof fixings causing flexing, often exacerbated by high *internal* pressures due to a broken door or window on the windward side damaged by flying debris. *See p 5-5 for possible way of shielding windows.*

There are two relatively easy and economical ways in which to give some restraint to your metal roof decking:

1 If the metal roof decking is fixed by nails rather than screws, then it would be wiser to hold the roof down by a crossed wire system which transfers the stresses to the bottom of the whole building structure. Using high tensile fencing wire is economical, but stainless steel cable would be stronger, with turnbuckles on the roof surface so that good tension can be maintained *(see diagram below)*. This is quite easy and quick to fix.

If the building is long, then areas A and B could still be weak and extra restraint may be advisable in the centres.

2 Experience has shown that where roofing has been fixed with screws, the repeated cycles of pressure and suction causes failure of the roofing metal at the screw head with consequent failure of the whole roof.

Specially designed washers are now available from Buildex which distribute the suction load over a larger roof area and are known as **Corri-lok** for corrugated steel roofs and **Square-lok** for square rib roofing.

However, it is of little value making the decking secure to the battens or purlins if they, in turn, are not secured to the trusses or beams below, so a top inspection is required. Most likely they will be nailed, so the battens or purlins will need to be wired or strapped down securely — if you have access.

Finally, do not under-estimate the power of wind on large roof areas — that final gram of precaution could be worth tonnes of anguish.

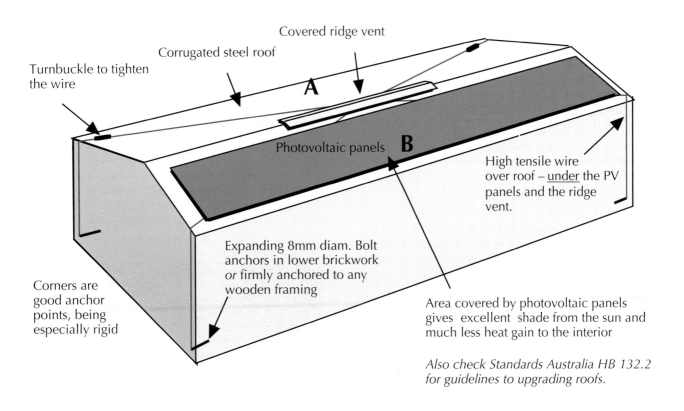

Covered ridge vent

Corrugated steel roof

Turnbuckle to tighten the wire

A

B

Photovoltaic panels

High tensile wire over roof – <u>under</u> the PV panels and the ridge vent.

Expanding 8mm diam. Bolt anchors in lower brickwork *or* firmly anchored to any wooden framing

Corners are good anchor points, being especially rigid

Area covered by photovoltaic panels gives excellent shade from the sun and much less heat gain to the interior

Also check Standards Australia HB 132.2 for guidelines to upgrading roofs.

12-7.1 Diagrammatic arrangement of a simple wire restraint system on the Mawson roof

Food facts

A meat eater's diet is responsible for about 1.5 tonnes more CO_2 per year than a
      vegetarian's diet,

Producing a kilogram of beef requires about 100,000 litres of water,

There is 55% less iron and
      7% less magnesium in rump steak today than there was 60 years ago
      because of the use of artificial fertilisers,

There is 24% less magnesium
      27% less iron
      47% less calcium in vegetables today
      because of industrial farming,

In 2005, 98% of the global fish catch was unsustainable,
      of which
      a third was used for fishmeal
      of which
      about two thirds was used to fatten other animals,

Up to 5kg of wild fish are needed to produce 1kg of farmed salmon.

Green Futures

It's always been done this way

Apathy

Conservatism

Why?

You're crazy

It won't work

It's never been done before

Nothing should ever be done for the first time

Why not?

It looks different

Luddites

Why should I stick my neck out?

It costs too much

The payback is too long

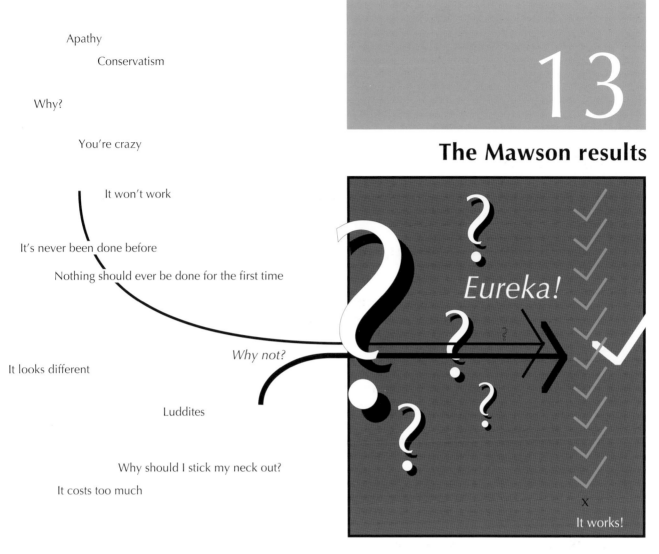

13

The Mawson results

Eureka!

It works!

13-2 **How do we evaluate the results of retrofitting?**

How do we evaluate the results of retrofitting?
— is the effort and expense worth it?

The 'pay back' period is rarely a valid indicator of the value of retrofitting actions.

How often do you hear somebody say that the pay-back period of their new swimming pool is X years? How can you possibly calculate the value of enjoyment, happiness, comfort, convenience, sustainability, clear skies, clear rivers, unpolluted land, leaving something for those who come after us — and a clear conscience?

Consider the following triple bottom-line evaluations of our Mawson experiences and make your own judgement:

ENVIRONMENTALLY	FINANCIALLY	AESTHETICALLY

Photovoltaic panels

From switching the panels on in August 2000 to the end of September 2009, the panels have *reduced* our emissions by 29.54 tonnes of CO_2-equivalent gas put into the atmosphere by the coal-burning generators supplying the grid (1kWh = 0.968kg CO_2e).

The shading effect on the roof has also made a significant contribution to the internal coolness of the house on hot days, resulting in *no* need for a polluting air-conditioning system. Six extra panels were added in December 2005 to increase generating output and to create more shade.

Over 9 years, the PVs generated 30,548kWh = an average of 9.22kWh/day, reducing costs by ~$3665.

Consumption over 9 years was 32,310kWh = 9.74kWh/day x 12c/kWh = $1.17/day. We paid $211 over 3315 days = 6.4c/day.

The PV array has thus contributed 94.66% of our electricity needs, for a net outlay of $19,000 on a DIY basis for a 2.94kW system.

The FIT should now reduce the pay-back period to 8.75 years, so by 2018 the system will have been paid off with several years life left (but nobody really knows!).

The large area of panels and their relatively low angle make them look more integrated into the building form, compared to adding a few panels which usually look 'stuck on', particularly if they are mounted at angles higher than the roof itself.

An extra six panels in 2005 made the array look even more like an integral part of the roof.

Several comments have been received as to the acceptable appearance of the Mawson array.

A successful exercise from all three points of view. (It is no longer the biggest PV array in Canberra.)

Adjustable sunshades over northern and eastern windows

Northern

Summer — 100% northern shading of summer sun entry.

All sunshades have significantly reduced the need for artificial cooling, and permit maximum penetration of daylight (due to its refractive weave), yet *retain full view through windows at all times*. The fabric allows rain to fall through to the garden below.

Winter — 95% (maximum possible) warming sun in northern rooms.

Eastern

Summer — shade does not exclude all low-angle sun, but it is not intense at that time and not a problem. Very effective after about 9am, when the sun becomes hotter.

Winter — early-morning low-angle sun very welcome. We have found no need to adjust the screen angle from horizontal.

There have been no wind problems. *They have maximised environmental benefit by reducing pollution from use of electricity for air conditioning.*

The exclusion of unwanted sun in summer has helped significantly to eliminate any need for air conditioning. This has meant a considerable saving on capital and running costs.

Over the cool season, the heating effect of winter sun penetrating the northern interior could conservatively amount to 9MWh of beneficial sun — or $6 worth of electrical heat every winter day.

The two large, clipped-on, hemmed, and eyeletted white Coolaroo shadecloth sheets are easily fixed every October, and removed and stored every April, taking only ten minutes with a stepladder, no tools being needed.

They cost about $900, much less than pivoted frames and with virtually no maintenance. If starting again, I now feel I would install spring roller blinds with the white Coolaroo underneath the gutter, as this is the easiest answer in the long run.

In summer, the Coolaroo shadecloth permits maximum entry of *visible light*, which is a delightful contrast to the gloom of the usual canvas roller awning. Darkness does not equate to coolness, and the extra *refracted* light enables rooms to be used to the full without the need for supplementary electric light.

The shade over the eastern window permits the enjoyment of the bush view which other forms of eastern shading would obscure.

It also permits entry of the low-angle winter sun, which is very delightful in early morning.

It is visually similar to the northern shades, adding to the integrity of the house's appearance, and it suits the external house design.

The full penetration of low-angle winter sun in all northern and eastern rooms is very beneficial, contributing greatly to our feelings of wellbeing and cheerfulness.

Adjustable sunshades are worth it for this reason alone.

ENVIRONMENTALLY	FINANCIALLY	AESTHETICALLY

Combined reflector/photovoltaic panel over southern bedroom window

Warms the bedroom by ~8° in winter and generates 274kWh/year of electricity — the total equivalent of 1.3 tonnes of CO_2e over one year.

The use of a very dark bedspread keeps the bed warm.

Over the 6-month heating season, ~1.13MWh of heat enters the main bedroom. This is the current equivalent of $147 of electrical heating per heating season + $27 of electricity generated over the year.

The psychological effect of sunshine entering a southern window is very uplifting, and almost worth doing just for this effect.

To a person confined to bed with illness, it would be a wonderful tonic.

Tracking heliostat reflector outside southern dining room

Reflected sunshine enters the room at 90° during sunshine hours, warming the room several degrees.

Internal temperature on a cold sunny day is frequently 24°.

~2.657 tonnes of CO_2e is saved every winter. Sunshine penetration hours are longer than with the fixed reflectors.

Not a recommended heating solution for the uncommitted — largely a research project.

Calculations indicate an input of 2.745MWh of heat = $356 of electrical heating per heating season.

A tiny amount of electrical energy from the photovoltaics drives the system automatically.

Some glare is evident when using the room at lunchtime, but it is quite tolerable when compared to the substantial benefits. It also reflects low-angle sun at breakfast time, which is very welcome.

The heliostat serves as a garden sculpture — a factor often commented on by visitors. The unit is switched off in the non-heating season.

Heat-storage wall

Added concrete wall absorbs heat from heliostat (61° recorded), preventing overheating of room in daytime and warmer winter evenings.

An expensive addition of mass — ~$500 concrete slabs, and a lot of fiddly labour — but *effective*.

No cost/benefit figures available.

Automatic thermal balancing — no action needed from occupants, just *set and forget; an ideal situation*.

Combined ceiling/ridge vent/lights

This integrated system helps to keep the house cool in summer and to provide daylight in dark areas of the house — when curtains are closed on hot days.

It saves electricity by making air conditioning unnecessary — a great reduction of CO_2e emissions and heat pollution now producing heat islands from air conditioners.

It further saves electricity which would otherwise be needed for lighting. *Highly effective.*

Capital and running costs of air conditioning are eliminated.

2009 estimates vary between $2700 for a small wall-mounted air-conditioning unit to around $10,000 for a ducted system, plus running costs of around $1/day, depending on the size of the house and how often it is used.

(By not installing an air-conditioning system, the capital contribution would go a long way toward installing a photovoltaic system.)

Noiseless, non-polluting removal of warm air, *natural cooling*, and *natural daylight* has resulted in much more pleasant conditions.

Internal temperatures are often around 8–10° cooler than outside, and 12° has been recorded. The roof/ceiling lights make the interior well-lit all the year round.

Very livable summer conditions internally and highly desirable socially. The panic for air conditioners is social madness.

Dishwashing greywater onto garden

The prototype system using aerobic bacteria was eventually abandoned because:

1 Tank and pipe sizes were too small, causing overflow after a party wash-up, otherwise OK.

2 I was too lazy *(or too busy writing books like this)* to give the necessary time to cleaning out a mucky system.

3 At 85, I no longer have the energy to build a Mk 3 system.

But it did work well for several years, and is worth developing!

No financial benefit to us because of Body Corporate's (BC) single meter for 17 houses.

All BC units should have separate meters to ensure equity of usage and charging. We use 80L/person/day, but our BC figures indicate that others in our group use much more — but this *includes* common areas which consume unsustainable amounts of water and maintenance.

It made us feel as though we were doing the right thing in using waste water in garden areas where water is needed.

Even in the hottest summer, there was no smell from the system, and so far there appears to be no deleterious impact to the soil structure. It has remained moist, and the plants are thriving.

The planter-box geraniums are an all-year-round delight.

ENVIRONMENTALLY	FINANCIALLY	AESTHETICALLY
Conservatory		
The efficiency of the rest of the house is adequate, and turning our ventilated garden room into a conservatory for more heat was too expensive at the time.	A natural convective process would produce convected heat with *no* financial running costs. The gain would not justify the cost in this case.	The garden room is a very pleasant outdoor eating place with large rocks and large plants.
Water heating		
We opted for a Quantum heat-pump system in 2000 because of frost and shade on the only available roof space — it extracts its heat from the surrounding air without reliance on the sun. No CFCs are used in its heat-transfer system, and it was the best solution at the time for this situation. It has worked well.	Its installed cost was around $3400 (similar to a solar tank on the roof) and its running cost has been reasonable, using about 1.8kWh/day average of PV-generated electricity = 21c/day. The newer compact heat-pump models would have been more efficient in the Canberra climate, but were not available at the time.	Invisible on our 10° pitched roof, and colour-matched to the roof anyway. We were not prepared, for visual reasons, to tilt large absorber panels at the optimum 35°, so the Quantum unit is aesthetically superior. The compressor does make a little noise, but its location in the workshop is no problem.
Space heating		
The house was bought in 1985 and had electric in-slab heating using 14.5kW, which we have not used since 1986. It was very expensive to use and *environmentally very polluting*. The passive measures we have taken keep us reasonably warm in winter — 19–24° with topping up in the cooler evenings from a natural-gas heater.	Natural-gas heating is significantly cheaper to run than electric heating, producing only one-quarter of the atmospheric pollution. Comparative space-heating costs over a heating season have been: In-slab electricity: ~$1000–2300 (if used) Natural gas: ~$92	Natural gas is not as effective as in-slab heating, but its response time is quicker and more flexible. Heat is produced as and when required, which can't be done with in-slab electric elements and their long response time. The fan noise is a little obtrusive when it starts up, but we soon become unaware of it.

Using rainwater to flush the WCs — *item omitted from this upgrade*

It was a good idea, at the time before plastic tanks came into existence, to use old oil tanks (described in previous editions) — but *hysteresis* between the pump and the float valve proved too troublesome. *I include this note in the hope that others might learn what not to do.*

The two WC cisterns have now been modified to a very simple lift-and-flush system *(see p 11-17)* which reduces flushes to about 1–3L as appropriate. Even that is potable water (too good for the purpose), so I am currently working on a roof-mounted UV system which will purify two qualities of water for the bathrooms: one suitable for flushing the WCs, and a small quantity that is suitable for potable use — yet to be tested!

Double glazing		
4mm fixed glazed panels have worked well (approx. 70% of a sealed DG unit). Silica-gel crystals enclosed in cavity have prevented any condensation.	No heat-loss figures available, but calculable. Cost on DIY basis: about $1000 for 25 large panes of glass = average $40 each (1992). Cost of sealed DG units were much higher at that time — they are coming down in price.	Benefit unperceived, but there must be some. We would notice it if the glass was removed. Traffic noise reduction on south side of house in winter.
Boston Ivy sunshading on eastern wall		
Prevents heat absorption by east-facing wall in summer and permits heat absorption in winter. Effective, natural, and automatic system — 'plant and forget'.	No figures available, but could be calculated. Absolutely free of cost. *Good value for 'money'.*	Visually very pleasant at all times. Lack of water resulted in die-back.

ENVIRONMENTALLY

Overhead vine sunshading

The ornamental vines now form canopies over the north-west entry and the north-east courts, protecting the garden underneath from the hot summer sun, establishing a reservoir of coolness which flows into the house when it is opened up around 6pm. This flushes out any residual warm air in the house and cools the structure down, ready for another hot day. In winter the vine loses its leaves, and permits entry of the sun to warm the interior of the house.

Leaf fall makes good compost.

Trees and shrubs

Deciduous Box Elders have been planted on the north side. They provide much-needed shade in the hotter months, yet permit full winter-sun penetration. They are moist trees and are fire-resistant. They will not grow so tall as to shade the photovoltaic array.

Eucalypts on the adjacent reserve are now growing tall and will soon shade part of the PV array.

However, they do provide some shade for the eastern window on summer mornings, which is quite acceptable.

Ivy, sedum and star jasmine provide good shady ground cover over several areas and contribute to the useful reservoir of coolness in the courts.

Leaf fall creates good compost.

'Lawn' areas

All our previous lawns have now been transformed into coarse, wood-chipped areas. The 'loss' of cool air within the grassy sward has gone unnoticed, and the shade from the overhead vine has enabled the wood chips to stay cool.

The amount of water and fossil fuel saved is enormous. We would not even consider going back to a labour- and resource-intensive lawn with all its polluting disadvantages.

The evidence from the 2003 fire in Canberra seems to indicate that, although there was some burning of these woodchip mulches, they did not seriously support fire as much as previously thought.

FINANCIALLY

No figures available, but known to be an excellent contributor to summer coolness in the house — particularly when purging the house in the early evening.

Cost of overhead straining wires was very small, using existing pergola and stakes in embankment.

Nil establishment cost and good environmental benefits make these plantings very valuable in the thermal functioning of the house, making the initial and running costs of an air conditioner unnecessary.

Incalculable financial benefits:

No watering
No mowing
No fertilising
No maintenance
No weeding
No scarab grub infestations
No coring
No pollution from exhaust fumes
No lawn mower (we sold it)
No noise
A more consistent, Australian appearance
No time lost — worth at least $1000 a year to me!

The only thing we have 'missed' is the exercise of mowing, but we get it elsewhere, so it's no loss.

A top-up load of wood chips seems to be necessary every five years or so.

AESTHETICALLY

The cooling effect is palpable and visually very enjoyable — creating the effect of walking 'into' a cool garden, rather than 'onto', making a welcoming entry to the house.

It is particularly beautiful in autumn when the leaves turn magenta. Visitors often comment on the pleasant effects.

Good exercise when pruning the vine in July.

No noise from air-conditioning equipment.

Leaf fall in autumn creates great beauty and shows how nature can work in harmony with human needs. It is really symbiotic.

One of the delightful aspects of living in Canberra is the change of the seasons, so evident in the deciduous trees and shrubs with their differing moods and colours.

There is no comparison between a consistent area of woodchips and a sparse, patchy, inconsistent apology for a lawn which is becoming the norm in a drought-ravaged area like this.

The natural ethos of Australia is not tidy and manicured as it is in England — it is rough and untidy, and the rough textured brown/grey appearance of a wood-chipped area fits much better into the reality of the Australian environment.

We should stop kidding ourselves with our nostalgia for 'the old country' — our climates are very different.

'You can't solve problems with the ways of thinking that created them.'

Albert Einstein

What if I live in a rented house?

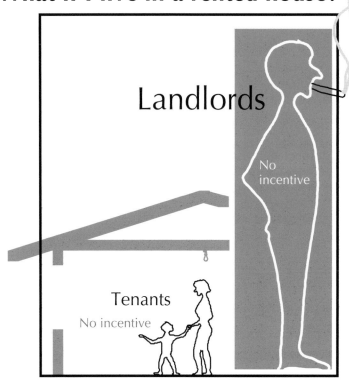

14-2   How tenants can reduce their fuel
bills and stay comfortable

How tenants can reduce their fuel bills and stay comfortable

An increasing proportion of the community now seem to be renting their living spaces — but it is often more difficult for them to keep warm in winter or cool in summer, quite apart from any altruistic desire about contributing to global sustainability.

Their rental properties are rarely state of the art in terms of comfort or convenience, and money for heating could often be in short supply. In colder areas, fuel poverty has resulted in increased deaths due to hypothermia.

Landlords currently have absolutely no incentive to provide effective insulation, solar hot-water systems, photovoltaics, or effective curtains, etc *unless the governments wake up to the enormous contribution that could be made to reducing greenhouse gas emissions in leased properties.*

It is inequitable that affluence places a person in a position to spend money to save money — eg, install photovoltaic arrays to generate their own electricity — whereas those who are not so affluent cannot do so. The rising cost of basic necessities such as electricity and gas also means that increasingly they cannot afford to keep warm in winter or cool in summer.

Having to pay rent further reduces their ability to gain a little more comfort.

So what can a tenant do at very little cost?

Keeping warmer in winter

1 Establishing a vegetable garden (assuming there is space available and you have a reasonable level of fitness) does not take a lot of money, but has several benefits:

- exercise (*warmth* and increased fitness and improved mental wellbeing
- more sunshine (vitamin D — very healthy)
- better nutrition from fresh vegetables
- no rules, regulations or hassles
- companionship with other gardeners
- a reason to get up in the morning
- lower cost of living

2 'Acquire' a lot of expanded polystyrene (XPS — the white, lightweight, open boxes used for transporting vegetables at the markets or at Woollies). Cut into flat slabs with a bread knife and placed about 100mm thickness over the plaster ceilings of the *warmest* rooms, it provides good insulation, and reduces heat loss and expenditure on fuel. The more the better.

3 If more XPS can be acquired, place it between the ground floor joists to reduce heat loss. Even crumpled up newspapers will be effective in this situation. Old bits of wire netting, plastic film, even stiff cardboard from the dump can be used to hold the insulation in place and reduce heat loss.

4 Transferring used washing-up water to the garden in a bucket will help to reduce the water bill — but let the water cool down *inside* the house before taking it outside, as every bit of heat inside helps, in winter.

5 On sunny winter days, get hold of some old bricks or small paving slabs, lay them in the sun for a few hours (sheltered from the wind), and put them under your feet when watching TV. They will stay warm for quite a while. If you can paint them black it will improve their heat absorption.

6 Heat a brick in the same way. Wrap it in cloth or newspaper *after* heating and put it in your bed after sunset in winter. 'Tent' the bedclothes so that the heat from the brick can circulate around the enclosed space, taking the chill off them.

7 Cut strips of stiff cardboard and glue them to the top of the curtain track to reduce any cooling of warm air between curtain and window *(see p 5-8)*.

8 On sunny days in winter, close the windows to retain residual heat and open the curtains to admit the warming sun. Close the curtains when the sun leaves the window, as heat gain then reverses into heat loss.

9 An investment of 'Raven' stick-on draught-stripping around doors and windows would be recouped very quickly by reducing fuel bills. Your landlord might even pay for it if you are prepared to apply the stripping. Otherwise long strips of newspaper stuffed into the cracks could be just as effective, but keep the windows closed.

10 If you have an old wooden floor at ground level where all the boards have shrunk and opened up the joints, you most likely have a major heat loss in winter due to the intrusion of cold air from under the floor structure. (If you have acted on item **3** in this section, you will have eliminated most of this problem, but the following technique would still be worth doing in a cold climate.) *(See also p **10**-5 on draughtproofing).*

If there is a woodworking place near to you, ask for a bag of fine sawdust (wood flour) from the area near the belt sander. They shouldn't charge you for it as they regard it as waste (it is really a valuable resource but don't tell them!).

Here's where you might have to experiment a bit.

You could try mixing the wood flour with water to start with and push the resultant putty into the cracks as much as you can. Let it dry thoroughly over a few days and see how much shrinkage has taken place. If there is a visible crack and the surface is a bit loose, you might have to buy some linseed oil and use it instead of the water. Don't forget the gap between the floor boarding and the skirting!

It is a laborious job, but has the potential of being *very* effective in keeping the room warmer in winter.

Alternatively, if you can afford or acquire a thick rug of a good size this could reduce the penetration of cold air. Lay a sheet of plastic underneath the carpet to improve its airtightness.

Reducing your electricity bills

1 Heat losses from exposed hot water piping can be quite substantial, particularly if they are in the roof space — and could be adding to your electricity bills.

Consider wrapping them in layers of newspaper *which trap air between the layers* rather than being tightly wound. This will increase the insulating efficiency.

If you feel generous enough to buy commercial pipe lagging, the Bradford black foam plastic would be one of the best, but you are unlikely to recoup your investment in reduced electricity bills unless you aim to be a long-term tenant. Ask your landlord to contribute if you are willing to supply the labour.

...*with hardly any outlay*

2 Your hot-water cylinder/tank may be up in the roof space or in a cupboard, and even though the external surface may feel cool to the touch it is quite likely that you are losing expensive heat.

Cylinders in the roof space could be wrapped around with two or three layers of old blankets, or carpet underlay (either the crumbed plastic foam variety or just underfelt), which can very likely be found at your nearest recycling place or at a carpet salesroom as offcuts or re-usable pieces. They may well let you have it for free, as it could save them a trip to the dump.

Offer to collect it all, and what you don't use for wrapping around your hot water cylinder you can put into the ceiling space. You can't put too much in.

Again, don't wrap it too tightly around the cylinder as the *air spaces* within its structure do the insuulating — if they are compressed to the point of non-existence they are of no value — and air space is free.

Cylinders in cupboards could be treated in the same way if you have sufficient access to get your arms and hands around it.

If not, try crumpling up old newpapers and stuffing them in the spaces. This also traps air in lots of little pockets, and restricts convection and radiant losses. Don't pack it too tightly.

Don't forget to cover the top of the cylinder with a double thickness, as that area is its weakest link. Even stuffing the spaces with broken bits of expanded polystyrene will be reasonably effective.

3 While fiddling around with the cylinder have a look at the thermostat, which is usually behind a screwed on plate. SWITCH OFF THE ELECTRICITY AT THE MAIN DISTRIBUTION BOARD FIRST and USE A TORCH!

If it is set at around 70ºC, your heat losses could be higher than is necessary. If the thermostat has an adjustable gauge you could re-adjust it to a lower figure such as 55º or 60ºC. This will minimise the heat losses, but possibly increase the volume of hot water used. Its a balancing act, but worth trying.

4 Glueing slabs of XPS on the sides and top of the refrigerator will reduce the amount of electricity or gas needed to keep food cold.

If its not your fridge make sure you can get the XPS off again without leaving any glue marks when you leave, or ask your landlord if he would like the insulation left there. Use Blu-Tak if you will have to take it off again.

5 If there is any choice, use natural gas to boil the kettle rather than by electricity — it is easier on the environment and on the pocket.

6 Take shorter showers to reduce the amount of energy needed to reheat cold water. Long showers are an expensive way to get warm.

7 If you can afford to buy 'Winter Windows' *(a cheap form of double glazing* — clear plastic sheets applied to the inner side of windows of the warmer rooms), some saving in fuel bills can be expected, but it would take a few years to break even.

In the meantime, however, you would feel more comfortable.

Keeping cooler in summer

1 On hot, sunny days in summer, close the curtains and all the windows to reduce heat intake by radiation.

2 Around sunset or when the outside air is cooling down, open up all the doors and windows to allow the cooler external air to blow through the house so that the structure can cool down. Keep them open as long as you can with any degree of security — until breakfast time next morning, and close up again as soon as it seems to be getting warmer than inside.

3 If a long-term tenancy is likely, planting a few cuttings of self-adhering Boston Ivy at the foot of east, west or north walls will, in about three years, produce a clinging, shady growth to a wall that becomes unbearably hot in summer. The shade produced on the wall will have a significant effect on the amount of heat absorbed, and the room behind will stay cooler. If the vine shows tendencies of growing over the roof, encourage it — it is extremely useful there, too, but it may prove too hot for the plant to thrive *(see p 12-5)*.

4 Another long-term solution would be to plant some quick-growing *deciduous* trees which could shade your northern windows in summer when fully grown, and let the winter sun in to warm the interior of the house. It may not take all that long for effective height and foliage to grow — Box Elders (*acer negundo*) grow fairly quickly, and could be useful in about 3–4 years *(see p 12-3 and 12-4)*.

It is a prolific seeder, and you shouldn't have any trouble finding self-starting seedlings. Even if you don't benefit from it, the next tenant may bless you for its shade — don't plant it any closer than about 5–6 m from the window, as they can grow up to 10m high with a corresponding spread *(see p 12-4)*.

5 Before you leave, give your landlord a list of the improvements you have made to the house — and tell him that you have improved the Energy Efficiency Rating of his property (and its resale value). He might even be kind-hearted enough to give you a week's rent, but will probably increase the rent as a thermally improved property for the next person.

Apart from having had a more comfortable time, you will have the warm fuzzy glow of knowing that, even as a tenant, you have made your contribution to reducing the greenhouse gas pollution problem — every little bit counts.

STOP PRESS

Help is at hand: a non-profit group called *Just Change* initiated a partial solution in 2008; and now, in collaboration with the federal government, programs are available Australia wide to negotiate contracts with landlords and tenants to help financially with installing ceiling insulation, low-flow showerheads, compact fluorescent bulbs, draught stoppers, and window treatments, etc.

Contact: **www.justchangeaustralia.org**

'The impacts of global warming are such that I have no hesitation in describing it as a weapon of mass destruction.'

Sir John Houghton,
former chief executive of the UK Meteorological Office

15

Who benefits and who pays?

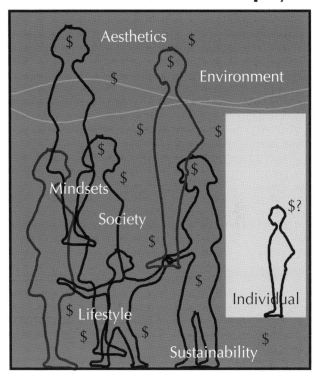

15-2   **Why should I retrofit?**

15-3   **Retrofitting & lifestyle**

15-4   **Which retrofit project should I do
        first?**

15-5   **How can we finance retrofitting?**
        'Solarisation' *An affordable proposal by
        Dr Andrew Blakers*

15-7   **Technoclutter**

Why should I retrofit?

Society's needs or mine?

The time has undoubtedly come when the driving force to reduce consumption and pollution arises from *the needs of the planet* rather than from our own need for *more effective comfort or convenience* in our homes.

How do we place a value on saving water or reducing our consumption of electricity or making our existing house cooler in summer — and how do we compare society's needs with our own, so that we can decide what to do first?

There are dollar values applicable to each retrofitting action, and we now have to weigh up their worth to society — as well as to ourselves.

Most of us already have very good-quality water laid on to our houses, but we literally throw most of it away down the drain. It isn't *right* or *logical* or *sustainable* — there *must* be a better way.

There is a large degree of altruism in conserving water because we are all in the same boat. Our population continues to increase, but our rainfall is decreasing — and without water we can't grow food.

Our environment and our lives are at risk, so it isn't personal comfort, or convenience, or saving money which is really driving us to take on such a project — it is the thought that:

- we are doing 'the right thing' for the environment and for future generations;

- we are striving to show that there is a more sustainable way of living which should be the norm rather than the exception; and

- we are helping to delay or even obviate the need for new dams to be built.

On *p 11-14* I used these inputs to produce a comparative analysis which shows that some measure, however imprecise, may be used to help us evaluate differing options on a more rational basis.

It has one further advantage — it can help to compare *subjective* opinions with *objective* facts to some extent.

The method has the capacity to show up significant differences between the items under consideration. Small differences are of no real help. Such a method may also help us decide between installing a rainwater system or a photovoltaic system, and confirm, or otherwise, any previous subjective opinion we might have formed.

Who is going to design and construct the new thinking?

There are many enquiring minds in this country — people who can think of better ways of doing things and have the initiative, the time, the skills, and the money to try out their ideas. Many of these people are 'Do-It-Yourself'ers, and the alternative technology movement is full of enquiring people who ask 'Why not?'

One problem they often face in trying out their new ideas is breaking through the legislative minds of our planning and design authorities. In previous years, authorities have applied the building regulations in a rigid way, which has often stifled lots of good ideas.

However, in recent years we have seen a new crop of administrators who are willing to talk things over with people with new ideas, who have some understanding of the need for sustainability, and who even encourage different ways of doing things.

This is indeed refreshing but, on the other hand, you will find some tradesmen 'who have always done it this way' and won't contemplate alternative ways.

Those who have to rely on tradespeople need to have the knowledge and the courage of their convictions to insist on the outcomes they wish to achieve. You will need to give clear instructions if you are to end up getting value for money.

The alternative (aka *'appropriate'*) technology movement is gaining respectability very rapidly (albeit belatedly from the 1960s when Fritz Schumacher first coined the term). Knowledge and new ideas are surfacing all the time — even insightful old knowledge and concepts are achieving timely recognition.

Regrettably, there is one section of industry which is not moving with the times — the housing industry, with its developers and builders who are marching to a different drumbeat, who seem to be more concerned with fashion, space, cost, and profits than with providing for the *real needs of living*.

The homeowner who wishes to retrofit would be well advised to talk to the Alternative Technology Association, which has branches in every Australian city, or to the Australian Solar Energy Society (AuSES), which is an allied group.

Members of these groups know who is working in any specific field, and can put you in touch with an advisor, who can explain the options and help you find a solution which suits your needs.

What is important is that your needs for retrofitting are seen in *your* context, with *your* priorities, *your* specific needs; but any solution should be the result of a holistic evaluation which *also* bears the needs of *society and the planet* in mind.

The field of retrofitting is a relatively new and integrative art and science, and it is inadvisable to rush into installing, say, a rainwater-harvesting system without considering a wider range of many small factors which may bend your solution one way rather than another. For example, does your house lend itself to a tank system? Will your washing machine work efficiently at a lower pressure than the current water pressure?

Having designed your particular system with your advisor, and produced some preliminary drawings and a performance specification, you will be in a far better position to find and discuss it with a sympathetic contractor who can put your ideas into reality.

Like many other things in life, it can be a false economy not to get the best advice. It can often save you money in the long run by integrating two essentials: knowledge and experience — both of which are still fairly scarce in this stimulating new field of retrofitting.

Retrofitting and lifestyle

Synergies

Retrofitting and your choice of lifestyle are synergistic in that they work together toward an improved future.

If you have chosen to retrofit your house to save energy for the sake of the environment, it is more than likely that you have already made some changes to the way you live, being sensitive to the way your actions improve or degrade the environment.

Many books have been written about the way we live and its effect upon the environment, so I won't go into detail. It is enough to provide a simple checklist to see how far we as individuals have changed since we became environmentally conscious.

It does concern me that although lifestyle changes are talked about more and more in the press, on radio and television, I'm not sure how many people are taking it seriously enough to actually do something about it.

'Doing the right thing' will undoubtedly affect our *comfort*, our *convenience*, our *hedonism* and also our *wallets* — four very strong forces which work against its adoption. As I witness the behaviour of others I often wonder how we will effectively get this message across — to the point where *enough* people will be convinced *to do something positive*.

I wonder about what my grandchildren will say when petrol becomes so expensive as to make their cars useless. Electric cars are now a reality, and can easily be charged from PVs on the roof — so why not? Other fuels will eventually become available.

Humans have become so accepting of the fact that science, technology, big business and governments will provide all the answers that perhaps we don't stop to think about the cumulative actions of 6 billion people and what a small change by each of them could do to improve this planet.

Australians and Americans are right at the top of the world league in creating pollution to satisfy our hedonistic lifestyles. On the other hand, there are several millions who have been given no choice as to their lifestyle, and it would be unreasonable to expect them to make any real contribution — which lends more emphasis to letting 'the polluter pay'.

We *do* have a choice: we have bought our comfort, our convenience and our pleasures, almost all of which require polluting energy. So if we wish to continue with an acceptable lifestyle, it requires us to pay again to change to more sustainable ways.

In other words, sustainability does not always come cheaply or even completely — it costs money, such as for photovoltaics, which, in their use of raw materials, and their manufacture and transport, cause pollution and consume dirty energy. Life Cycle Analysis (LCA) is really needed on all of our 'improvements' so that we can make informed choices to be sure that we really are doing the right thing.

This book has been an attempt to show in a practical way that many things are possible by those of us with existing houses who are in a position to make lots of small differences add up to a more sustainable world.

If only for the sake of our grandchildren, I hope that we can all start to make a difference in the way we live.

A quick checklist

- Walk, ride a bike, take a bus, instead of going by car.
- Think of the switch on the wall as one of the worst greenhouse polluters — switch it off!
- A hot meal consumes more energy than a cold meal.
- Invest in a solar water heater — enquire about all the grants now available.
- Check on your roof to see if it is suitable for installing a photovoltaic array. *(See p 7–5.)*
- Start a couple of compost bins.
- Try vegetarian cooking — it's certainly healthier.
- Do you *really* need to cut down a tree *every* day to read the daily news?
- If you must buy newspapers, spread them on your lawn and cover with wood chips. See how quiet it becomes and how your water bill reduces. *(See p **12**-6.)*
- Reflect on the virtues of southern reflectors. *(See p **6**-2.)*
- Check ceiling insulation - is there enough? *(See p **9**-2.)*
- Check air infiltration through your floor. *(See p **10**-5.)*
- Got an old heating-oil tank on the outside wall? Convert it to supply your garden. *(See p **11**-22.)*
- Install dual-flush cisterns — or convert. *(See p **11**-17.)*
- Old enough to remember 'Dig for Victory'? — try 'Digging for Sustainability'. Start a vegetable garden.
- Bask in the winter warmth and the summer coolness with sunshades over your northern windows. *(See p **5**-3.)*
- Make your curtains airtight, and lose less heat. *(See p **5**-8.)*
- Switch lights and stand-by LEDs off when not needed.
- Install long-life compact fluorescent or LED lamps.
- Install water-saving AAA shower heads *(See p **11**-4.)*
- Try one-minute showers, and use less soap and cleansers.
- Don't leave the tap running when you clean your teeth.
- Use both sides of A4 paper before you recycle.
- Wash up in the sink instead of a dishwasher, and put the grey water on the garden — not the sewer. *(See p **11**-19.)*
- And, of course, recycling ... can it be better organised?

15-3.1 **Separate boxes for paper, jars for re-use, plastics and glass, soft plastics (to Woolworth's bins) and above, aluminium bits which get compressed into blocks and sold to the metal recyclers. All stored in the laundry on their way out to the wheelie bins**

Which retrofit project should I do first?

It's all very well to say what *needs* to be done, but there are so many factors to be juggled — how on earth do you decide which to do first, assuming you do have some money to invest in retrofitting …?

Many times in my life I have faced problems with bewildering lists of factors which need reconciling — some very factual, others extremely subjective and woolly which defy any quantification.

On several occasions I have used a management technique called 'weighted rank ordering' for resolving diverse problems such as which car to buy, selecting a block of land, buying a house or, in this context, which retrofitting project should be tackled first.

Any project which involves significant expenditure of time or money deserves a thorough analysis — it helps to preserve your sanity and, having completed the analysis, it gives peace of mind, knowing that you have done your best to resolve the problem.

Some of the factors I have had to resolve in designing and constructing the retrofitting projects described in this book have been:

How much money can I afford to invest in retrofitting?
Is a Return- on-Investment analysis relevant here when individual contributions for society's benefit are what might be needed?

Will I have to borrow or do I have enough saved?
Am I too old to take on a loan? What else would I otherwise be doing with my money?

Am I competent to do it all myself?
Can I design it myself?
Do I have the skills and the equipment?
Will I need to get somebody else to make it?

Am I willing to take it on?
Do I have the time? the energy? the commitment?

Am I healthy enough to carry it through?
Projects like constructing a photovoltaic array can be quite demanding and can stress the body's capacity, probing every weakness.

Why am I even considering such a project?
Am I doing this purely to save future recurrent expenditure, to do my bit toward reducing greenhouse gas emissions, or just to try out a new and promising idea?

Can I use renewable materials?
Should I feel guilty about using non-renewable materials?

Is there a better way of doing it?
Can the problem be resolved by eliminating the problem?

Will the components be suitable for re-use or recycling when the project has reached its economic use-by date?

Is it more important to save fossil-fuelled electricity or to save rainwater?
Photovoltaics or water tanks?

An examination of our *real* motivations are always a good start to problem-solving.

The resolution of complex issues is somewhat beyond the real scope of this book on sustainable modifications to existing houses, so I propose to issue it as a separate paper which can be downloaded from my website:

<www.derek.wrigley.design.id.au>

If you can't see it on the website send me an email, which will stimulate me into action:

dwrigley@cyberone.com.au

Other papers on sustainable house design will also be available on the site.

How can we finance retrofitting?

'Solarisation' – *an affordable proposal by Dr Andrew Blakers*

Director, Centre for Sustainable Energy Systems, Faculty of Engineering and Information Technology, Australian National University, Canberra

The turnover of building stock (demolition followed by new construction) is low. Even if all new buildings have excellent energy ratings, there is only a slow reduction in average greenhouse intensity. Mass retrofitting of buildings is the only way in which rapid reductions in greenhouse gas emissions can be achieved in the building sector.

Mass retrofitting of roof, wall and floor insulation, draught proofing and solar water-heaters to existing buildings ('solarisation') will yield large greenhouse gas reductions. In a typical brick veneer house the cost of thorough solarisation is about $8,000. The reduction in energy bills pays for solarisation well within the lifetime of the solar water-heater and insulation.

The barriers to mass solarisation are the need for up-front capital and the lack of information on the part of building owners. This paper suggests a practical and commercially attractive method of removing these obstacles.

Australians move houses frequently. An investment in solarisation is often not recognised in the sale price of the house. There is no incentive for a landlord to invest in solarisation because they do not pay the energy bills.

There is no incentive for a tenant to invest in solarisation because they do not own the house. How to pay for solarisation, up front? The key to an effective solarisation funding model is that the debt belongs to the house, not the homeowner.

I propose the following mechanism for funding solarisation. Consortia would be established (e.g., 'Solarisation Pty Ltd'), comprising a solar water-heater company, a house-insulation installer, a billing agency, and a financier.

Solarisation P/L would contract its members to retrofit solar water-heaters, insulation and draught proofing in houses and commercial buildings. The company could also install double-glazing, gas heaters and photovoltaic systems.

The house owner would not be required to put up the cash. Instead, Solarisation P/L would recover its investment (at normal commercial rates of return) over 8–12 years through quarterly bills to the house owner. This is equivalent to the way in which electricity companies recover their investment in a new power station.

House owners (and tenants) would enjoy reduced overall energy costs (comprising gas, electricity and the solarisation quarterly repayments) and improved thermal comfort and noise insulation. A much better greenhouse outcome per dollar would be obtained than from 'green electricity'.

The uptake will be high if Solarisation P/L provides a fast, efficient turnkey service for a range of energy technologies and services — a single visit by an assessor skilled in all of the energy technologies, followed by a well-managed and rapid implementation including easy financing. A low-cost financing option is to draw additional funds from a mortgage.

Solarisation P/L would construct alliances with insulation and solar suppliers that includes the supply of equipment and services at a substantial discount to reflect reduced advertising costs and increased sales volume.

It would be very helpful if the state government were to pass legislation to allow the debt for solarisation to be easily attached to the house (without incurring a second mortgage) rather than the house owner.

The debt would need to be disclosed each time a house was sold — like disclosing rates or electricity bills or the House Energy Rating. This legislation is not essential, but would be helpful because the risk of default would be almost eliminated, allowing Solarisation P/L to charge a low interest rate on the debt.

Companies involved in solarisation would benefit from a low-risk investment, because the equipment to be installed has a long guarantee period and the debt is against the house rather than house owner.

Gas and electricity companies would experience reduced sales of energy. However, solarisation would provide replacement revenue and profits. They would have an opportunity to 'lock-in' customers for long periods (an important consideration in the era of contestability), and would acquire a large supply of RECS from the solar water-heaters.

Solarisation of 100,000 homes in Canberra over a decade would be worth around $80 million/year and would lead to the creation of about 800 new jobs. Electricity utilities would benefit from mass solarisation through a reduction in peak loads, because better insulation would reduce the space heating peak-load in winter and the air-conditioning peak-load in summer, while solar water-heaters would have gas or off-peak electric boosting.

Solarisation would also help energy companies (e.g., in NSW) cope with any government requirements that the greenhouse intensity of their products must decline each year.

A large majority of local government districts in Australia have no gas, coal or electricity production. In these districts there are few economic losers from tough greenhouse targets. On the contrary, there are many winners. Solarisation is more labour-intensive than electricity or gas production, and most of the jobs are local. Tenants living in uninsulated homes will be big winners, since it gets around the problem that the landlord has no incentive to invest in energy efficiency because the landlord does not pay the energy bills.

Solarisation is one of the rare occasions when employment, social, economic and environmental objectives are aligned — and is therefore politically attractive, particularly at a local level.

Government moral support would be valuable, in order to give credibility to this new idea. A modest initial government subsidy could also accelerate uptake. In return for a modest subsidy Solarisation P/L would promise to solarise a specified number of buildings to a specified standard (e.g., five stars).

Solarisation – *Dr Andrew Blakers* *(cont)*

The government might also include a tender provision that rewards local manufacturing. Alternatively, councils could offer modest revenue-neutral rate relief that is linked to the star rating of a building.

Initial solarisations could focus on the items with the most clear-cut financial benefit. This would increase the probability that the scheme would be commercially successful. In approximate order this would be ceiling insulation, draught proofing, house zoning and low-flow shower heads, followed by solar water-heaters and wall and floor insulation, followed by photovoltaic systems and double glazing.

Solarisation will create a substantial number of new jobs in the local community. The scheme fits very well with the building energy-rating scheme in several states. Early solarisation companies will be well placed to dominate the national solarisation market that is likely to develop in a few years' time.

The risk will be low because of the debt being secured against the building, and being repayable within the guarantee period of the equipment. Large reductions in greenhouse gas emissions are likely.

Solarisation can be tested on a small scale in a few suburbs or in a regional centre. Early adopters could be the 2–3% of customers who purchase 'greenpower'. Housing trusts for low-income tenants and upper-income, busy professionals are two other groups of potential early adopters.

The key to successful solarisation is that the service be provided by well-known companies offering a very smooth, no-fuss service — e.g., one phone call, one house-assessment visit, one contract, rapid and trouble-free installation of insulation and equipment, and good after-sales service.

Why haven't governments adopted this excellent suggestion?

Pass it on to your local MP ———————————— *However, there are now many grants available through federal, state and local governments to encourage potential retrofitters to take action to save energy, reduce pollution, save water, etc.*

Google will bring up many possibilities …

Technoclutter – *the creeping ugliness*

In describing all the ways in which we can achieve more comfort by the use of natural energies we should be conscious of a **creeping visual problem** which, if we are not careful, will at some point make us wonder at our lack of foresight.

We have all seen the sprouting of television antennae on our roofs, followed by dish antennae for satellite broadcasting, hot-water absorber panels, some with close-coupled tanks, air conditioners, evaporative coolers — and now photovoltaic panels and reflectors are beginning to make their appearance.

15-7.1   **The roof is becoming a visible junkyard** *

Fortunately, roof top *radio* aerials have now become unnecessary through increased efficiency of indoor aerials and, in some areas with strong television signals, indoor aerials are quite adequate.

Solar devices, however, need direct contact with the incoming radiant energy. Roof tops are the obvious location, being higher than most bushes — although, unfortunately not free from all trees — and offering some safety from damage and loss.

However, we should be aware of the negative effects of *cumulative* techno-clutter on this convenient and visually obvious location.

The main problem is the ultimate visual appearance of the streetscape. If the street runs east-west, half of the houses will face north to the street, and they will have their techno-clutter on the street side of their roofs.

This could create a lot of ugliness if there is no aesthetic control over location and integration with the existing form of the building.

15-7.2   **Couldn't this have been better integrated ?**

15-7.3   **Air-conditioning units rarely make any attempt to integrate into the architectural form. Visible plumbing and no colour matching compound the ugliness.**

Morning shade on the panels from this tree ?

15-7.4   **Badly oriented houses sometimes force owners to place solar absorbing panels at inappropriate angles to the roof form — but surely it didn't get design approval?**

Present and future

To minimise this creeping ugliness we need a strong, unifying discipline which integrates the necessarily individual pieces of technology into the architecture – both functionally and aesthetically — so that we can be one step closer to truly sustainable, autonomous and good-looking housing. We are still in the early stages of developing these new bits of technology, and industry has to talk to architects about how these can be successfully integrated into architecture.
This is vital if the public are to be persuaded to adopt these measures toward a sustainable future.

The UK environmental industry is worth over £8.5 billion a year, rising to more than £10 billion by 2010 — out of a global environmental market worth around £400 billion a year.

Green Futures

Unless we change direction we are likely to end up where we are going.

Old Chinese proverb

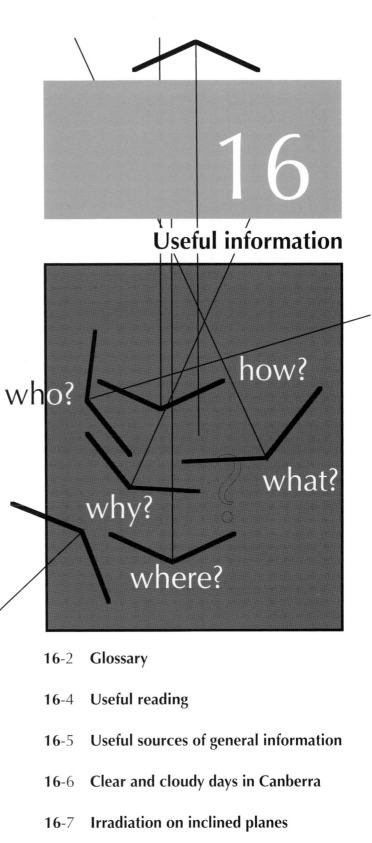

16

Useful information

16-2   **Glossary**

16-4   **Useful reading**

16-5   **Useful sources of general information**

16-6   **Clear and cloudy days in Canberra**

16-7   **Irradiation on inclined planes**

16-8   **Solar plotter 1**

16-9   **Solar plotter 2**

16-10 **Checklist**

16-15 **Is housing design going in a sustainable direction?**

Glossary

Active The gaining or losing of heat from one substance to another by the use of some artificial force derived from fuel, *eg air-conditioning system.*

Albedo Part of the incoming radiation (say through a window) which has been *reflected* from external objects rather than direct radiation from the sun.

Altitude In this context, the angle in between the sun and a horizontal line as seen from a particular point on earth. Eg. the sun's altitude at noon at the summer solstice of Dec. 22 is ~78° — its highest altitude for the 35° latitude (Canberra).

Ambient In this context, the surrounding space relative to a particular object, eg: the ambient temperature of the surrounding air is 20° relative to a Trombe wall which might be at 40°.

Amorphous One particular type of photovoltaic panel made using a deposition process, which is a little more shade and heat tolerant, but usually slightly less efficient per sq.m. in producing electricity and usually a little less costly.

Array A collective term for a group of any number of PV panels.

Azimuth The angle in degrees starting from 0° at *true* north, of an object such as the sun, in relation to a particular point on earth. Eg. in the southern hemisphere the azimuth of the sun at local noon is always 0° from any point. In the northern hemisphere azimuth would be 180° at local noon. In the context of a house in the southern hemisphere, the orientation of the main 'northerly' elevation is (say) 10° west of north or 350° azimuth.

Black water Used water (effluent) from toilets (water closets, WCs) containing urine and faeces. Strictly speaking, soiled nappies washed in the laundry tub would create black water.

Capacity In thermal dynamics the ability of a material to absorb and store heat energy and give off that heat at a later time when ambient temperature falls *(see Trombe–Michel wall).*

Conduction Movement of heat through a substance by direct transferrance from one particle to an adjacent particle without any movement (as in Convection)

Convection Movement of heat in a fluid substance (gas or liquid) by the application of heat, causing a decrease in density of particles with resultant tendency to rise vertically, assisted by a downward movement of cooler heavier particles, thus setting up a convection current or loop movement. This loop movement transfers the gained heat to cooler substances around the loop, resulting in heat transfer or loss.

Crystalline An alternative type of photovoltaic panel made from solid silicon, with differing characteristics to amorphous. Less shade and heat tolerant, more efficient per sq.m., but a little more costly.

Ecology Study of the relationship between organisms and the environments in which they live.

Environment In this context, the sum of conditions surrounding and sustaining all living organisms — *natural* things such as soil, air, water, atmosphere and *artificial* things such as buildings, roads, etc.

Equinox Points on the calendar when days and nights are of approx. equal lengths. In the southern hemisphere the autumnal equinox occurs about March 21 and the vernal equinox about September 23.

Grey water Any effluent or 'waste' water from a house which does not contain faecal matter — usually accepted as used water from showers, baths, basins, sinks, tubs. The washing of soiled nappies could be cause for concern under certain circumstances.

Heliostat A mechanism which automatically follows the sun's apparent movement across the sky from east to west to utilise the insolation for some useful purpose. Some mechanisms track the movement optically; others use timing mechanisms.

Insulation Material that inhibits or resists the flow of heat through the material. The greater its resistance the higher is the R number *(see R).*

Insolation The amount of solar radiation which reaches the Earth's surface from the sun. It varies with the seasons and the latitude, being greatest in summer when the sun's rays are more direct (nearer to vertical) and least when more tangential in winter. The insolation is greatest at the equator, least at the poles.

Inverter A device which transforms the direct current (DC) electricity from the photovoltaic panels (PV) into more useful alternating current (AC) to match the Australian standard electricity of 220–240 volts.

Mass In thermal physics, the ability or capacity of a building material to absorb heat energy from the warmer surrounding air by radiation, convection or conduction, and to release it by the same processes when the surrounding temperature drops below the temperature of the mass.

Magnetic north Azimuth bearing in degrees as shown by use of a magnetic compass. Every point on earth has its magnetic declination (aka variation) which is the difference in degrees between true north and magnetic north. In the case of Canberra, magnetic north was 13.7° east of true north in 1996 and moves 0.05° east each year = 14.1° in 2004. In Sydney in 2004 magnetic north was 12.475° east. This degree of precision is not critical for our purposes, but it is important that true north is used in all solar calculations.

Orientation The way in which rooms and the whole house are placed in relation to the compass, view, sun, prevailing winds and site features.

Passive The gaining or losing of heat from one substance to another by natural transfer rather than by any mechanical means which relies on energy input derived from fuel, *eg a building's ability to absorb solar radiation directly from the sun.*

Photovoltaics Composite semi-conductor materials, usually in panel form, which have the capacity to absorb solar radiation of heat and light wavelengths and transform it into direct current (DC) electricity, which can be collected for purposes useful to humans.

R A measure of the efficiency of an insulating substance in which R4 is more efficient than R1. It is a commercialised version of the scientific equation of 1/r.

Radiation The emission of energy as particles or waves, e.g., heat and light, as from the sun, received by earth as solar energy. This radiant energy can travel through space or a vacuum.

Retrofitting Dictionaries describe R. as 'repairs and maintenance', but increasingly it is being taken to mean the art and science of *modifying* an existing building with the aim of improving its *environmental* performance, *e.g., adding insulation to reduce heat losses, to reduce the consumption of fossil fuels and to reduce the emissions of greenhouse gases which are contributing to global warming.*

Solar energy Electromagnetic radiation from the sun in the forms of visible light, infrared and ultraviolet wavelengths which are absorbed by the earth, human structures and its surrounding atmosphere, resulting in global climate patterns of varying temperatures, wind, rainfall, waves and clouds.

Solstice Twice during the year when the sun is farthest south or north of the celestial equator — usually taken in the southern hemisphere as June 21 for the winter solstice and Dec 22 as the summer solstice.

Specific heat The quantity of heat required to raise the temperature of a substance by one degree C, measured in joules per kilogram of mass per degree C. *(see Capacity)*.

Sustainability Capable of being continued indefinitely. In this context, doing minimum or no harm to our environment; using resources that can be created as fast as they are used; an impossible concept given current population growth and expectations, but one which we have no alternative but to aim for.

Tilt Angle of inclination of an absorber panel from the horizontal. Sometimes used synonymously with *altitude.*

Trombe–Michel wall A high-density wall built inside a window in order to receive and store radiant energy from the sun with the aim of radiating or convecting that stored heat energy into the room when the internal ambient temperature falls below the temperature of the wall.

True north Shown as ⌃N̑ throughout this book, it is the reference point of all geographical and solar calculations. It can be taken for the purposes of this topic as the azimuth position of the sun at local noon standard time on any day of the year. To be accurate, noon for a given location will be midway between local sunrise and local sunset as published in the local newspaper.

It may vary from standard 'clock' noon, but this does not affect solar design calculations arising from the topics covered in this book, where good margins of practical tolerance exist.

Useful reading

Consumers Guide to Effective Environmental Choices
Practical advice from the Union of Concerned Scientists, USA
Michael Brower & Warren Leon, 1999

Copper Corrosion
(http://www.agric.nsw.gov.au/reader/ac2-corrosion.htm)

Ecohouse 2
Roaf, Fuentes and Thomas
A design guide to ecological housing with good analysis and examples. *Architectural Press, 2003*

Factor 4
Weizsacker & Lovins, Rocky Mountains Institute, USA
How to do twice as much with half the resources — an inspiring guide to future possibilities.*(Bookshops or Allen & Unwin as above, 1977)*

Green Futures
The journal of Forum for the Future — an excellent way of keeping in touch with environmental matters overseas. About A$50 + airmail postage. Worth every cent.
Published 6 x per year.
Subscriptions : email < greenfutures@circa-uk.demon.co.uk>

Greeniology
Tanya Ha, Planet Ark

A very well-researched and readable book on how to be green and make a contribution to living well, yet making a difference to your time on Planet Earth.
A complementary book to the one you are now reading.
(Bookshops or <www.allenandunwin.com>)

ReNew
Journal of the Alternative Technology Association
Full of practical articles of low energy experiments carried out by members, critical reviews of new technologies and where to get them.
The ATA Bookshop also publishes many helpful books and booklets on several of the topics covered in this book. List is available from:
(<www.ata.org.au/>

Sunshine and Shade in Australasia
Ralph Phillips
Technical Report 92/2. Reprinted 2002.
Written by my colleague of the 1950s, this seminal book explains the movements of the sun from anywhere in Australia and helps you to understand how sunshades work. A helpful book for DIYs.
(CSIRO Publishing, (<publishing.sales@csiro.au>)

Solar energy & building
Steve V.Szokolay, University of Queensland,
A seminal guide to the utilisation of solar energy. An excellent technical source book on solar basics.
(Probably out of print. 1975 Architectural Press, UK)

Solar Greenhouse Book
James McCullagh
A thorough analysis of how greenhouses work — very useful for designing conservatories.*(Probably out of print. 1978 Rodale Press, USA)*

Sustainable Water from Rain Harvesting
Rod Wade, Environmental Conservation Planning P/L
A thorough, but commercial analysis of what you need to know and what can be supplied to harvest rainwater effectively.*<www.rainharvesting.com.au>*

The Autonomous House
Brenda and Robert Vale. A seminal work on the design of near self-sufficient houses in England.
Thames and Hudson, 1975

The Complete Bushfire Safety Book
Joan Webster
A timely and well-researched book on how we should be designing our houses for safety in bushfires. There are many lessons to be learned from it.
(Bookshops and Random House Australia)

The *New* Autonomous House
Brenda and Robert Vale.
A welcome update on their 1975 book. Essentially English context, but convertible to Australian conditions. *Thames and Hudson, 2000*

Warm House — Cool House
Nick Hollo. Covers the basic facts about heat transfer in houses, with many examples to illustrate the principles relating to new house designs and to existing houses. *Choice Books, 1995*

Waterwise House and Garden
Allan Windust, 2003
A very detailed explanation of how to save water. *Landlinks Press, PO Box 1139, Collingwood, Vic. 3066.*

Your Home
Published by the Australian Greenhouse Office, which explains in simple language some of the things that can be designed into a new home. Free.

Your Home — Technical manual
A more technical explanation of the basic physics behind low-energy houses. Published by the Australian Greenhouse Office.
(<www.greenhouse.gov.au>)

Rainwater Tanks — guidelines for residential properties in Canberra
By ActewAGL, Environment ACT and ACTPLA
A guide from the supply and regulating authorities on the safe design of tank systems of various sizes. Based on water consumption rates as existing — no allowance seems to have been made for voluntary reduction of water consumption. Useful graphs for determining tank sizes.
(<www.actewagl.com.au)

Water and sewer pipes —rules for building over or near Actew Corporation water and sewer pipes
By ActewAGL
Easements for future access must be maintained in case of sewer pipe failure. Vital information to those wishing to place new water tanks around the house.
(<www.actewagl.com.au>)

Useful sources of general information

There has been such an explosion of information on the subject of retrofitting and sustainable design by all Australian governments, industries, and commercial organisations that it has become impossible to adequately cover the field in any detailed and helpful way.

Also, many firms shown in previous editions of this book have changed their contact details or simply disappeared, while the internet has become a major source of information on almost any topic.

Knowing *how* to obtain the relevant information to suit your needs has become almost as important as actually resolving your needs, so I can only advise on a few sources that I have found useful in some generic way:

GOOGLE
Using the 'I'm feeling lucky' button can be quicker, but full search results allow you to select the 'Pages from Australia' option which can increase relevance.
<www.google.com.au>

ALTERNATIVE TECHNOLOGY ASSOCIATION
Membership is strongly advised, as the magazine *ReNew* is informative and practical for those who want to be sustainable. It has excellent articles and a directory of useful Australian suppliers. Specialist technical writers will answer readers' questions. Back issues are available on the Web.
<www.ata.org.au>

CLEAN ENERGY COUNCIL
If you need to find an accredited photovoltaic designer/installer in your area.
<www.solaraccreditation.com.au/acccec/consumers/findaninstaller.html>

GREEN PLUMBERS
If you need an accredited plumber who has been trained and accredited to understand sustainability issues and install appropriately.
<greenplumbers.com.au>

GREEN PROFESSIONALS
The Green Building Council of Australia has a list of Green Star Accredited Professionals (mainly concerned with star rating of commercial multi-storey buildings, and hence not too relevant to single-storey houses).
<www.gbca.org.au/ap-list.asp>

FEDERAL GOVERNMENT'S ONE-STOP LIST
This list informs you about energy, water, waste, and transport issues in the home, together with information on rebates, grants, and loans to make buying more affordable. Typical calculations of various systems are given to assist you to weigh up the options available.
<www.livinggreener.gov.au>

BUILDING REGULATIONS
The national Building Code of Australia applies to all housing (substantial payment required), together with local building codes/guides. Consult your local council.
<www.bcaillustrated.com.au>

Clear and cloudy days in Canberra

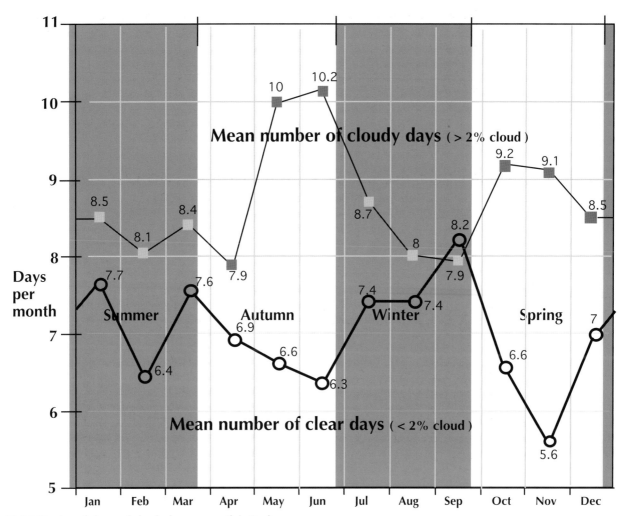

16-6.1 Number of clear and cloudy days per month in Canberra
Source of data: Bureau of Meteorology, Canberra, 2004

Our atmosphere is changing

The statistics in the graph above may be of use to those wishing to optimise their absorption of solar radiation.

A quick glance at the number of cloudy and clear days will show that Canberra is a good solar city, having solar radiation available for a high proportion of its daytime hours. Add to that its clear atmosphere at an altitude of about 560m, free from industrial pollution, and we have a location waiting to take full advantage of free solar radiation.

However, the topic of *global dimming* was raised around 2004, although it now seems to have dropped out of public discussion.

Airborne particles, aerosols, water vapour, and contrails from aircraft are undoubtedly affecting the thermal balance of our planet, and cloud cover seems to be increasing.

This must have some effect upon our reliance on solar devices and their absorptive area; and, of course, on the form, orientation, and size of our roofs, which are rapidly becoming much more significant elements in our building design — they are no longer a means of simply keeping the weather out.

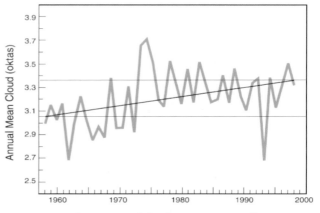

16-6.2 Annual average total cloud cover over Australia 1957–1998
Source: Bureau of Meteorology, Canberra

Graph **16**-6.2 seems to indicate a rise in total cloud cover of about 0.245% p.a. which, while being rather small, would suggest that in determining areas of photovoltaic and other radiation-absorbing panels, we should be thinking bigger rather than smaller, unless technology manages to increase collection efficiencies.

Irradiation on inclined planes

These useful figures will enable you to assess the efficiency of a photovoltaic array fixed at angles of tilt or azimuth *other than* the optimum 100% by facing due north and at 35° Canberra inclination (or tilt) *(see bold box at top of chart)*. Similar charts have been calculated for other locations around Australia.

Example: An array fixed directly onto a tiled roof at 22° pitch (inclination/tilt) at 15° west of north (azimuth 345°) will receive approximately 98%. Tilting it further to 35° would only receive an extra 1% of radiation, which would not be worth the effort, cost, or loss of aesthetics.

This chart is very useful in evaluating alternative locations of panels and reconciling them with effort, cost, and aesthetics as shown in the above example.

Annual daily irradiation on an inclined plane expressed as percentage of maximum value for Canberra

Plane azimuth (degrees)	Plane inclination (degrees above horizontal) Latitude (degrees north or south of the equator)										
	0	**10**	**20**	**30**	**35**	**40**	**50**	**60**	**70**	**80**	**90**
0	87	94	98	100	100	99	96	90	83	74	64
10	87	94	98	99	99	99	96	91	83	74	64
20	87	93	97	99	99	98	95	90	83	74	64
30	87	93	96	98	98	97	94	89	82	73	64
40	87	92	95	96	96	95	92	87	80	72	63
50	87	92	94	94	94	93	89	84	78	70	62
60	87	91	92	92	91	90	86	81	75	68	61
70	87	90	90	89	89	87	83	78	72	66	59
80	87	89	88	87	86	84	80	75	69	63	56
90	87	88	86	84	83	80	76	71	65	59	53
100	87	87	84	81	80	77	72	67	61	56	50
110	87	86	82	78	76	73	68	62	57	51	46
120	87	85	80	75	73	69	63	58	52	47	42
130	87	84	78	72	70	66	59	53	48	43	38
140	87	83	77	70	67	62	55	49	44	39	35
150	87	82	76	68	65	60	52	45	40	35	32
160	87	82	75	66	63	57	50	42	36	33	29
170	87	82	74	65	62	56	48	41	35	30	28
180	87	81	74	65	62	56	48	40	34	30	27
190	87	81	74	65	62	56	48	41	35	30	28
200	87	82	74	66	63	57	50	42	36	32	29
210	87	82	75	67	65	59	52	45	40	35	32
220	87	83	77	69	67	62	55	49	43	39	35
230	87	84	78	72	70	65	59	53	48	43	38
240	87	84	80	74	72	68	63	57	52	47	41
250	87	85	82	77	76	72	67	62	56	51	45
260	87	86	84	80	79	76	71	66	61	55	49
270	87	87	86	83	82	79	75	70	65	59	52
280	87	89	88	86	85	83	79	74	68	62	55
290	87	90	90	89	88	86	82	77	71	65	58
300	87	91	92	91	91	89	85	81	74	67	60
310	87	91	93	94	93	92	88	83	77	70	61
320	87	92	95	96	95	94	91	86	79	71	63
330	87	93	96	97	97	96	93	88	81	73	63
340	87	93	97	98	98	98	95	89	82	74	64
350	87	94	98	99	99	99	95	90	83	74	64

This chart is part of the Installation Guidelines for grid-connected solar systems prepared for the **Business Council for Sustainable Energy** which are available to BCSE members and accredited personnel. It is printed here by kind permission of BCSE**.**

Solar plotter 1

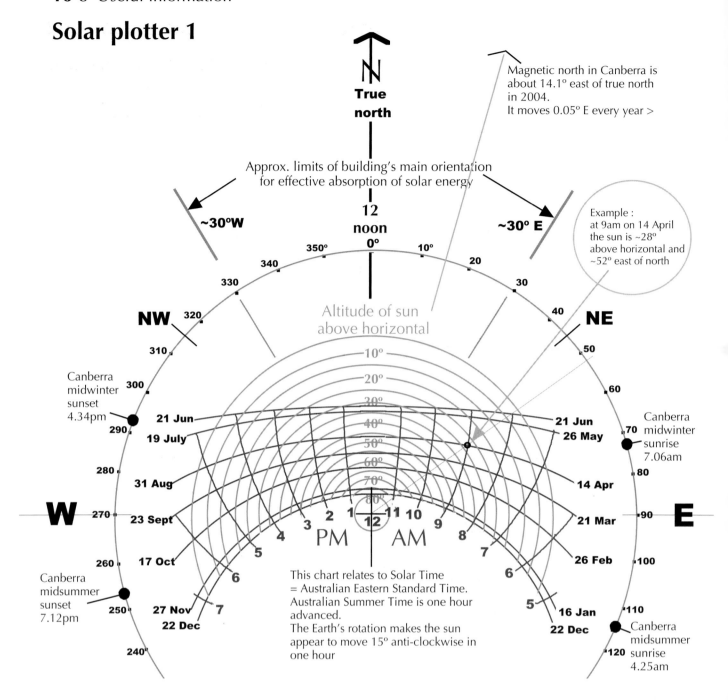

True north

Magnetic north in Canberra is about 14.1° east of true north in 2004.
It moves 0.05° E every year >

Approx. limits of building's main orientation for effective absorption of solar energy

~30°W

12 noon
0°

~30° E

Example : at 9am on 14 April the sun is ~28° above horizontal and ~52° east of north

NW

NE

Altitude of sun above horizontal

Canberra midwinter sunset 4.34pm

21 Jun
19 July
31 Aug
23 Sept
17 Oct
27 Nov
22 Dec

Canberra midsummer sunset 7.12pm

21 Jun
26 May
14 Apr
21 Mar
26 Feb
16 Jan
22 Dec

Canberra midwinter sunrise 7.06am

Canberra midsummer sunrise 4.25am

W

E

PM   AM

This chart relates to Solar Time = Australian Eastern Standard Time. Australian Summer Time is one hour advanced.
The Earth's rotation makes the sun appear to move 15° anti-clockwise in one hour

Chart calculated for latitude 35° south, but is approximately useful for shaded area shown on map below:

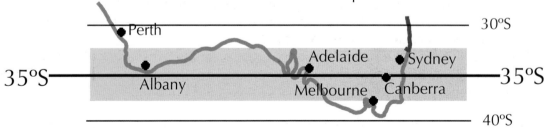

Perth
30°S

Adelaide   Sydney

35°S   Albany   Melbourne   Canberra   35°S

40°S

This chart can be used for determining sun angles at any time of day for any north-facing building, window or solar-absorbing device.

For building orientations other than north the combined use of a transparent building template makes the design of adequate sunshades a little easier — use in conjunction with Solar Plotter 2 >.

The original solar chart was devised by Ralph Phillips in 1983 and published in the CSIRO book *Sunshine and Shade in Australasia*. Redrawn by Derek Wrigley with permission from CSIRO 2002.

Solar plotter 2

Follow the instructions below to determine the effectiveness and efficiences of proposed solar devices on any building

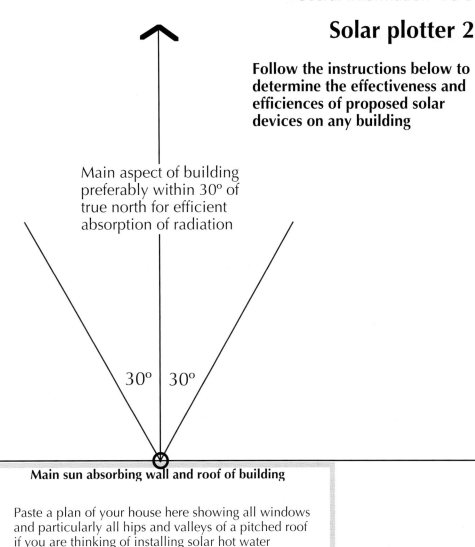

Main aspect of building preferably within 30° of true north for efficient absorption of radiation

30° | 30°

Main sun absorbing wall and roof of building

Paste a plan of your house here showing all windows and particularly all hips and valleys of a pitched roof if you are thinking of installing solar hot water heaters or photovoltaic arrays. Note also any large trees on east, north and west and plot to scale - this will help to locate any shading on the roof at any time of day and to determine optimum shade free locations

Notional building outline

1.   Make a plain photocopy of this page on A4 paper. Also a paper copy of **Solar Plotter 1**.
2.   Paste a photocopy of your building plan *(scale not critical, but should fit on this page)* on the photocopy of this chart with its northerly elevation just under the horizontal line, approximately centred on the small circle,
3.   Make a second photocopy of this *composite* page on *transparent* photocopying film,
4.   Place small circle of composite transparency diagram on centre point of **Solar Plotter 1** and rotate transparency to *actual* orientation of the building,

This will now show the actual relationship of the building to the sun at any time of day or month and will show the altitudes and azimuths of the sun more easily on east, north and west elevations, enabling more accurate sunshade design for windows, location of effective placing of photovoltaic panels on your roof and also reflectors on the *southern* side of your building.

Using the irradiation chart on p **16**-7 with roof pitch and azimuth angles you will now be able to calculate the efficiency of your proposed photovoltaic array.

Checklist

The following practical checklist will help readers to *buy* a new house, *design* their own dream home, or *retrofit* their existing house if they wish to:

* change their lifestyle;

* live happier, healthier lives;

* have much lower running costs;

* reduce their impact on the world;

* effectively prioritise their retrofitting list;

* reduce their pollution of the atmosphere;

* consume fewer non-renewable resources;

* effectively save many thousands of dollars;

* leave a better world for their grandchildren; and

* help to create a better society which works with nature — not against it.

I suggest that the four following pages be photocopied, producing one set for each house being assessed, to enable comparative evaluations.

These sheets can also be downloaded from the Nature and Society Forum website **<www.natsoc.org.au>**

Nature and Society Forum
A&NZ Solar Energy Society (ACT)
Alternative Technology Association (ACT)
ANU Emeritus Faculty

House address ....

Agent's name and contact..

A practical checklist for

SELECTING A MORE COMFORTABLE HOUSE WITH LOW RUNNING

COSTS *and saving our environment*

This checklist is relevant to **one** house only and its purpose is to enable prospective buyers to easily compare a few houses for effective use of the sun, economical use of energies and of water.
You will need a compass and a measuring tape.

Please read first :

Your home is probably the most expensive purchase you will ever make. Careful thought now can save you a lot of time, money and future discomfort and the resale value will likely be higher if you have selected wisely.

A quick sketch of the block and the house may help to remind you of its features when you are comparing. Don't forget to put the compass north point on this sketch, bearing in mind that true north is 13° west of compass north. .Add the block and section number and any significant trees which might shade the roof now or in future.

Climate change is generally predicted to result in hotter, drier and more extreme weather throughout southern Australia and *it is already happening*. Modern housing needs to adapt to these challenges.

This checklist can be used in all areas in Australia approximately south of a line from Perth (WA) to Newcastle (NSW), having cool to cold winters and warm to hot summers. It is not likely to apply to areas further north or very hot inland areas without some reconsideration based on the local climate.

The checklist can be used to broadly assess an *existing* home, a *new* project home, or a *new* house plan in relation to your comfort in such a house and its effectiveness in using energy. *It does not cover* all the more personal factors in choosing your home - such as location, number of bedrooms, proximity to shops/school/transport, affordability and finance which you will be considering. The five most important issues for reducing energy consumption in a house in these more temperate areas of Australia are :

* *orientation* with adequate north facing glass to admit the warming winter sun,
* *shading* to exclude hot summer sun,
* *insulation* to minimise heat loss and heat gain,
* *internal mass* (brick or concrete walls) to stabilise internal temperatures throughout the year.
* *ventilation,* to assist the heating and cooling of the house and its occupants.

The checklist is simple to use, with little technical knowledge required. However, considering the large amount of money involved it is certainly in your interests to inform yourself on aspects you may not fully understand. Further reading on all the questions is suggested on the back page.

How to use the checklist

1   Fill in a separate copy of this checklist for *each house* you wish to consider more closely.
         Obtain more copies from the web <www.natsoc.org.au> or feel free to photocopy this checklist.
2   Fill in the house and agent details in the box at the top of this page.
3   For EACH QUESTION in this checklist circle either **Y** (Yes) or **N** (No) in the right hand margin.
4   Circle **F** (Fixable at a later time) *only* if the listed conditions can be satisfied.
5   Consider your circled answers - **Y, N** or **F** using the guide in the box HOW TO ASSESS...on back page.
6   Compare your answers with those from other houses you may be interested in.

ORIENTATION

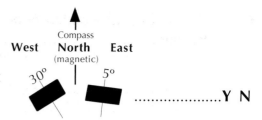

Q1 **Does the long side of the house (with windows to the main living areas) face between 5 degrees east of compass north and 30 degrees west of north?** ....Y N

*This is the most important question - if your answer is **NO** this house will not be able to use the winter sun for warmth. The more it is outside these limits the more expensive it will be to run and it will not be possible to fix in the future. You should seriously consider if it is worth buying this house.*

WINDOWS

Q2 **In all *northern* living areas, is the window area larger than half the floor area?** ......Y N F
If NO, solar heating is likely to be inadequate. It may be fixable, but is likely to be expensive.

Q3 **Will low angle winter sun be able to enter these *northern* rooms for most of the day?** ....Y N F
*Circle NO if there is possible shade from existing evergreen or non-removable trees (particularly if on neighbouring land), neighbouring houses, verandas or large eaves (see Q4) + **F** if it is likely you will be able to <u>remove</u> the cause of the shading.*

Q4 **Can high angle summer sun be excluded by external shading devices from these *northern* rooms for most of the day?** ....Y N F
*Eaves should start near the top of the window and project horizontally no more than 20% of the window height. Eaves should preferably extend beyond either side of the window. Circle NO if there are no eaves or shading devices, + **F** if it would be possible to fit overhead sunshades extending about 1m out from the window or a pergola about 3m from window for deciduous creepers.*

Q5 **Are *eastern* or *western* windows shaded *externally* from low angle summer sun?** .... Y N F
*If NO, there could be excessive heat gain and some control will be needed, at least to <u>western</u> windows + **F** if full shade control could be fitted later. <u>Internal</u> curtains/blinds <u>do not</u> reduce heat gain.*

Q6 **Is each *southern* window in a bedroom or daytime living area smaller than half the floor area?** ....Y N F
*If NO then external reflectors are not likely to be effective. Circle **N+F** where <u>larger</u> than half, if :*
- southern reflectors could be fitted about 1.5 to 2m outside these windows, and
- there is no gable roof above the window (see reading list 2, page 6-2...)
*Note : southern reflectors can reflect heat **and** sunlight into these usually sunless rooms in winter.*

Q7 **Are all windows well sealed against draughts?** ....Y N F
*If NO, circle **N+F** if windows can be easily sealed. Wooden sash windows are very hard to seal. For more information on window seals, pelmets and curtains see Reading List 1 and 2.*

Q8 **Are windows to bedrooms and living areas double glazed?** ....Y N F
*If NO, circle **N+F** if there is at least 20mm thickness of framing inside the existing glass to allow for DIY double glazing, or if a supplier confirms that commercial double glazing can be fitted.*

FLOORS AND INTERNAL WALLS

Q9 **Does the house have a concrete slab floor, with a polished finish or covered with tiles, brick, slate?** ....Y N
Timber or carpet over concrete reduces its ability to store solar heat. Rugs are acceptable if removed out of the sunlit area during sunny winter days. This is usually not fixable. If NO, skip Q10.

Q10 **Is the concrete slab insulated around its exposed external edges?** ....Y N
This may be hard to see - if so, ask the house agent. It is hard and expensive to retrofit.

Q11 If a traditional wooden floor, has it been insulated underneath to a minimum R2 rating? ....Y N F
*If NO, circle **N+F** <u>only</u> if there is adequate underfloor access to allow for fitting insulation.*

Q12 If a wooden floor, are there internal brick walls in *northern* rooms? ....Y N
If NO, these rooms will be hotter in summer and colder in winter, even if the floor and walls are insulated. This situation is not usually fixable.

EXTERNAL WALLS AND DOORS

Q13 Are all external walls insulated to a minimum R2 rating? ....Y N F
*If NO, circle **N+F** <u>only</u> if cavity walls can be filled with injected insulation. Ask the agent.*

Q14 Are all external doors well sealed against draughts? ....Y N F
*If NO, circle **N+F** if doors can be easily sealed. Some sliding doors and older wooden doors are hard to seal. Modern aluminium sliding doors are usually adequately sealed.*

CEILINGS AND ROOFS

Q15 Are all ceilings insulated to a minimum R3.5 rating? ....Y N F
*If NO, circle **N+F** <u>only</u> if there is adequate access to roof space to install insulation.*
Ceilings which are parallel to the roof are often inadequately insulated and expensive to fix.

Q16 Is the roof lighter in colour than a standard terracotta tile? ....Y N F
*Dark roofs absorb too much heat in summer, but can be painted, circle **N+F** if this is likely.*
Air conditioners, however, are expensive to buy as well as expensive and polluting to run. Their large scale adoption is very bad for the environment.

Q17 Is there reflective foil below the tiles or metal roof? ....Y N F
*It is difficult to rectify this omission, but can be done if plenty of space. Circle **N+F** if likely.*

SOLAR ABSORBERS ON ROOFS

Q18 Are solar *hot water* panels fitted on a near north facing roof?... .... Y N F
If NO, and you think it is likely you will be installing a solar hot water system in future, then you will need the following type of roof:
> *- the northern facing roof which has a slope of between 15 and 30 degrees*
> > *(a normal tiled roof is usually about 22 degrees), <u>and</u>*
> *- there is a space about 2 metres by 2 metres to install solar hot water panels on this roof, <u>and</u>*
> *- that particular roof area is free of shade for most of the time on sunny days.*
> *If this roof satisfies all three conditions, then circle **N+F***

Q19 Are solar *photovoltaic* panels fitted on a near north facing roof? ....Y N F
If NO, and you think it is likely you will be installing photovoltaic panels in future, then you will need the following type of roof :
> *- the northern facing roof has a slope of between 15 and 30 degrees, <u>and</u>*
> *- there is enough rectangular space to install solar PV on this roof (typically 20 to 40 sq.m, check panel sizes with an accredited supplier), <u>and</u>*
> *- this roof area is free of shade for most of the time on sunny days.*
> *If this roof satisfies all three conditions, then circle **N+F***

HEATING, COOLING AND VENTILATION
*The format of Q20/21 is different to produce positive, low energy, low pollution **Y** answers*

Q20 If reverse cycle or evaporative airconditioning is *NOT* fitted, circle **Y** ....Y N F
Refrigerative systems use a lot of electricity and evaporative also use lots of water - both undesirable.
A well oriented, constructed, insulated, ventilated and shaded house should not need cooling.

Q21 If in-slab heating is *NOT* fitted, circle **Y**... ......Y N F
It is expensive to buy and run and too polluting to use. Gas heating is preferable.

Q22   Is natural gas heating installed? ....Y N F
*NO?, circle **N+F** if natural gas can be connected (check with the local gas company).*

Q23   Is there at least 1 square metre of roof *ridge* ventilation?...............................Y N F
*NO?, circle **N+F** as ridge vents can usually be fitted to normal pitched roofs, and do not need to be closable if the ceiling space is well insulated. It is difficult to retrofit a ridge vent to sloping ceilings.*

Q24   Are there closable *ceiling* vents *(totalling at least 1 square metre)* which let hot summer air into the roof space *(and out through the ridge vent)?* ....Y N F
*NO?, circle **N+F** as vents can be fitted to any ceiling, but MUST be easily closable. One vent could be over the refrigerator. Vents can also double as skylights (see Reading List 2, page 10-2).*

LIGHTING

Q25   Are compact fluorescent light fittings installed throughout the house? ....Y N F
*NO? Circle **N+F** if 240v halogen downlights installed. Circle **N** only if 12v halogens which cannot be exchanged for 240v compact fluorescents. Confirm voltage with the agent.*

WATER SUPPLY, PLUMBING AND DRAINAGE

Q26   Is laundry and bathroom grey water re-used for a second purpose *(ie. garden)*?....Y N F
*Circle **Y** if connected to a treatment unit, or directly into a percolation pipe in the garden subsoil? Circle **N** if connected to the sewer. Circle **F** if a diverter can be fitted to the laundry tub which gives a fall to garden level with an extension hose. Confirm with the agent.*

Q27   Are there adequate water tanks for domestic use? ....Y N F
*Circle **Y** if there is at least 4000L storage per person with a fail-safe mains connection. This should supply about half your consumption, if careful. Circle **N** if there is less than the above or no room around the house to install adequate tanks. Circle **F** if this (or more)storage can be retrofitted later.*

Q28   Are metal leaf guards fitted to all gutters? ....Y N F
NO? Circle F as leaf guards are easily fitted. They improve rainwater quality and reduce fire risk.

HOW TO ASSESS YOUR Y N F ANSWERS ◄——————— Totals:☐☐☐

All YES answers? *Somewhat unlikely, but if so, it seems that this house is designed for your comfort with low running costs and lower impact on the environment!* **Put it at the top of your list!**

Some NO answers? *Consider each NO answer carefully in relation to your needs. Every NO answer is likely to make the house less energy efficient, more expensive to heat and cool and less comfortable to live in.* **The more NO answers the more this house will be increasing climate change.**

For each FIXABLE answer, *consider whether you can fix it yourself (and when) or if you will need professional help. Consider the likely cost in relation to the potential long term gain.* **Turning every NO to YES helps everybody and the environment.**

READING LIST

1   **YOUR HOME *Technical Manual,*** *pub. Aust. Greenhouse Office,<www.yourhome.gov.au>*
2   **MAKING YOUR HOME SUSTAINABLE,** *A guide to retrofitting, Derek Wrigley, pub. Scribe Melb.*
3   **WARM HOUSE COOL HOUSE,** *Nick Hollo, Pub. Aust. Consumers Assoc. Sydney.*
4   **CLIMATE CHANGE NEEDS HOUSING CHANGE,** *pub. Nature and Society Forum, Canberra*

This brochure has been co-authored by Derek Wrigley,OAM, Emer.Prof. John Sandeman, OAM, and Simon Fisher, with guidance from the Solar Housing Group of Nature and Society Forum, including representatives of the ANZ Solar Energy Society and the Alternative Technology Association. It is the hope of these organisations that by free distribution and permitting photocopying that the buying public can be empowered to choose more carefully, obtain better value for money and, most significantly, *reduce the emissions of greenhouse gases that are damaging our planet.*

Please address any comment/query to Nature and Society Forum <office@natsoc.org.au> Tel: 02 6125 2526 Website: <www.natsoc.org.au>

Is housing design going in a sustainable direction?

The visual evidence on the ground says that it is not, yet there are rising voices in the community saying that we cannot continue to plunder the earth to ensure comfort and convenience in *unsustainable* ways.

None of our existing or recent new homes can work without the importation of large amounts of non-renewable polluting fuel — electricity, gas, petrol, oil, kerosene — all derived from diminishing resources. These houses are unsustainable, and may well become unlivable unless new fuels or better utilisation of natural energies are achieved.

Brenda and Robert Vale, in their 1975 seminal book *The Autonomous House (see p 16-4)*, showed us a way to design houses which can use natural energies to achieve internal comfort and convenience.

That was a quarter of a century ago, and yet the design of houses offered for sale in the 21st century show few signs of integrating more thermally efficient construction techniques and other research into thermal efficiency.

The car industry and its customers have benefited enormously from research into better and safer vehicles, and the buying public has recognised and accepted these improvements. So, it must be asked, why hasn't the design of our new houses shown a similar degree of improvement?

What is really needed to change direction toward *sustainable* housing?

We need urgent, perhaps mandatory, involvement of qualified 'green' architects and designers in *all* housing design *(it all starts with design because we can no longer afford poorly conceived, unsustainable designs)*.

We need developers and builders to recognise the enormous potential benefits of sustainable housing to themselves, to their customers, to all the industry suppliers, *and to the environment* — and to support this urgent need by appropriate action. (The Housing Industry Association has made a good start in establishing its GreenSmart training program, but why has it not been put into practice by its members?)

We need a buying public which recognises the benefits of *sustainable* housing and is prepared to be more outspoken. (Australians are usually very accepting of new technology and, judging by the comments received from Solar House Day visitors, they would welcome a new direction from the housing industry.)

We need the mortgage and real-estate industries to recognise the urgent need for *sustainability* criteria to be at the top of the shopping list, to make it financially easier for purchasers to do the right thing for the environment, and to recognise and promote the concept that a sustainable house is value-added. (Comparative running costs of houses could be promoted, which would undoubtedly favour the sustainable house.)

We need governments to *recognise* the *urgency* of the need to retrofit our existing stock of houses, and to provide real incentives to designers, builders, and house buyers to do the right thing by the environment. (The urgency of the situation would require some mandatory approach toward better design, better uptake of these designs by builders, and compulsory advertisement of indicators of thermal performance, running costs, and their environmental consequences.)

Could we look forward to some enlightened developer/s building houses which:

- are more reasonably sized, *in keeping with the trend for smaller families*;
- control, admit, store, and release the sun's freely available energy, when needed, *to a useful level*;
- ventilate naturally, quietly, and with no running costs, *without using any non-renewable energy*;
- never exceed 26° inside in hot summers, *without air conditioning*;
- never go below 13° in cold winters, *minimising or even eliminating the use of non-renewable energy*;
- collect and rely on their own rainwater;
- generate all or most of their own electricity;
- provide all of their hot water from the sun;
- rely on daylight to light all interiors, *without electricity*;
- collect, treat, and reuse all their own wastes;
- reduce their emissions of carbon dioxide and other greenhouse gases to the absolute minimum;
- satisfy needs, rather than wants;
- create no health problems for their occupants;
- use low-embodied energy materials and use fewer non-renewable resources;
- have much lower running costs than have been usual; and
- are a delight to live in?

Such houses would not only create better internal and external environments, but would, as a by-product, result in happier people and a much happier society. Reports from around the world indicate that 'There is a clear lack of connection between rampant consumerism and a happier life'. *(Green Futures)*

A conclusion drawn from those reports was that bigger and more expensive houses may not increase customer satisfaction, reinforcing Schumacher's 1960s statement: 'The West has not learned when enough is enough.'

We should support our government's carbon tax for the very fundamental reason that we cannot continue 'fouling our own nest'. We have to bite the bullet and pay to correct our past mistakes. We must realise that we have been living beyond our means, and that it cannot continue. Let me put it quite bluntly: would you pee in your water tank if it was your only source of drinking water?

There is an enormous need for ecological education of all members of society and for us all to *do* the right thing *now* — for the sake of our grandchildren, who will inevitably have to pay the bills we have put on the credit card.

It is worth repeating again that *unless we change direction we are likely to end up where we are going.*

Time is *not* on our side.

This book is all about taking action in a clean and renewable way which is as sustainable as possible. If every householder in Australia took some action it would go a long way towards creating a sustainable future.

Show the housing industry that it can be done.